Feminist Solutions for Ending War

T0288182

Feminist Solutions for Ending War

Edited by
Megan MacKenzie and Nicole Wegner

Foreword by Swati Parashar

First published 2021 by Pluto Press
New Wing, Somerset House, Strand, London WC2R 1LA

www.plutobooks.com

British Library Cataloguing in Publication Data
A catalogue record for this book is available from the British Library

ISBN   978 0 7453 4287 0   Hardback
ISBN   978 0 7453 4286 3   Paperback
ISBN   978 0 7453 4290 0   PDF
ISBN   978 0 7453 4288 7   EPUB

This book is printed on paper suitable for recycling and made from fully managed
and sustained forest sources. Logging, pulping and manufacturing processes are
expected to conform to the environmental standards of the country of origin.

Typeset by Stanford DTP Services, Northampton, England

Simultaneously printed in the United Kingdom and United States of America

In loving memory of Teresia Teaiwa

Contents

Abbreviations and Acronyms

AU	African Union
CEDAW	Committee on the Elimination of Discrimination against Women
DDR	Disarmament, Demobilisation and Reintegration
ECAP	Estudios Comunitarios y Acción Psicosocial
FARC	Revolutionary Armed Forces of Colombia
FOWAC	Foundation for Women Affected by Conflict
ICAN	International Campaign to Abolish Nuclear Weapons
IDF	Israeli Defense Forces
IFI	international financial institutions
ILC	International Law Commission
IMF	International Monetary Fund
IR	International Relations
KCK	Kurdistan Communities Union
LGBT	Lesbian, gay, bisexual and transgender
LGBTQ	Lesbian, gay, bisexual, transgender and queer
NAP	National Action Plans
NATO	North Atlantic Treaty Organization
NES	North-east Syria
NGO	non-governmental organisation
PKK	Kurdistan Workers' Party
PTSD	post-traumatic stress disorder
PYD	(Kurdish) Democratic Union Party
RAF	Royal Air Force
SDF	Syrian Democratic Forces
SIPRI	Stockholm International Peace Research Institute
SSR	Security Sector Reform
TMM	Trans Murder Monitoring
TSA	Transport Security Administration
UN	United Nations
UNDP	United Nations Development Programme

WILPF   Women's International League for Peace and Freedom
WPS   Women, Peace and Security
YPG   (Kurdish) People's Protection Units
YPJ   (Kurdish) Women's Protection Units

Acknowledgements

This book was a collective effort, guided by a dedication to feminist ethics and praxis. We are grateful first and foremost to the contributing authors, for dedicating their time and sharing their knowledge.

This book project began just before the start of the Covid-19 global pandemic and during a time of renewed anti-racism movements and activism sparked, in part, by the ongoing killing of black men and women by police in Canada and the US, including George Floyd, Regis Korchinski-Paquet, Breonna Taylor and Rodney Levi. These global events required us to pause. We felt we needed to rethink the purpose and relevance of our scholarship and reflect on what types of academic work were useful and possible at this point in history. Early in 2020, we checked in with the authors, and revisited if and how we should move forward with this project. We were pleased that everyone remained committed to the book despite the pressures of homeschooling, caregiving, university sector cuts and precarity, and the emotional and physical impacts of living in a pandemic. We acknowledge and were conscious that many contributors are at early stages of their career and do not have fixed-term stable work, which we recognise adds extra stress, pressure, and drain.

Reading the chapter drafts and supporting authors in revising and completing the chapters was one of the best professional experiences either of us have had. During an otherwise difficult year, we found the chapters offered hope, drew attention to crucial issues of justice, and offered creative pathways forward. We are grateful to have learned from and been inspired by our engagement with the authors in this project.

We are also grateful to our community, colleagues, and wonderful students at the University of Sydney. Thank you also to Jakob Horstmann at Pluto Press, for his enthusiastic work advocating for this project from the beginning.

Foreword
Waging the War on Wars: Feminist Ways Forward

Swati Parashar, Professor in Peace and Development,
Gothenburg University, Sweden

Amidst the pandemic shutdown, this book came like a breath of fresh air. It has now become commonplace to think of the pandemic in terms of war, using the war metaphor to describe 'combating' the novel coronavirus and winning a decisive victory against it. While public health has now become a military campaign, actual wars happening out there (Yemen, Syria, Afghanistan and elsewhere) have been normalised to such an extent that unless the violence exceeds past statistics, they escape public scrutiny and attention. In these times, when we have accepted the realities and the discourses of war, removed the tag of exceptionalism and adopted its vocabulary in everyday parlance, to turn to the question of feminist solutions to ending war seems both exhilarating and daunting. The editors of this volume and the chapter authors have created a unique opportunity for us to centre, once again, the politics of hope in reimagining a world without the relevance and spectacle of wars. This reimagining is enabled through a recognition of differences in feminist knowledges, epistemologies and methods, in our understandings of wars as gendered violent encounters that have dominated most of human history.

First, this book raises an important question: what do we think of as war and what are its most compelling stories and memorialisations? War is an unaesthetic, cruel, violent and occasionally even redeeming activity for participants, victims, survivors and observers alike. It remains one of the most theorised and researched activities in politics, International Relations (IR) and cognate disciplines. War captures distinctive social formations, and foregrounds imagined communities and emotional orders, lived experiences, performing bodies and their relationship with one another. Feminists have intimate knowledge about the injuries of war and myths that perpetuate it. If it were not for feminist research and activism, we would not know the gendered seduction and emotions of war, or the sustained myths about its inevitability, its (dis)honourable codes of conduct, performativity, multiple forms of violence within violence, patriarchal dividends and quality of redemption. Our levels of analysis would not have gone beyond the state and international system to include complex war narratives, memory politics and the spotlight on warring bodies, who know more about wars than our minds know about them. We would not have a sense of our own embeddedness in wars 'out there', as consumers of the media, unintended victims, unsuspecting bystanders, and tax-paying contributors to the war machine and its frenzied narrative.

This feminist storytelling about war itself is the most radical act of dissent; remember when they did not want us to study/research war and write about it? We could mourn its victims, but could we have a politics highlighting its violence and failures, and demanding its end? Megan MacKenzie and Nicole Wegner, who conceptualised this project, are invested in the stories we tell about wars because these stories unsettle war myths and the normative assumptions about gender roles and hierarchies. The nature of war has changed, as the authors in this volume remind us, and how we count the injuries and deaths matter in how we foresee its end. In my own work, it is precisely in this feminist mode of dissenting storytelling that I have been invested in counting the famine dead as victims of 'slow violence' of wars. For, in that counting and acknowledging of the emaciated, feminised bodies as victims of deliberate violence and starvation, lies the solution to famine wars and reparative and restorative justice. This book offers a number of similar alternative stories of war, which explore a number of important questions, including: what is considered war and by whom; how and with what weapons are contemporary wars being fought; who counts as a casualty and why; which actors have material and discursive power; who has the monopoly of violence; and what insights can feminist collaboration organising and activism offer to prevent and end violence; how can this same feminist activism help to support lives in war zones and reconstruct and reorder broken communities, and heal individuals and societies, after the deathly destruction?

Mainstream knowledge about war have assumed it is inevitable, claiming that certain protagonists (states and their militaries) have a legitimate monopoly over violence. We have also been told that some (just) wars are necessary for a greater good and for the survival of the human race itself, wars that obliterate destructive forces, evil people and shifting enemies. Feminist research has challenged this view by bringing to light the violence that is structural, silent and often invisible, pervasive and beyond the immediate context. War victories and defeats both unleash more violence than exists in a pre-war scenario, often compounding the problem it sought to solve in the first place. Continuously highlighting this through rigorous and ethical feminist research has driven the point that war is neither a natural outcome of a preordained gender order, where men always make wars (aggressive, militarised masculinity) and women make peace (passive, peaceful femininity), nor always the logical outcome of pre-existing conflicts. The authors in this volume tell us wars can be prevented through consistently questioning their legitimacy and efficacy, through timely interventions by peace-seeking stakeholders, by emphasising generosity as opposed to 'loss of face', by focusing on stories that are backstage and invisible, and by developing alternative vocabularies where war and peace are seen as a mutually sustaining continuum and not as distinct temporal activities where one ceases when the other begins.

In my own work on wars and political violence, over a period of time, I have talked about radical knowledges necessary about war, that can make peace more accessible and democratic. Those who own the war story (usually men, victorious and claiming both moral and material superiority over the vanquished) also get to have the big voice in peace. Alternative storytelling (for example, of women as perpetrators and planners of war; of men as pacifist peace-makers) challenges the gendered order of war, thus rendering the conventional war story non-sustainable and unrepresentative. However, some of us working with postcolonial/decolonial/anti-race feminisms have also cautioned that this alternative storytelling about war cannot be premised on Western ideals and experiences. Promoting Western-style 'gender equality' through conventional institutions, politics and organisations, will not guarantee peace or the absence of violence. Decolonial feminist research demands engagement with and critical scrutiny of gender tropes, including the idea that better representation of women (which women?) automatically challenges gender hierarchies and violent masculinities. Feminists know all too well that 'gender equality' has been the mainstay of colonial civilisational projects and is certainly not a panacea in these times, especially if it becomes the war cry to emancipate women 'out there'.

This thoughtful collection provides an excellent insight into feminist thinking about war and its solutions. The authors not only retell stories about war and warring bodies with empathy, detail and diligence but also highlight the missed opportunities, erasures and silences in dominant war myths. The chapters also, perhaps unintentionally, reflect the anxiety and uncertainty of the times we inhabit, the enclosures we have built around ourselves, the framings which have been hard to reject and the vocabularies in feminist research and writings that we have normalised and accepted without querying further. In that, I wish some of the brilliant minds in this collection had looked beyond the fenced terrains of feminist inquiry around conventional terms: the state and non-state actors, civilian–military relations, international organisations, United Nations Security Council agendas and formal settings of peace. A radical crossing over, swimming against the tide is absolutely necessary in these times, to reclaim feminist curiosity and the spirit of homelessness. Mainstreaming impulses of feminism need to be challenged, and while that may not have been the mandate for this volume, it certainly can serve as the intervention to question feminist framings and terminologies. It is equally important to recognise that feminists are not alone in this struggle to find solutions to war, and we need to join forces with a range of activists and scholars who are engaged in these efforts.

It is important to interrogate how we normalise mainstream narratives and fence knowledge terrains for radical and alternative knowledges to emerge. The step towards this is a self-reflexive critical enquiry about our own situatedness and our privileges in the knowledge systems we seem to legitimise. Russ-Smith in this volume, for example, powerfully reminds us that, 'Non-Indigenous people must critically reflect, unpack and address their privilege and colonial legacies in order to even begin a process of decolonisation. This process is unsettling.... It is meant to be unsettling.' This can be the starting point we all need because when feminism gets all too comfortable, and loses its capacity to unsettle, our storytelling becomes predictable. We focus on perhaps forgotten characters, but not the circumstances that enable the gendered politics around these characters. A transformative storytelling would involve an unsettling of the self, a querying of privileges we carry, including the privilege of storytelling as academics, researchers and activists. As feminists we must get used to that position of discomfort, unsettling and annoyance. We are not in the business of pleasing the world out there, agreeing with established wisdom, borrowing the terms of reference from given knowledges. We have thrived only because we have created our unconventional frames of analysis and provided avant-garde visions. The comfort of our feminism needs to be unsettled.

Feminists know that in victory and in defeat, war produces the same results. During reflective moments and self-doubt that are so frequent for those of us studying war and peace, I turn to the Mahabharata (Great War), the popular epic from India. Several retellings of this ancient and highly complex war story exist in the popular domain, and the characters involved have been discussed at length. The war in this story lasts only for 18 days, whereas the story itself revolves around the lives of the protagonists entwined with ancestral and intergenerational politics across a few hundred years. The events leading to the war and the overtures of peace are significant. A feminist re-reading would suggest that unbridled patriarchal aspirations, militarism of the times and not paying attention to complex gendered relations breeds a culture of violence. The 'Great War' was avoidable and the text itself, the conversations that Krishna (God incarnate) has with both warring sides (Pandavas and Kauravas, who were also related in a kinship) as a mediator, includes advocating for peace, generosity and justice. Krishna's messages were subtle but important: there are no sides in war, all have something to lose; no war is completely ethical in its methods and moral in its outcomes; war is never the only solution to injustices, ambitions and aspirational masculinities. It is important to remember that Krishna does not choose battlefield bravery for himself always, preferring to be called *Ranchhor* or 'one who abandons the battlefield'. The feminist Mahabharat, thus, tells us that war is not a virtuous encounter between equal adversaries, it is entirely avoidable through empathy and peaceful reasoning, and ultimately there are no moral victories. For me, this is a peace story as much as a war one.

So, then, what is my take-away from this rich volume? That feminists do not have one or more solutions to war, feminist critical thinking and unsettling *is* the solution as the chapters in this book impressively convey. This is an uplifting and thought-provoking contribution in times when we are witnessing multiple kinds of wars, along with a global backlash against feminist thinking and gender activism. The ideas here leave us inspired as we bear witness to this risk-taking intellectual collaboration. The book does not answer all the questions and neither does it pretend to fulfil all its promises, but then, conversations have just begun …

In closing, it would be wise to remember these words of the Indian poet of radical ideas, Sahir Ludhianvi.

Jang to khud hi ek maslaa hai,
Jang kyaa maslon ka hal degi;
Aag aur khoon aaj bakhshegi,
Bhookh aur ehtiyaaj kal degi.

War is itself a problem,
It isn't the solution to any problem;
Today it will offer fire and blood,
And deliver hunger and want tomorrow.

Introduction to Feminist Solutions for Ending War

Megan MacKenzie and Nicole Wegner

War is studied within a range of academic subfields and commented on by endless policy experts and analysists. What unifies much of this work is that it is grounded in an implicit assumption that war is inevitable and a permanent part of global relations. The goals of much of war studies seem to be to predict, quantify effects and costs, scrutinise and improve military strategy, and measure power gains and losses. We treat this approach to war as a problem with serious global implications. We argue that if the study of war does not question the utility of war, and is largely absent of any attention or commitment to limiting and ending war, then such work can, and does, entrench ideas of war and militarism as normal and acceptable parts of social and political life.

Our solution to this problem is to draw on experts from around the world to explore feminist solutions for ending war. What we offer in this book is hope in the form of tools for reconceptualising war and imagining a world without it. As we explain in greater detail below, the focus is on feminist solutions because, drawing on the work of bell hooks, we understand war to be a complex failure that is the product of an international system shaped by patriarchy, militarism, white supremacy and capitalism. As a result, feminist solutions that acknowledge and address this complexity are required.

This book started from a desire to face the complexity of war with a sense of hope and a vision that peace is possible. After teaching and researching war and security for over a decade, I (Megan) felt it was necessary to regroup and try different approaches to studying war in order to avoid overwhelming myself and my students. While teaching issues like rape in war, I would inevitably see students almost physically lean back as they became overwhelmed by the magnitude of the issues and the seeming lack of any pathway forward. In 2018 I hosted a small workshop entitled Feminist Solutions to Ending War and organised a senior undergraduate unit with the same title. The intent of both was to centre feminist solutions in our analysis of war. There was a commitment not to be simplistic or delusional in the quest for solutions, but to keep the attention on solutions even while acknowledging the complexity of war. Students and scholars seemed to embrace this approach and the conversations that were generated in this class and at the initial workshop continued. In 2019 we (Nicole and Megan) began working together and we were united in our unabashed commitment to doing work and generating conversations aimed at ending war. This book is a product of that commitment.

This book is also a product of the context and time in which it was written. While we understand that global politics is never dull, the time during which we were writing and editing this volume was shaped by events that were repeatedly described as 'unprecedented' and historic. As the authors were completing their chapters, vast swaths of Australian land were ravaged by bushfires, producing toxic air in most major cities, displacing 18,000 Australians and killing nearly half a billion animals. The World Health Organization declared a global pandemic, as the SARS-COV-2 'coronavirus' spread rapidly throughout the world, resulting in the deaths of nearly 2 million individuals (at the time of writing). The virus has laid bare global racism and inequality, the impacts of weak and underfunded social and health services, with black and marginalized communities at increased fatal risks from the virus.

While the virus spread rapidly across the world, in the United States, George Floyd, an unarmed Black man, was asphyxiated by four police officers in Minneapolis, Minnesota, prompting national and international protests, many met by brutal militarised state security responses. Black Lives Matter and other anti-racist movements pointed to the legacy of police killing and brutality towards black men and women in the US and Canada, including the recent deaths of Regis Korchinski-Paquet, Breonna Taylor and Rodney Levi. Similar violent force in the past year was used against civilian protesters at anti-authoritarian rallies in Hong Kong, Algeria, Iraq, Bolivia, India, Nicaragua and Russia. Detailed claims of Australian soldiers killing

Afghan civilians have surfaced. Military forces and militarised police forces have been used against civilians around the world and billions dedicated to military budgets, even as nations struggle to provide adequate medical resources to civilians in a global pandemic. Media images have shown nurses around the world wearing garbage bags as personal protection gowns and face masks they have reused or bought themselves while military and police forces show up to civilian protests with gas masks and shields.

As editors, we recognise that these events inevitably shaped why and how we wrote this book, and that we have experienced and witnessed them from a place of extreme privilege. We edited the book with a commitment to feminist politics and ethics. Given the global circumstances, we were aware that authors wrote their chapters while dealing with multiple pressures, including caring for and worrying about loved ones, home schooling children, and facing illness and unemployment. Feminist methods and ethics required us to acknowledge these circumstances and adjust our editorial practices, which included checking in with authors regularly, shifting deadlines, and offering different types of support to ensure that the chapters were not an additional burden during an already intense time. We tried to ensure that the process of writing this book, even in light of a pandemic, could be inspiring and supportive. In many of the conversations we had during this time, authors expressed a revived commitment to this book, and told us that in the current context, bold feminist solutions for ending war seem more important than ever. We agree.

Although this book was written at a time of intense global insecurity and uncertainty, it is grounded in hope. We seek to look boldly at the world and not simply critique what is, but propose what *could be*. This book aims to offer pathways forward to a more peaceful and equitable world. What we advance in this book are solutions (broadly conceived) for ending war and promoting sustainable peace. The purpose of the book is to inspire readers to consider the possibility of life without war and political violence, and to engage with a number of possible pathways to peace. It also asks readers to rethink what constitutes war and what peace is and how we can attain it.

This book does not rely on a single definition or ideal of feminism. Nor is feminism merely used to critique mainstream scholarship or accounts of war and political violence. In short, this is not a book promising peace if we just 'add' women. Instead, in each chapter the authors draw on their own expertise and experience to offer unique definitions and theorising of feminism and war, which shape their unique solution to ending war and political violence. These solutions include economic restructuring, arms abolition, centring Indigenous knowledge, memorialising war differently and incorporating the voices of diverse actors in seeking strategies for ending war. Ending war requires challenging complex structures, but the solutions found in this edition have risen to this challenge.

In addition to answering the overarching question, 'How can we end war?', some of the sub-questions that the book will address include: How might the stories we tell about war perpetuate or prevent it? What can we learn from feminist activism and feminist theory in order to prevent war and violence in the future? What are the obstacles to preventing war and violence and what signs exist that feminist work can remove or overcome these obstacles?

In this introduction, we do not present an extensive summary of each of the chapters. It would be difficult to provide a summary that would do justice to the richness of the chapters and we want to let the authors speak for themselves. In the remainder of the chapter, we outline the understanding of 'feminism', 'ending', 'war' and 'solution' that influenced our approach to editing this book. We also highlight the ways that contributing authors offer distinct understandings and theorisations of these same concepts. We encourage readers to engage with the diverse theories, definitions and solutions offered in the chapters that follow and consider the ways that the solutions might be complementary, overlapping and opposing.

WHAT DO WE MEAN BY 'FEMINIST'?

Feminists have long theorised the connections of gender and war, outlining how multiple relations of power are reproduced through war. They have also studied how the effects of war are intensely shaped by gender, race and class, with impacts that extend long into the so-called post-war periods. How individuals experience war, whether they might support or oppose war, and how they manage to survive and thrive in the 'post-war' period are shaped by gender, race, class and location. The contributors to this volume offer solutions that draw from a range of feminist, queer, Indigenous, and postcolonial theories. While we acknowledge and value the diverse understandings of feminism offered by the authors of this volume, it is important to clarify the approach to feminism that grounded our thinking in putting together the book.

We draw on bell hooks' definition of feminism, and her approach to addressing the connections between patriarchy, white supremacy, capitalism and militarism. bell hooks describes feminism as 'a movement to end sexism, sexist exploitation, and oppression' (2014, 1). Throughout her work, she discusses 'white supremacist capitalist patriarchy' and uses the phrase 'to remind us continually of the inter-locking systems of domination that define our reality' (1997, 7). For hooks, it is impossible and futile to study militarism in isolation from patriarchy, racism, and capitalism because they all 'function simul-taneously' (1997, 7). This aligns with Carol P. Christ's work, which treats patriarchy as an 'integral system created at the intersection of the control of women, private property, and war – which sanctions and celebrates violence, conquest, rape, looting, exploitation of resources, and the taking of slaves' (Christ 2016, 216). Similarly Johan Galtung declared 'the liberation of all oppressed peoples necessitates the destruction of the political-economic systems of capitalism and imperialism as well as patriarchy' (cited in Combahee River Collective 1977). Rather than treating war as a confined political event that can be observed, predicted and studied in isolation, these approaches situate war within a complex system of patriarchy, white supremacy, capitalism and militarism.

This understanding of feminism and the demand to consider these interlocking forms of oppression requires a departure from simplistic ideas that adding women to the study, practice, or analysis of war will necessarily lead to more peace. We do not believe that 'adding women and stirring' is sufficient to disrupt the interlocking systems of oppression and exploitation that perpetuate conflict and warfare across the globe. Women participate in, support, and benefit from war and militarism in ways that some feminist peace scholarship does not acknowledge or account for. Assuming that electing more women, hiring more female soldiers, or generating a female-led foreign policy will lead to peace not only perpetuates a simplistic and binary understanding of women as inherently peaceful but also mystifies the ways that women contribute to current forms of war and militarism. Again, we draw on hooks, who disputes the assumption that women are agentless, and therefore inherently peaceful:

> In keeping with sexist thinking, women are described as objects rather than subjects. We are depicted not as laborers and activists who, like men, make political choices, but as passive observers who have taken no responsibility for actively maintaining and perpetuating the current value system of our society which privileges violence and domination as the most effective tool of coercive control in human interaction, a society whose value systems advocate and promote war. (1995, 60)

We believe that feminist solutions for ending war must acknowledge the ways that women – particularly white women in positions of power – have benefited from war, imperialism and militarism.

Just as it is simplistic to assume that 'adding more women' will lead to peace, we do not assume that men are the sole source of war and militarism. While many acts of war and practices that perpetuate insecurity are led by men, we agree with hooks that 'all men do not glory in war, that all men who fight in wars do not necessarily believe that wars are just, that men are not inherently capable of killing or that militarism is the only possible means of safety' (hooks 1995, 59). Feminist solutions for ending war must consider the ways that war and militarism create conditions in which some men – particularly Brown and Black men – are treated as inherent threats and whose death and harm are all too often treated as inevitable if unfortunate 'collateral damage' to security operations.

Moving beyond an understanding of war as 'man made' and solvable by 'more women' opens space for the types of complex and hopeful solutions to ending war we seek. If war is understood as a practice embedded in patriarchy, white supremacy, capitalism

Introduction

and militarism, complex solutions are required to end war. It first
requires that we rethink the inevitability and utility of war as well as
the ways that war is an extension of the everyday forms of violence
that have become acceptable and normalised in society. hooks makes
clear how her approach to feminism requires radical rethinking and
radical solutions to ending war and militarism: 'to fight militarism
we must resist the socialisation and brainwashing in our children that
teaches passive acceptance of violence in daily life, that teaches us
we can eliminate violence with violence ...' (1995, 63). In addition,
resisting war is not simply about condemning military operations.
It requires that we take a close look at our own complicity in global
practices that perpetuate the strong hold of militarism, capitalism,
and colonialism. For example, white bourgeois women in the United
States often benefit from imperialist conquest as consumers of widely
available cheap commercial goods. Ending militarism requires
examining our consumption patterns and then actively working
towards wealth redistribution. Cynthia Enloe's (2004) examination of the militarisation of sneakers and the processes that lead to
'cheap labour' in many global factories reminds us that capitalism,
imperialism, and militarism work in tandem, even outside spaces we
consider to be 'war zones'. Women who oppose militarism must be
willing to withdraw all support for war, 'knowing full well that such
withdrawal necessarily begins with a transformation in our psyches,
one that changes our passive acceptance of violence as a means of
social control into active resistance' (hooks 1995, 63–4).

While reading this book, we encourage readers to consider the
various ways that feminism is defined and theorised in this book. For
example, in chapter 3, scholar and activist Sarai Aharoni maps both
the power and perils of feminist peace activism. Aharoni distinguishes
between 'women's politics' and 'feminist politics', explaining that
there is no inherent 'peaceful' nature of women that motivates them
to organise, but that lived realities have certainly influenced women's
desire to seek alternative politics focused on peace. Aharoni shows
that disagreements and failures can be productive and highlights
ways that women peace organisers can create meaningful space for
self-care and solidarity in their challenging work. In chapter 2, Heidi
Hudson bridges a feminist ethics of care with African Ubuntu-inspired

7

feminisms to advocate taking collective responsibility for war. Rather than essentialising gendered roles or simplifying Ubuntu philosophy, Hudson demonstrates how mutual responsibility is a practice for all genders in creating conditions for peace and for ending conflict.

For some authors, the value or role of feminism is questioned in their solutions to end war. For example, in chapter 1 Jess Russ-Smith opens with an Indigenous vision of war and peace as a Wiradyuri woman. She challenges settler futurity and the idea that colonial dominance is inevitable. Russ-Smith centres Indigenous knowledge as a cosmology, not a 'tool' or 'lens' for Western feminists to engage with superficially. Eda Gunaydin offers another challenge to Western feminism in chapter 5, where she explores jineological theory and practices implemented by Kurdish women's liberation movements in her chapter. Gunaydin argues that Kurdish women articulate a feminism that is radically different from Western feminisms, particularly in the emphasis on anarchist and anti-capitalist ideals. In chapter 6, Cai Wilkinson acknowledges the tensions between queer and feminist theory and praxis, and offers a queer analysis of security practices. Drawing on examples and powerful testimonials, Wilkinson shows the ways that queer visions of security trouble the assumption of 'peaceful' and 'secure' everyday spaces such as border crossings, public bathrooms, and bedrooms.

WHAT DO WE MEAN BY 'WAR'?

Just as the chapters do not offer a unified definition of feminism, they also do not offer a singular conception of what constitutes 'war' or peace. As editors, we aim to identify common-sense ideas about war that persist in many Western societies, including that war is an inevitable, temporal, necessary political act. We ask readers to consider the politics of such mythologised ideas. We reject commonly held ideas about war, including the concept of war as politics by other means. We dispute that war is necessary, brave, useful. We reject the notion that war is always a final resort, after all other political options have been exhausted. In creating our own definition of war, we draw on Carolyn Nordstrom's (2004) approach to war as a complex and expansive political process, and her concept of 'vanishing points'. She defines vanishing points as 'the points where the normative (what should be) intersects with reality (what actually is)'. She goes on to argue that research on war:

> should illuminate both sides of this intersection: the ideals we hold as a society and the unfolding realities as people live them, regardless of how they might contradict our stated laws and values. In point of fact, research may uphold a division that considers only the normative, as if it were reality. That which contradicts normative ideals is ignored, and becomes invisible to formal analysis. (Nordstrom 2004, 163)

Vanishing points can be re-illuminated when we explore myths about war. These myths can be disrupted by using more complex definitions of war and violence, by speaking to different people with varied experiences about war, and by asking different questions about war.

Drawing from Nordstrom and hooks, we define war as a complex failure shaped by patriarchy, militarism, capitalism and white supremacy. War is a complex failure because war rarely achieves the political outcome for which it was declared, and the effects of war are unbounded and endlessly destructive. War is a complex failure because, rather than a calculated last resort, war is often hasty and reactionary. War is a career choice, a multi-billion-dollar industry, and a never-ending series of policies. War is a complex failure of human ethical and moral commitments to each other. War is a complex failure to create political solutions that would enhance the capacity for humans and animal species not only to thrive and survive, but also to live in a safe environment that is protected and respected. War is a complex failure situated within, and a product of, a patriarchal, white supremacist, capitalist and militarist system. Any solution to war must acknowledge and address this complexity.

In addition to naming war as a complex failure and rejecting key myths of war, we reject the idea of the unknowability of war. We reject the assumption that civilians must commit unrestricted support for war and soldiers in exchange for their presumed ignorance of the pain of war. It may be true that most Western citizens do not know the details of the activities done in their name in wars and occupation overseas, but civilians in war zones *know* war, they experience it and have knowledge about war that matters. When war is treated as a political operation led by militaries, soldier experiences are fetishised and presumed to be the primary means to know and understand war. Furthermore, the public understands soldier experiences to be 'off limits' and private, largely as a result of gendered norms. 'Good soldiers' are constituted as stoic hyper-masculine heroes who should keep their stories and trauma deep within. At the same time, civilian experiences of war and insecurity are often cast as 'anecdotes' or context to war, rather than constituting a valid account of war.

We reject the idea that individual experiences of war are simply anecdotes to be superseded by data on civilian casualties, military budgets, and statistics. Stories and context matter. Solutions to war must account for these stories in order to address the complexity of war, and to acknowledge the experience of war. Such solutions will be radically different from current military strategies, which prioritise vague and technocratic plans of coercive credibility, balance of power, strategic defence, and mutually assured destruction. These strategies sustain war; they are not solutions and ways to peace.

We encourage readers to consider the implications of treating war as a complex failure. We also encourage readers to map the varying and complex definitions of war offered in this text. In chapter 7, Ray Acheson reminds us of the ever-present war that centres around the production of nuclear weapons and the metaphorical and physical violence associated with nuclear bombs and the nuclear industry. Nuclear war is not only the exchange of missiles but also a conflict over whose opinions, knowledges and experiences are credible in discussing the bomb. Acheson explains that current patriarchal, capitalist, militarist and colonialist systems are sustained in discourse on nuclear weapons. In chapter 1, Jess Russ-Smith focuses on 'war on Country', or the long-standing political project to colonise and erase Indigenous peoples and their ways of knowing and being. Her conceptualisation of war breaks open traditional notions of war as combat between two uniformed institutions and helps us to recognise the ways that Indigenous lives have been subject to martial control. War, for Indigenous peoples, is ongoing and relentless. For many

Indigenous communities, the ongoing forms of everyday violence on people and country constitute war. In chapter 8, Yolande Bouka also considers war and intervention as extensions of colonial and imperial violence. Drawing on Black Feminist and anti-colonial thought, she asks readers to 'reimagine the world as one where Black and Brown people's lives matter', and argues that considering the experiences of Black and Brown people – particularly women – would fundamentally challenge global justifications for war and intervention.

WHAT DO WE MEAN BY 'ENDING'?

Feminists have long been critical of the temporality of wars and the assumption that peace 'happens' when formal war fighting stops. Ending wars, understood as complex failures, requires thinking outside the 'official' delineations of fighting and considering the ways that war and violence seep into the everyday. Ending war asks that we consider what is left in the rubble of violent practices and how to move forward from the ashes. In chapter 9, Sertan Saral considers the ways that the ends of wars have been memorialised and how these memorials serve to romanticise the war period while simultaneously erasing colonial violence on the lands in which the memorials are built. In chapter 10, Roxani Krystalli considers experiences of former female combatants in Colombia and the challenges they face in times of 'peace'. For many of her interlocutors, war was not a traumatic black-box experience, but provided opportunities for friendship, meaning and authority. She considers the effects of 'ending' war on these women and their identity.

Imagining a world without war creates space for considering radically different ways of organising society. Rather than strategising about the cessation of formal wars, in chapter 11 Keina Yoshida proposes living in harmony with nature as a solution for peace. Yoshida suggests that the destruction of nature is a root cause and catalyst of many wars; therefore, to end war we must end the ecological domination and destruction of nature and reconceptualise our relationship to land, forests, rivers and oceans. In chapter 12, Carol Cohn and Claire Duncanson challenge the sustainability of ending war without adequate economic planning for peace. Cohn and Duncanson outline the relationship between capitalism and war and see post-war contexts as windows of opportunity in which new economies of care and ecological sustainability can ensure meaningful and sustainable peace.

WHAT DO WE MEAN BY 'SOLUTIONS'?

Our understanding of feminism and war demands solutions for ending war that are complex, comprehensive and interested not only in silencing guns, but in dismantling wider systems of oppression that limit people's everyday security and sense of health and serenity. We are particularly interested in solutions that embrace the notion of sharing responsibility, power, and accountability with regard to ending war. Feminists have long understood that peace is more than the cessation of 'official' fighting. For many feminists, peace involves dismantling interconnected systems of patriarchy, colonialism, racism, capitalism, nationalism – recognising that these hierarchical structures work in tandem in perpetuating exploitation that underpins global conflict. Dismantling these systems is a tall order. As Laura Shepherd reminds us in chapter 14: 'Preventing violence is complex, ending war much more so.' Therefore, in the chapters to follow, the authors offer various tangible solutions to addressing the complex and interconnected challenges associated with war and political violence. These solutions are sometimes complementary and sometimes competing. For example, some authors emphasise a strong role for the state, while others suggest dismantling state structures. We embrace the diversity of these solutions and encourage readers to consider what approaches they can envision and if, whether and how they might consider incorporating these solutions into their everyday practice.

The contributors to this volume offer a range of important solutions for ending war, and also explore the potential benefits of, and limitations to, these proposed solutions. For example, in chapter 14 Laura Shepherd offers a seemingly simple, yet profound solution to war: listen to women. Outlining the politics of the Women, Peace, and Security agenda of the United Nations, Shepherd demonstrates how women can offer unique solutions to war from their historical knowledges about war and peace, their historical practices involving peace organisation, and their ongoing practices of making connections across complex areas and geographical distances. In chapter 13, Thomas Gregory offers a solution that challenges how war casualties are counted. Demystifying the concept of 'collateral damage', Gregory demands we consider not the quantitative human costs of war, but the qualitative experiences of those touched by it. In chapter 4, Diksha Poddar and Shweta Singh challenge the notion of 'solutions' and argue that learning the contextual complexities of localised conflict is key to understanding how conflict can be ended and peace can be fostered. They resist the notion of universal 'solutions' to ending war and instead urge us to focus our attentions on quotidian practices, such as education for peace as a pathway to ending war.

CONCLUSION

There are several overarching themes that run through this edited collection. The first is the finding that women and marginalised people and communities have unique lived experiences in relation to war and violence. These experiences are often ignored, erased, or unaccounted for in descriptions of war and insecurity, as well as efforts to reduce war and political violence. These knowledges and lived experiences should be reflected on and taken seriously if we seek to promote sustainable and wholistic peace. The second theme of this volume is the conclusion that ending war requires much more than examining violence against 'women' or exposing gender inequalities. Several chapters consider structures that underpin the processes of war and violence and hinder meaningful peace, including issues of colonial oppression, ecological exploitation, heteronormativity and homonormativity, state and nationalist racism. Their authors seem to agree that to end war, we must challenge and dismantle multiple hierarchies. A third theme across chapters involves the practice(s) and ethics of care and caring as central to the human experience. Far from the vapid neoliberal idea of resilience and 'me time', these chapters acknowledge the ways that humans are interdependent in relation to each other and to non-human life in the natural world, despite long-standing onto-epistemological assertions within mainstream IR that actors are rational, individual and self-serving. The chapters in this book demand that our relationships to one another, to our environment, and to our future require that we take seriously practices of relationality and care/community building if we seek to end war for good.

As shown by the contributions in this collection, ending war is no simple task, and it requires hope. Hope is radical. Hope makes space for acknowledging violence and oppression and taking responsibility for a role in transformative change. We hope that you find the following chapters inspire and challenge you. We have found great joy and hope in reading the brilliant contributions to follow and hope that you will too.

REFERENCES

Note: URLs accessed 21 June 2021.

Christ, Carol P. (2016) A new definition of patriarchy: Control of women's sexuality, private property, and war. *Feminist Theology* 24(3): 214–25.

Combahee River Collective (1977) *The Combahee River Collective Statement.* Available at: https://americanstudies.yale.edu/sites/default/files/files/Keyword%20Coalition_Readings.pdf

Enloe, Cynthia (2004) *The Curious Feminist: Searching for Women in a New Age of Empire.* Berkeley, CA: University of California Press.

hooks, bell (1995) Feminism and militarism: A comment. *Women's Studies Quarterly* 23(3/4): 58–64

hooks, bell (1997) Cultural criticism and transformation. Media Education Foundation Transcript. Available at: www.mediaed.org/transcripts/bell-hooks-Transcript.pdf

hooks, bell (2014) *Teaching to Transgress: Education as the Practice of Freedom.* Abingdon: Routledge.

Nordstrom, Carolyn (2004) *Shadows of War: Violence, Power, and International Profiteering in the Twenty-first Century.* Berkeley: University of California Press.

1

Giyira: Indigenous Women's Knowing, Being and Doing as a Way to End War on Country

Jessica Russ-Smith

Indigenous knowledges are not a tool of, or for, Western feminism, but are an entire cosmology that produces radically different ways of thinking, writing, and understanding war and violence. Given that this chapter draws on Indigenous knowledge, readers should expect to be challenged by what will inevitably be unique ways of phrasing the problem of war and the potential for solutions. For example, for reasons I will elaborate, I focus on 'war on Country' to capture the ways that colonial violence has continued to impact Indigenous peoples and Country, and as a Wiradyuri woman I centre Wiradyuri women's knowledge and teachings as a pathway toward peace and survival. Specifically, this chapter explores Wiradyuri ways of knowing, being and doing as an Indigenous feminist solution to ending the war on Country. It is imperative to understand that Indigenous knowledges cannot be owned, nor should they be expected to be fitted and edited in ways that fit Western models and expectations. Indigenous knowledge has potential for shaping and influencing peace solutions and for understanding how to end the colonial war on Country that Indigenous people and land continue to be subjected to.

This chapter aims to explore these ideas through discussion of the following core themes: colonisation as an act of war, decolonisation, white possessive logics and futurities as violence, Indigenous futures and giyira. This chapter will be using the 2019–20 Australian bushfires to further illustrate the key arguments. These fires are a war on

Country and an act of colonial violence based upon colonial relationships to land. Colonial relationships to land reflect possessive logics of ownership and use of land as a commodity (Moreton-Robinson 2015), which vary significantly from Indigenous relationships of care and love of Country. Australian politics and society have long ignored Indigenous knowledges and relationships to land. This active ignorance and exercise of white colonial power have led to more intense violations of Country, including catastrophic fires.

For Indigenous people, Country is all things. It is the land, water, people, animals, ancestors, stories, songlines and sovereignty. I am a Wiradyuri woman from the Wambuul (commonly known as the Macquarie River in New South Wales, Australia), and my positioning and experience as a Wiradyuri woman is central to the core themes discussed below. This chapter is centred around the Wiradyuri concept of 'giyira' which means womb and future (Grant Snr and Rudder 2018). Giyira illustrates the ways that our past, present, and future are connected. This concept is useful for exploring the ways that solutions to war on Country require attention to past, present, and future violence, as well as commitment to future Indigenous communities and respect for past and present knowledges. Through a Wiradyuri yinna (woman's) lens, the war on Country will be explored to propose ways through which we can weave peace within our ways of knowing, being and doing which will directly impact our future generations. I use the terms 'knowing, being and doing' together to reflect the ways that Indigenous cultures insist on a deep connection between knowledge, identity, and praxis (Moreton-Robinson 2015). Colonialism continues to cause great wounding and violence across many spaces and Indigenous knowledges.

Central to this discussion is the idea that Indigenous and Wiradyuri women's ways of knowing, being and doing require us to think differently about time and place. Western and dominant understandings of time and place reflect colonial logics of power and ownership that directly affect ways of knowing, being and doing in relation to Country. If we want peace in the future, we need to think about past and present violences and their legacies and acknowledge the importance of Indigenous knowledges as key to weaving a future of peace. The acknowledgement of, and respectful engagement with,

Indigenous knowledges must be central to efforts to sustainable processes of peace-building (Adeogun and Muthuki 2017). Through the exploration of grandmother and granddaughter relationships that are significant to Wiradyuri way of life, I propose ways through which colonial violences of land can be transformed. Wiradyuri women and our wombs are the grass we use to weave, and the future generations are the baskets, the transformations of our weaving.

Relationships are fundamental to Indigenous cultures. Within Wiradyuri culture, and many Indigenous cultures, women play an important role in these relationships. Wiradyuri way tells us that the relationship between grandmother and granddaughter is of unique significance. Through our grandmothers we are given and taught our stories, songlines, totems and responsibilities. Grandmothers and granddaughters share an indescribable and intrinsic connection. Wiradyuri ways of knowing through grandmother and granddaughter challenge Western conceptions of time and space. The relationship between grandmother and granddaughter is not solely related to living grandmothers and their living granddaughters, but also relates to the grandmothers and granddaughters that are our ancestors. I am a granddaughter not only to my two biological grandmothers, but to generations of women before me. I am also a grandmother, even though I have not given birth to a child and therefore a granddaughter has not been 'birthed' in a medical sense. Within my womb I hold the ovum of my future children and their children. My body is both grandmother and granddaughter, my body is a space of relationship to future and past. My being is guided by the understanding that I am a grandmother and a granddaughter, that I have responsibility to care for the past and the future. My role in addressing war and violence is embedded within the notion of effecting change beyond my lived life, as I am to live in my present guided by the following question, '*What kind of ancestor do I want to be for my granddaughter?*' This approach to being reflects the importance of future and relationship within our culture. My body symbolises the past and the present, my body is the grass being woven. What is being woven is dependent upon my actions. An absence of action now, or an absence of respect and care in our actions now, feeds the war on Country as it directly impacts the time and space our granddaughters will live in. Therefore, *baladhu giyira, baladhu giyira, I am womb, I am future.*

This chapter presents an Indigenous and radical rethinking of war, violence and peace. So, as the author I invite you to engage with this chapter through deep critical reflection of self, knowledge and learning. Deep critical reflection and listening for Wiradyuri people requires vulnerability, respect and openness. For Wiradyuri people, listening deeply is a central part of our culture that requires continuous self-reflection. A commitment to learning and listening to the ideas expressed in this chapter is also a commitment to respecting self and others. Therefore, this invitation to respectfully engage with these knowledges discussed below is of great importance, as our knowledges cannot be taken out of context and require deep respect. As you read, I encourage you to reflect on the following questions: How can you as a reader reflect upon 'being, knowing and doing' – or the ways that you know, are, and do? How do you think these ways impact how you do or do not engage with Indigenous knowledges respectfully? What does deep listening look like for you?

WAR ON COUNTRY

In Australia we are currently fighting a war that deeply violates the past, present and future. War on Country refers to the colonisation of land and the ongoing colonial practices towards Country. These are extremely violent and require solutions that can save and nurture our future. Colonial understandings see land as a commodity which can be owned, bought, traded, sold, and an object to which any action can be committed if it leads to an economic benefit. This understanding of Country is the foundation of colonial violence, as it sees Country as inferior, voiceless, powerless and therefore an object which can be owned. This colonial logic reflects what Aileen Moreton-Robinson (2015, xii) refers to as white possessive logics: 'White Possessive logics are operationalised within discourses to circulate sets of meanings about ownership of the nation, as part of common-sense knowledge, decision-making, and socially produced conventions.' In contrast to Indigenous relations to Country, settler colonial states, including Australia, see Country as a source of property and capital to own; from this view, Indigenous peoples are seen as an obstacle to settlers' claiming the resources of Country (Tuck and Yang 2012). These white possessive logics of Country are an action of war, as they aim to perpetuate and reinforce colonial and white superiority.

White possessive logics of Country have led to land being used, abused and violated in the name of money and power. These violences include the cutting down of sacred birthing trees for new roads, destroying sacred sites for mining, drilling land for oil, clear-cutting forests for agriculture, and the exploitation of many sacred sites for tourist pleasure, such as climbing Uluru. These weapons of war are carving a grim future, or lack of future, for our future generations of people, animals and plants. Indigenous ways of being, knowing and doing are critical and essential for preserving and caring for our future. For Wiradyuri people, Country is fundamental to our way of life, wellbeing, and future (Green 2018). Country is all living and non-living things; it is our bodies, our relationships, the ancestors, the land, animals and plants. Solving the war on Country is about shifting colonial logics to an understanding that reflects Indigenous ways of knowing, being and doing, which emphasise being in a relationship to, with and through Country. Indigenous peoples' relational being with Country must be acknowledged, nurtured and listened to if we hope for a future.

Towards the end of 2019, multiple catastrophic fires began burning across various areas of Australia; these were the frontiers of a war on Country. The fires have killed or displaced over 3 billion animals, with some native species potentially extinct, and unprecedented heat waves and fires continue into 2020 and 2021 (Australian Parliamentary House 2020; UN Environment Programme 2020). Country, homes, animals and people have been destroyed by the force and violence of the fires. These fires in Australia are one army of colonial violence and settler futurity, that is, logics that sustain settler power and bodies while attempting to erase Indigenous people and Country. Fires are burning, destroying and erupting upon Country. The fire is not a metaphor for colonial violence or war. It *is* colonial violence. It *is* war. The perspective I am presenting here is that fire is a multidimensional being that can have its own agency and can be used, or misused, within relationships of power. Culturally, fire holds great significance in sacred practices. This is sacred knowledge and therefore further details cannot and will not be shared in this context, but is important to note that Indigenous peoples have deep knowledge and a series of practices associated with fire that have been repeatedly marginalised and ignored by Australian governments and society. In relation to colonial violence, fire has been used as weapon to exert power, and therefore fire is also an extension of colonial policies that have been attempting to erase Country both literally and metaphorically for centuries. In these contexts, fire is colonial violence as it is part of the colonial relationship to land that reflects possessive and hierarchical logics.

The more of Country that burns, the more colonial violence displaces and dislocates people, animals, plants and Country from one another. As the fire burns, Indigenous people are violently dislocated from our mother and wounded. The fire attempts to erase Country, it erases our ways of being as Indigenous people as we *are* Country. We are not separate beings to Country, nor do we just exist in a relationship to Country. We cannot own Country, because Country is not an object. We cannot possess Country because we do not exist in a relationship of power over Country. We *are* Country. We, as Indigenous people, are an expression and part of Country. The violence of fire does not metaphorically impact Indigenous people, it literally harms us. By us, I do not just mean individuals or communities but also our ancestors, songlines, stories, and futures, all of which are part of our bodies. As the fires burn, salt and acid are poured into the open wound, with violence so deep it makes our ancestors cry. As Indigenous peoples, these cries echo in our bodies.

Historically, colonial war has violently torn through land by invasion in attempt to dislocate Indigenous peoples from the land. The impact of colonial violence in the present does not just impact Indigenous peoples and communities, it re-opens the wounds of past violences as it continues the war on Country, which is a war on Indigenous ways of knowing, being and doing. Therefore, the fires re-open wounds of the past, pulling apart the scars which are on our bodies and skin. Colonial logics and actions such as ignoring Indigenous knowledges, prioritising extraction, and disconnection from land have all fuelled these fires. These fires perpetuate colonial logics that attempt to erase Indigenous sovereignty through erasing Country.

Indigenous peoples' ongoing sovereign relationship to Country may appear threatening to white and non-Indigenous people: it is a reminder that colonists do not in fact own the land, that the land is not to be owned. Our relationship to Country is an embodied relationship that extends beyond space and time. Colonialism has desperately been trying to erase Indigenous relationships with Country through various weapons of war, from massacres in the Australian frontier wars to the destruction of sacred lands and resources for profits, to the forced removal of Indigenous children from their families and Countries, to the contemporary bushfires. The relationship Indigenous people have with Country reminds us that the fire can be resisted and the future can be protected. Indigenous cosmologies resist colonial violence and war, as explored in greater detail below through my analysis of Wiradyuri women's relationships of grandmother and granddaughter. Indigenous ways of knowing, being and doing, can be a way to prevent and heal from colonial violence and nurture the future.

DECOLONISING KNOWLEDGES: SHIFTING FROM SETTLER FUTURITY TO GIYIRA

For Indigenous people the past, present and future are interconnected. Understanding and analysis of the past is crucial for developing meaning and understanding of contemporary contexts and structures. However, discussions of the future are equally as important when attempting to end the war on Country. Core to ending the war on Country is shifting from 'settler futurity' to giyira. This shift involves decolonising and transforming hierarchies of knowledge and examining structures of privilege and power that sustain white/Western knowledges as superior while dismissing Indigenous knowledges. The continuation of dominant discourses and structures, epitomised by white supremacy, that sustain colonial violence will only further place Western systems of knowledge as superior. We cannot continue to position white and Western knowledges as the benchmark system through which peace and solution must be explored. If this hierarchy of knowledge continues, the war on Country will continue and our future is endangered.

Settler futurity refers to a future where settler power and bodies are sustained and preserved, while Indigenous bodies are erased (Baldwin 2012; Tuck and Gatzambide-Fernandez 2013; Goodyear-Kaʻopua 2017). Settler futurity is an understanding of the future as a separate, disembodied and disconnected time and space. It is important to note that settler futurity is not merely an idea or theory, but is an active agent in contemporary and past society. Settler futurity frames Indigenous people and culture as a thing of the past, and therefore positions the future to relate to and centre around settler, colonial and white identities. Settler futurities reassert colonial narratives of Indigenous people as savages and a race that cannot survive time (Goodyear-Kaʻopua 2017). Settler futurities are actioned now in the present in ways that forcibly violate Indigenous relationships with Country in a hope to erase Indigenous people.

The ignorance and neglect of climate change by white politicians and citizens represent settler futurities and are purposeful and strategic actions of the war on Country. The absence of caring for Country in a way that sustains and enriches Country for our grand-daughters and their granddaughters are examples of colonial violence. This inaction does not come from not knowing, but rather a space of knowledge hierarchy that sees Indigenous ways of knowing, being and doing as invalid, wrong and relating to the past. Through the fire, settler futurity aims to erase evidence of Indigenous knowing, being and doing through violently destroying the being that is central to our survival, Country. Indigenous knowledges, and in particular Indigenous women, are key in shifting settler futurity logics and practice; our bodies symbolise Indigenous futurities through giyira. Our bodies resist settler futurity as they loudly and unapologetically protest that Indigenous people are here and will continue to live through our ways of caring for Country. As Goodyear-Kaʻopua (2017, 187) states, 'in many ways the Indigenous person's most powerful weapon against further destructions and exploitation is simply staying and surviving'. Decolonisation is a solution to war; however, it cannot succeed unless Indigenous women, our sovereignty, voices, knowledges and bodies, are central to this transformation.

Discussions about, and solutions to the war on Country cannot be abstract or guided by catch phrases. Decolonisation is not a metaphor, it is a process of continued action. Tuck and Yang assert the dangers in decolonisation being taken as a metaphor:

> When metaphor invades decolonization, it kills the very possibility of decolonization; it re-centres whiteness, it resettles theory, it extends innocence to the settler, it entertains a settler future. Decolonize (a verb) and decolonization (a noun) cannot easily be grafted onto pre-existing discourses/frameworks, even if they are critical, even if they are anti-racist, even if they are justice frameworks. The easy absorption, adoption, and transposing of decolonization is yet another form of settler appropriation. (Tuck and Yang 2012, 3)

Decolonisation used as a metaphor echoes white supremacist logics as it proposes a white/settler innocence, excusing guilt and responsibility for the actions of war. This can be seen within institutions, including universities, where a wave of energy toward the inclusion of Indigenous people and knowledges has occurred; however, the methods of doing so have often maintained knowledge and racial hierarchies. The inclusion of Indigenous scholars and knowledge has been called an 'addition of diversity' to the dominant white structure (Green et al. 2018). Yet, these 'inclusions' are not genuine actions of justice, rather they are tokenistic, offensive and further the maintenance of colonial power by maintaining existing hierarchies of knowledge. Tuck and Gatzambide-Fernandez (2013, 73) describe this re-inscription of colonial violence by arguing that 'white curriculum scholars re-occupy the "spaces" opened by responses to racism and colonisation in the curriculum, such as multiculturalism and critical race theory, absorbing the knowledge, but once again displacing the bodies out to the margins.'

White and non-Indigenous people must critically reflect, unpack and address their privilege and colonial legacies in order to even begin a process of decolonisation. This process is unsettling (Fanon 1963; Tuck and Yang 2012). It is meant to be unsettling. Decolonisation disrupts space, fuelling discomfort. Decolonisation calls upon each person to be, know and do in a way that unsettles all fibres of their being. Decolonisation calls for us to think of our role to nurture now, like a womb, and to nurture the future for those who will come after us, our future.

CARING FOR COUNTRY: INDIGENOUS FUTURITIES

Indigenous futurities reflect a relationship of care with Country that nurtures our future generations. Through our relationships to, with and through Country, colonial violence and the war on Country can be transformed. Indigenous people believe that the past, present and future are connected. This interrelationship of time differs from Western logics that see time as linear. Indigenous understandings of time and place reflect the notion that all things, past, present, future, living and non-living always exist in relationship. As Bryan Kamaloi Kuwada (cited in Goodyear-Ka'opua 2017, 184) states:

> We are trying to get people back to the right timescale, so that they can understand how they are connected and what is to come … we are operating on geological and genealogical time … The future is a realm we have inhabited for thousands of years.

Indigenous futurities therefore do not signal a new solution to ending war. Instead, they reflect a constant existence that can be engaged with to create safe and healthy Country for our granddaughters and their granddaughters. Indigenous futurities are a conception of the future as a realm that we are already a part of. This links directly to the concept of giyira, which means womb and future, and emphasises the relationship between past, present, and future (Grant Snr and Rudder 2018). Country and our bodies as Indigenous women are the womb, but we are simultaneously the future as it is through the womb that new life is created and nurtured. Therefore, the state of our future depends upon the way in which we treat or mistreat Country now, as the health of the womb determines the health of the future. Colonial violence aims to destroy Country, in turn wounding the womb and wounding the future. Indigenous ways of knowing, being and doing provide space to transform colonial relationships with land, through a culture that is based upon respect, love and care for Country.

Indigenous relations to Country reflect a relationship of connection and deep care. For Wiradyuri people, caring for Country is a part of our culture, as Wiradyuri woman Sue Green (2018, 141) states:

> the role of caring was not just situated with one person and an individual was not seen as being someone who was specially cared for, but rather everyone was cared for and everyone played a role in caring and nurturing the family and community.

Caring for Country in this way presents a powerful solution for ending colonial violence and the war on Country. Indigenous futurities, including giyira, assert our sovereignty as Indigenous people, which shifts dominating colonial discourses about the future (Goodyear-Ka'Opua and Kuwada 2018, 50). Indigenous knowledges, specifically the importance of women and futurity, highlight powerful ways of thinking, being and doing that can end colonial violence and the war on Country.

Giyira, womb and future, is a being and action of past, present and future. This chapter takes particular focus upon the future through a Wiradyuri women's lens. This positionality challenges notions of settler futurity, and emphasises a sovereign, decolonised and Indigenous understanding of future through women and relationships. I argue that, in order to solve the war on Country, we must look to the future through a lens of relationships, as opposed to one of settler futurity. In this context, future refers to our future generations, including our grandchildren, as well as the Country they will be in relationship with. Thus, discussions of giyira pose solutions to ending the war on Country as a collective consciousness of care for all things, including self, people and land, and is critical to the ways we be, know and do now in the present.

GIYIRA: WOMB AND FUTURE – I AM GRANDDAUGHTER, I AM GRANDMOTHER

In Wiradyuri way of life we learn that everything exists in a network of relationships. Through these relationships our ways of being in the world are influenced and transformed. In Wiradyuri culture we understand that relationships create and govern our being and future. As stated by Elder Uncle Stan Grant Snr and Dr Paul Rudder (2018, 8), 'the value of anything is also connected to an understanding of relationships between that item and its relationships, to people, events, [and] places'. In effect, our value and wellbeing as humans can only be seen to be of the same value as Country. If Country is respected and treated with care and love, our bodies too reflect this positive peaceful state. However, if violence and war is perpetrated upon Country, much like the devastating fires in Australia 2019–20, then our bodies too become wounded. Moreover, if our bodies as women become wounded then our future is in jeopardy. My body is future and womb, if my body is unwell, the future is endangered. When Country is harmed by colonial violence and war, our connections to story, history, songlines and being are also harmed. Colonial violence aims to erase Country, and therefore erase Indigenous women's bodies, as we are an extension of Country. Colonial violence aims to maintain and instil white supremacy and colonial legacies for the future. Therefore, Indigenous women and our ways of knowing, being and doing are key to preserving the future, as our bodies resist the power of white supremacy and colonial legacies which are weapons of the war on Country.

Giyira, as an expression of Indigenous futurity, allows for Wiradyuri relations of caring for Country to become embedded into societal discourse, disrupting violence and liberating our future granddaughters. Decolonising and transforming discourses and relationships to Country are key to nurturing and caring for the future. Transforming settler colonial relations to land emphasises the need for reasserting the role of humans as protectors or carers of Country (Goodyear-Kaʻopua 2017). In order to protect our future, we must ensure a future is likely; here the womb plays the most critical role. Giyiria is how Wiradyuri women protect, through our bodies, and ensure that our existence continues. This continuation is not just about the physical existence of our bodies, but rather the powerful message our bodies carry; *we are here, we cannot be erased, our granddaughters are here, our granddaughters cannot be erased*. Through our wombs, the future is here and continues to be nurtured as our future generations and the stories they carry will continue. Our wombs are an act of resistance to colonial violence, giyira is thus a way through which we can end the war on Country.

CONCLUSION

Colonial violence and the war on Country threaten the future. Indigenous ways of knowing, being and doing are the key to transforming violence, ending war on Country, and creating safe space for the future. Settler futurity is a dominant understanding of the future that gains its power through colonial weapons of war and violence actioned in the present. Settler futurity emphasises the erasure of Indigenous people and knowledges, while aiming to ensure a future that benefits white power and ownership over Country. Indigenous ways of knowing, being and doing, in particular Indigenous women, our bodies and knowledges, are key to solving the war on Country. Through the Wiradyuri concept of giyira, the importance of (1) considering the future and (2) our role in nurturing and caring for the present to ensure a safe future is explored. This chapter emphasises the importance of challenging and reconceptualising dominant understandings of time, land and relationships as central to the process of decolonisation. Decolonisation is the solution to war on Country. Shifting from settler futurity to Indigenous futurities expresses the importance of thinking and acting in order to create safety for our granddaughters and future generations. Through the knowing, being and doing of our bodies now we can end the war on Country and ensure a healthy future for our grandchildren. *Baladhu giyira, baladhu giyira. I am womb. I am future.*

REFERENCES

Note: All URLs last accessed May 2020.

Adeogun, T.J. and Muthuki, M.J. (2017) Indigenous approaches to peace building: Examining strategies employed by women in South Sudan. *Gender and Behaviour* 15(3): 9639–9651.

Australian Parliamentary House (2020) 2019–20 Australian bushfires – frequently asked questions: A quick guide. Available at: www.aph.gov.au/

About_Parliament/Parliamentary_Departments/Parliamentary_Library/
pubs/rp/rp1920/Quick_Guides/AustralianBushfires

Baldwin, A. (2012) Whiteness and futurity: Towards a research agenda. *Progress in Human Geography* 36(2): 172–187.

Fanon, F. (1963) *The Wretched of the Earth.* New York: Grove Weidenfeld.

Goodyear-Ka'Opua, N. (2017) Protectors of the future, not protestors of the past: Indigenous Pacific activism and Mauna a Wakea. *South Atlantic Quarterly* 116(1): 184–194.

Goodyear-Ka'Opua, N. and Kuwada, B.R. (2018) Making 'Aha: Independent Hawaiian pasts, presents and futures. *Dædalus, the Journal of the American Academy of Arts & Sciences* 147(2): 49–59.

Grant Snr, S. and Rudder, P. (2018) *A Grammar of Wiradjuri Language,* 2nd edn. Wagga Wagga: Restoration House.

Green, S. (2018) Aboriginal people and caring within a colonised society. In: B. Pease, A. Vreugdenhil and S. Stanford (eds) *Critical Ethics and Care in Social Work: Transforming the Politics and Practices or Caring,* Routledge: New York, pp. 139–147.

Green, S., Russ-Smith, J. and Tynan, L. (2018) 'Claiming the space, creating the future', *Australian Journal of Education* (Special Issue) 63(3): 256–265.

Moreton-Robinson, A. (2015) *The White Possessive: Property, Power and Indigenous Sovereignty.* Minneapolis: University of Minnesota Press.

Tuck, E. and Gaztambide-Fernandez, RA. (2013) 'Curriculum, replacement and settler futurity', *Journal of Curriculum Theorizing* 29(1): 72–89.

Tuck, E. and Yang, K.W. (2012) 'Decolonization is not a metaphor', *Decolonization: Indigeneity, Education & Society* 1(1): 1–40.

United Nations Environment Programme (2020) 'Why Australia's 2019–2020 bushfire season was not normal, in three graphs. Available at: www.unenvironment.org/news-and-stories/story/why-australias-2019-2020-bushfire-season-was-not-normal-three-graphs

2
One for All, All for One: Taking Collective Responsibility for Ending War and Sustaining Peace

Heidi Hudson

The chapter will advocate for feminist principles of solidarity and community that foster collective responsibility for war and peace. It theorises war and peace as a shared activity and responsibility. Despite efforts by critical and feminist scholars in the global North to challenge the narrow framings of (human) security, security discourses and practices continue to reflect individualist, abstract, and rights-based understandings of war and peace. The chapter will therefore consider an endogenous solution to ending war. Communal responsibility for war and peace can shift the focus from which warring parties or powerful individuals are accountable for ending wars. The feminist solutions in this chapter propose that war is an activity that we are all connected to in real ways, and therefore have a mutual responsibility to resist.

The chapter draws on an integrated reading of Ubuntu, African/ Ubuntu feminisms and feminist ethics of care principles. It makes a case for embracing collective responsibility as an integral step in globally ending war. Ubuntu/Ubuntu feminism has emancipatory potential to end war and human insecurity, because, at the epistemological level, it serves as a critique of Western modernity. I present Ubuntu – an African value system(s) and philosophy(s) of personhood – as a means to reconsider contemporary Western and neoliberal visions of peace and security. Ontologically, Ubuntu/ Ubuntu feminism offers practical suggestions to foster friendly and caring relations that have wide relevance for both preventing conflict and reconciling communities after conflict. Extending a normative framework that is based on liberal human rights to include Ubuntu-inspired, African-centred, feminist interpretations of community and human security drives home the recognition that the solution to ending war is not 'out there'; war is not just someone else's problem to solve; we all need to be active, caring participants in bringing about the end of wars.

I start by outlining the contributions of critical and Western feminist scholars to peace and security and highlight how their contributions have opened space for thinking about collective security. These approaches have not succeeded in dislodging the individual from the centre of how war, security and peace are analysed and theorised. In the second section I introduce Ubuntu as an African philosophy, showing how hospitality, identity and solidarity underpin a radical rethinking of who is responsible for war. In the third part, I discuss the peculiar relationship between Ubuntu feminisms and Ubuntu 'proper', showing how Ubuntu feminism amplifies human security. In the fourth section, I map out a related feminist version of human security that revolves around a global ethic of care. Taking the complementarity of Ubuntu, Ubuntu feminism and feminist care ethics into account, the chapter concludes with two elements of this singular solution of taking collective responsibility for ending war – taking collective responsibility for *being hospitable* to others, and from there, taking collective responsibility *to care* for others.

FEMINIST AND OTHER COLLECTIVIST ATTEMPTS TO MOVE FROM WAR TO PEACE

Despite the emergence of a climate of neighbourliness after the end of the Cold War, collective security arrangements have remained largely state-centric and focused on building military confidence, failing to translate collective security into collective responsibility. Human security emerged as policy tool and academic agenda for bottom-up, non-statist thinking about the absence of threat to human life, lifestyle and culture through the fulfilment of basic needs (UNDP 1994).

The global peace movement of the 1980s advocated for thinking about peace and security as an end state of 'one for all, and all for one'. Feminist contributions have moved understandings of collective security closer to collective responsibility by redefining power as 'the ability to act in concert' (Hannah Arendt in Hudson 1998, 73). Collective security is therefore dependent on collective responsibility as the means to prevent war and promote peace/security. Interdependence, mutual enablement and empathy are given preference over masculine-associated autonomy, self-help, individualism and competition. In practice, it requires a collaborative approach where the survival of one depends on the wellbeing of the other, and where collaboration is not motivated by individual interest. The practice of mutuality also requires situated thinking about security in terms of care and everyday concerns, within a particular community, and not in relation to isolated individuals. By deconstructing 'the human' in human security, feminists and critical scholars have challenged the assumed universalism of basic needs of protection ('freedom from fear') and empowerment ('freedom from want'). Yet, feminist human security scholarship has also been criticised for remaining stuck in individualist liberal approaches (Du Plessis 2019, 42).

The strong affinity between human security and human rights partly explains the failure to dislodge the liberal subject. Both human security and human rights speak predominantly to abstract autonomous liberal individuals rather than to communities in context. A case in point is United Nations Security Council Resolution 1325 on Women, Peace and Security, where the liberal pro-women language presumes universal rights rather than rights that are connected to the economic, social and cultural context in which they are claimed. These feminist limitations form part of bigger liberal peace practices such as Disarmament, Demobilisation and Reintegration (DDR) and Security Sector Reform (SSR), which assume a 'one-size-fits-all' set of post-conflict reconstruction initiatives. Similarly, for countries emerging from violent and protracted conflict, elections are rarely an expression of collective responsibility for ending war and sustaining peace, but rather vehicles of heightened competition and conflict.

Despite these shortcomings, and the fact that security scholarship in general has been slow in making a substantive theoretical and empirical connection between collective security and collective responsibility, critical-feminist work has nevertheless created openings for thinking about collective responsibility.

UBUNTU – 'I AM BECAUSE WE ARE'

In light of these remaining limitations, we need alternative, contextualised approaches to pursuing peace and ending wars. One option is to bring largely Western critical-feminist perspectives into conversation with the African philosophy of Ubuntu and African feminisms. When a person is praised as having Ubuntu, it refers to the fact that s/he is generous, hospitable, friendly, caring and compassionate. This particular version of relationality has many dimensions: First, it goes to the heart of what it means to be human, stating that one's humanity is bound up in the humanity of others – 'a person is a person through other people'. Second, shared humanity is grounded in a sense of belonging, or as Archbishop Tutu remarked: 'I am human because I belong, I participate, and I share.' Third, a person with Ubuntu affirms rather than fights others, because there is a sense of belonging 'in a greater whole [which] is diminished when others are ... oppressed' (Murithi 2006, 28).

Restoring harmonious relationships through collective agreement is an ancient worldview (Peacock 2019, 3) not exclusive to Africa, and should therefore not be linked to Africans in an essentialist way as being stereotypically collectivist. Ubuntu is often criticised for its ambiguous nature – its gender-blindness, associating caregiving just with women. While women are celebrated as mothers, they have little decision-making power outside of this private sphere (Manyonganise 2015). And although the philosophy and practice of Ubuntu is contested (Manyonganise 2015), it nevertheless offers a number of tenets that can aid in an understanding of collective responsibility. Two key facets of Ubuntu are relevant for the feminist objective of ending wars. The first is hospitality, or the practice of opening up your home to others. The second tenet concerns the conditions that make such hospitality possible, and revolves around identity – namely how you view yourself in this relationship of caring. In a third tenet, Ubuntu feminism also extends the principles of Ubuntu through a collaborative approach to gender relations. The fourth tenet of Ubuntu feminism relates to transcending gender binaries. In the following section I outline these four tenets of Ubuntu feminism and advocate for *Ubuntu-inspired feminism*. I then link my loosely-defined Ubuntu feminism to the two tenets of an *ethics of care* (its global reach and the salience of dependency) as a means to outline my 'collective responsibility' solution to ending war.

Ubuntu hospitality: Laying the foundation for sharing and caring

The Nguni saying *Siyakwamukela or wamlekile ekhaya* ('you are welcome') captures Ubuntu philosophical connections of hospitality to the idea of sharing. The African saying *izandla ziyagezana* ('hands wash each other') (Chisale 2018, 5) invokes the notion of 'sharing is caring', grounded in the values of co-responsibility for the mutual enjoyment of rights, creating mutual interests and giving mutual satisfaction. This hospitality also extends to the environment, holistically connecting past, present and future, connecting with ancestors in a web of 'ecological togetherness' (Seehawer 2018, 455, 456). Ubuntu can therefore support feminist solutions to ending war because, as a way of thinking, it underpins, for instance, the shared commitment of women's organisations, such as the Foundation for Women Affected by Conflict (FOWAC) in northern Uganda, supporting rape survivors.

Identity, solidarity and humility

What makes such hospitality or sharing possible? It is sustained by three interconnected factors – identity, solidarity and humility. Thaddeus Metz argues that the capacity for community is dependent on the ability to identify with others, and displaying solidarity with them (Metz 2011, 533). But identifying with a group is not enough – there must be an expression of solidarity, a recognition of shared interests and mutual responsibility before care or mutual aid can materialise and produce mutual benefit. Solidarity thus coheres around sympathy for the group or having a genuine interest in each other's wellbeing (Metz 2011, 538). Solidarity means one cares about other people's human security. Ubuntu is also about becoming more fully human, without being selfish (Molefe and Magam 2019, 315–16), knowing full well that this process of becoming is always perpetual. Ubuntu therefore necessitates humility in recognising one's own shortcomings and the need to rely on others. It also underlines that no identity is ever final and is only sustained through relationships with incomplete 'others' (Nyamnjoh 2015, 1–2). And it is therefore through this combination of identity, solidarity and humility that a deep relationality (the musketeer principle) begins to override people's status as discrete individuals compelling them to support one another during times of war.

Living the reality of care and community

African feminisms (Kolawole 2002) arise out of the concrete realities of African women's lives. Their lives are pivoted on daily, gendered practices of responsibility, caregiving and community building during times of war and peace. Fatma Ibnouf (2020), in her study on wartime care work and peace-building in Africa, hones in on the everyday structures that sustain lives during violent armed conflict and, specifically, care work performed by women. She draws attention to the unpaid and less visible care work that women do in conflict and post-conflict/peace-building contexts such as Darfur, western Sudan. It is often forgotten that it is exactly through this role as care workers during conflict that women actually earn their place as valid protagonists in peace-building processes. Most often it is women who take on the responsibility to keep life going (for all) during and after the conflict. There is therefore a direct link between women's responsibilities to care for life and their commitment to end war. This connection is important – not to essentialise women's commitment to peace, but rather to revalue care and peace by making it a collective commitment. Ubuntu-feminist principles of responsibility revolve around the family/community. It is a holistic approach concerned with the wellbeing of the whole community, both male and female. The implications of this are that you cannot end war from a distance through standardised international recipes; experiences of war and conflict are local, immediate and integrally linked to the interdependence of men and women in their social and spatial contexts.

Community and security as inclusive to all genders

African-feminist understandings of social justice contend that social transformation for all can only be achieved through women cooperating with men – not by reversing gender roles (Ogundipe 1994). By extension, ending war becomes a shared responsibility that recognises differential gendered experiences of war, and equally important roles for both men and women in making peace. It recognises how both men and women, through gendered expectations, are responsible for conflict/violence. For instance, in Uganda, masculinity is associated with ownership of cattle, a norm that in the past has driven many men and boys to participate in cattle raiding, which in turn sparked violent conflict between communities. Women also promote conflict by encouraging men to partake in raids. When environmental and economic conditions make some tribes dependent on cattle for their livelihoods, competition increases. Conflict potential is further raised because scarcity of cattle impedes men's ability to pay bride wealth, thereby also affecting their sense of masculinity (Watson et al. 2018).

For collective responsibility across gender divides to take root, we need to first unlearn individualist thinking about what makes us feel (in)secure and then we need to understand that both conflict and peace are influenced by gender norms. For Ubuntu feminism, binary gender separation is not a given; its point of departure is not to reify sexed distinctions, instead offering an opening for thinking about root causes in multidimensional terms that transcend gender stereotypes of peaceful women and violent men.

In practical terms, to sensitise all genders to address the need for security means that women must work *with* men to eradicate the oppression of women through the creation of dialogical spaces between them. Part of this process of affiliation starts with the recognition that men have enjoyed the benefits of the patriarchal dividend at the expense of women. The next 'step' would be for men to recognise that Ubuntu is their construction and that they have defined it in rather narrow terms, thereby marginalising women. This common understanding should then be used as the basis from which notions of community, and gender roles and responsibilities, can be renegotiated.

Whereas the feminist notion of intersectionality (Crenshaw 1991) is constructed around a negative relationality of interlocked oppressions, Ubuntu feminism embodies a positive relationality of shared security and the 'freedom to relate' (Du Plessis 2019, 44). This is a radical departure from the understanding of human security as freedom from want or fear. Conceived as such, Ubuntu feminism offers us an understanding of human intersubjectivity that looks for commonalities across genders instead of looking for sameness with a particular group. This drive to 'reach out' or relate therefore works against seeing all men as violent perpetrators and women as eternal victims (Du Plessis 2019, 44). Ubuntu feminism extends Ubuntu's notion of collective responsibility towards a more inclusive form of relationality where gender is not always primary and sometimes has to subject itself to the bond between men and women against racism, imperialism and war. It is this element of strategic/pragmatic fluidity that imbues Ubuntu feminism with the ability to make ordinary beings engage in 'extraordinary' acts of kindness during conflict. The story of a Sierra Leonean boy soldier who demanded a chicken at gunpoint is a case in point. While he was waiting, the woman of the house gave him a biscuit and water: 'Later my neighbours criticized me for giving him the biscuit. I said I didn't care if he was a rebel or not. He's still somebody's child' (Cockburn 2007, 42).

A GLOBALLY CONNECTED UBUNTU? CARE AS THE ETHICAL AND PRACTICAL BASIS OF HUMAN SECURITY

Although Ubuntu and Ubuntu feminism do not speak directly to human security, their emphasis on care and community may address the gaps within dominant security perspectives in respect of gendered human security. Within state security perspectives, women are subject to biopolitical control of their bodies, sexuality (reproduction) and labour (production) for the benefit of others. In a people-centric approach, a connection is made between women's vulnerability/insecurity and the lack of development, making women the 'faces of development'. A gendered human security is therefore conflated with a women-centric human security, and the woman in question is the bearer of universal rights to protection and empowerment (Du Plessis 2019, 45–7). What is clearly missing from this thinking is the complex and interconnected context within which these individual rights are being exercised or infringed upon, and how this relates to the global context.

In the analysis of Ubuntu and Ubuntu feminisms, I have largely pitched the encounters at the community/local and private level, in the everyday where family, marriage and motherhood enact themselves. But this runs the risk of depicting care as a responsibility that is localised in the home. It is necessary to make more explicit connections with the realm of global security politics. For this purpose, I draw on Fiona Robinson's (2011) theory on the ethics of care related to human security to extend my Ubuntu-feminist approach to war and peace. Her relational ontology approach (similar to Ubuntu) suggests that dependence and interdependence are fundamental to human existence (Robinson 2011, 4). The aim should be to understand the nature of the relationships as well as locating the political, social and economic sources from where the relationships originate. Robinson (2011, 10) argues that relationships of domination and exclusion emanate from existing structures of power and inequality, ranging from local (e.g. the household) to global structures such as the global political economy, and consequently impact directly on the practices of care. Care is therefore not only a private matter confined to the family or local community (as depicted in Ubuntu and Ubuntu feminism respectively) but is also a global political issue that is central to the survival and security of people. How states 'care for' their citizens through decisions about the distribution of resources has a direct impact on human security (Robinson 2011, 3). How families and communities care for one another equally has a direct impact on state security.

Robinson offers insights for understanding *security as dependence*. She maintains that we should rethink dependency:

Our view of security in global politics would change once we recognise and accept not just interdependence among states but the ways responsibilities and practices of care grow out of relations of dependence and vulnerability among people in the context of complex webs of relations of responsibility. (Robinson 2011, 4)

Similar to Nyamnjoh, Robinson (2011, 11) argues that dependence should not be seen as something that needs to be overcome. It is a 'normal' aspect of human existence and interaction with other vulnerable human beings. These insights should be integrated into security theory in non-paternalistic ways.

With such a radical redefinition of the primacy of dependence, the relational qualities of security come to the fore. These include, first, the understanding that feeling secure has to do with a sense of belonging/attachment and knowing that others are there to provide support (Robinson 2011, 7). Second, the human subjects of human security are understood as 'human-beings-in-relations' (Robinson 2011, 10), who function within networks of shared responsibility. Third, such a relational ontology presumes that human rights are much more powerful if viewed as relational and collective and located within the wider context of care (Robinson 2011, 11–12). In contrast, the dominant human rights perspective of human security focuses on autonomy and individual responsibility. Women as bearers of universal, abstract, inalienable rights and entitlements can only have human security if they are protected and empowered within a context of autonomy. Therefore, under conditions of poverty, a woman's right to independence hinges on the level of protection against threats to personal security (usually by and from men as police, aid workers, fathers, husbands and partners).

Robinson's relational ethic of care theory displays a substantive degree of normative overlap with the epistemologies of Ubuntu and Ubuntu feminisms. But more importantly, it extends the principles of Ubuntu and African feminisms in significant ways by making explicit links between human relations and (human) security, and by recognising the political nature of relationality. Robinson reminds us to think of gendered human security as a deep appreciation of human interdependence, intersubjectivity, connectedness and relationality.

A ROADMAP OF SORTS FOR ACTION

We need to read Ubuntu (as an African philosophy), Ubuntu feminism (as an extension and corrective to Ubuntu) and the theory of a global ethic of care (as a challenge to the co-optation of human security as complementary to state security) in conjunction. In so doing, we can begin to see how the feminist combination of Ubuntu and human security helps us to take seriously collective responsibility, changing the way we understand war and peace-building. Two broad 'solutions' to end war and ensure sustainable peace emerge from an integrated reading of the three perspectives.

Take collective responsibility for ending war and sustaining peace through hospitality

A 'one for all, all for one principle', present in all three above philosophical approaches, advocates that all citizens (global or otherwise) must collectively share the responsibility for ending war. Nyamnjoh (2019, 3) states that being inhospitable is tantamount to declaring war as it rejects the bond of allegiance and solidarity. In this context, hospitality becomes a tool to achieve a sense of collective responsibility, as inspired by Ubuntu, Ubuntu feminism and ethics of care.

Ubuntu offers us a new vocabulary in relation to war. We learn that war, human insecurity and human rights violations constitute grave degradations of people's capacity for hospitality. Deprivations (want) or poverty seriously hinder people's capacity for communal relationships because they deprive them of the ability and dignity to share or take care of others (Hoffmann and Metz 2017, 158, 159). The obverse – peace or freedom – is therefore not about 'freedom from fear or want' (human security speak), or freedom from interference of others (liberal speak) but about interdependence and collective responsibility.

In addition, we learn that offering hospitality to strangers or travellers is a deliberate choice. Ubuntu feminism reminds us that making peace is not an accident, but requires a deliberate intervention or change of heart; for example why women are included and/or excluded from the peace table. In a patriarchal and violent environment, the reality is that women have to be 'invited' by men who display a change of heart, 'allowed in' by men who understand that men and women are collectively responsible for war and for ending it. And then the hard work begins not only to change behaviour but also the gendered norms that drive the behaviour.

Finally, we learn that hospitality involves communal human encounters (Waghid and Smeyers 2012, 15) – relationships of accountability and responsibility. Working from the principle of solidarity, identifying with others and sharing lives of mutuality and reciprocity, Ubuntu offers very particular applications for when war ends. When post-conflict restorative justice processes are instituted, hospitality forms the 'meeting point' where 'the dominant (violent) one [becomes] answerable to the one against whom violence is perpetrated' (Waghid and Smeyers 2012, 14).

To illustrate how collective responsibility might be operationalised, I draw upon a traditional structure of *Inkundla/Lekgotla*, a group mediation and reconciliation forum. This process of conflict resolution, using various stages of collective responsibility, demonstrates how peaceful transition from war into sustainable peace can be 'actioned'. The first stage involves fact-finding where the views of victims, perpetrators and witnesses are heard and perpetrators encouraged to acknowledge responsibility. In stage two, perpetrators are encouraged to demonstrate genuine remorse. During the third stage, perpetrators are encouraged to ask for forgiveness; victims are asked to show mercy. The fourth stage is where the perpetrator is expected to pay an appropriate compensation or reparation for the wrong done; amnesty is granted, but not with impunity; and in the final, the fifth stage, the process is consolidated by encouraging the parties to commit themselves to reconciliation. It is a public participatory process, but also one where there is a public display of support (and communal responsibility) for both victim and perpetrator, who is never alone but always accompanied by family and friends (Murithi 2006, 30–31).

This step of hospitality involves actions of opening up and engagement; inviting parties to your home, the peace summit/*lekgotla*, as opposed to excluding them from such private and public spaces. This provides the foundation for deep care to develop. Collective responsibility conceived as restorative and hospitable can therefore complement the punitive edges of conventional justice.

Take collective responsibility for ending war and sustaining peace through practising a feminist care ethic

The above depiction of reconciliation, however, runs the risk of presenting the process as uncomplicated. This is certainly not the case, as the construction of community solidarity does not take place in a vacuum where individual interest is absent. For this reason, we must include an ethics of care to ensure that the causes of war/conflict are resolved, rather than simply leading to a cessation of armed violence. This involves a community-centred collective understanding of mutual care.

Ubuntu feminism's cooperative stance in relation to men for the sake of the community/family, together with Robinson's elevation of dependence and vulnerability as key to achieving human security force us to think of security in relational terms. As previously discussed, externally imposed solutions such as SSR and DDR often fail because they do not address underlying grievances. Operationalising an ethic of care as a global practice is therefore proposed as a means to move from addressing symptoms of war to root causes. To move beyond abstraction, we need to remember that security threats and root causes are related.

Relations of care are rooted in everyday experiences of (in)security. By introducing human subjectivity and human relations of dependence and vulnerability into human security thinking one begins to see the actual human (and natural environment) entanglements. This relationality expands human security's rights-based focus on discrete individuals who are deemed insecure and unprotected because they do not have rights. We must focus on mutual responsibility for both conflict and peace. In conventional security approaches, we fail to see marginalised groups in society and how relations of power threaten human security (Robinson 2011, 8). An alternative Ubuntu-feminist framing helps us recognise that it involves not only collective responsibility for ending war, but also for creating a peace where community care/hospitality is valued equally, rather than being a task or role of a particular gender.

In this contribution, I proposed to operationalise this ideal through an integrated reading of Ubuntu, Ubuntu feminisms and a feminist global ethic of care for human security (a globally connected version of Ubuntu). Each strand of thought offers a particular piece of the collective responsibility puzzle. By combining the specific insights of Ubuntu on hospitality, Ubuntu feminism on cooperative relations with men/gender relationality, and feminist security theory on its global application, this roadmap or tool provides us with a more textured understanding of gendered human security. A serious engagement with collective responsibility would change the way we understand war, and has implications for peace that we are yet to contemplate fully.

REFERENCES

Chisale, Sinenhlanhla S. (2018) *Ubuntu* as care: Deconstructing the gendered *Ubuntu*. *Verbum et Ecclesia* 39(1): 1–8.

Cockburn, Cynthia (2007) *From Where We Stand: War, Women's Activism and Feminist Analysis.* London: Zed.

Crenshaw, Kimberlé (1991) Mapping the margins: Intersectionality, identity politics and violence against women of color. *Stanford Law Review* 43(6): 1241–1299.

Du Plessis, Gretchen Erika (2019) Gendered human (in)security in South Africa: What can Ubuntu feminism offer? *Acta Academica* 51(2): 41–63.

Hoffmann, Nimi and Metz, Thaddeus (2017) What can the capabilities approach learn from an *Ubuntu* ethic? A relational approach to development theory. *World Development* 97: 153–164.

Hudson, Heidi (1998) A feminist reading of security in Africa. *ISS Monograph Series* 20: 22–98.

Ibnouf, Fatma Osman (2020) *War-time Care Work and Peacebuilding in Africa: The Forgotten One.* New York: Palgrave Macmillan.

Kolawole, Mary M. (2002) Transcending incongruities: Rethinking feminism and the dynamics of identity in Africa. *Agenda* 54: 92–98.

Manyonganise, Molly (2015) Oppressive and liberative: A Zimbabwean woman's reflections on *Ubuntu*. *Verbum et Ecclesia* 36(2): 1–7.

Metz, Thaddeus (2011) *Ubuntu* as a moral theory and human rights in South Africa. *African Human Rights Law Journal* 11: 532–559.

Molefe, Motsamai and Magam, Nolubabalo (2019) What can Ubuntu do? A reflection on African moral theory in light of post-colonial challenges. *Politikon* 46(3): 311–325.

Murithi, Timothy (2006) Practical peacemaking wisdom from Africa: Reflections on Ubuntu. *Journal of Pan African Studies* 1(4): 25–34.

Nyamnjoh, Francis B. (2015) Amos Tutuola and the elusiveness of completeness. *Stichproben. Wiener Zeitschrift für kritische Afrikastudien* 15(29): 1–47.

Nyamnjoh, Francis B. (2019) Ubuntuism and Africa: Actualised, misappropriated, endangered and reappraised. Africa Day Memorial Lecture, 22 May, University of the Free State.

Ogundipe, Molara (1994) *Recreating Ourselves*. Trenton, NJ: Africa World Press.

Peacock, Robert (2019) Overview of concepts in victimology. In: Robert Peacock (ed.), *Victimology in Africa*, 3rd edn. Pretoria: Van Schaik, pp. 3–18.

Robinson, Fiona (2011) *The Ethics of Care: A Feminist Approach to Human Security*. Philadelphia, PA: Temple University Press.

Seehawer, Maren Kristin (2018) Decolonising research in a Sub-Saharan African context: Exploring Ubuntu as a foundation for research methodology, ethics and agenda. *International Journal of Social Research Methodology* 21(4): 453–466.

UNDP (United Nations Development Programme) (1994) *Human Development Report 1994*. New York: Oxford University Press.

Waghid, Yusef and Smeyers, Paul (2012) Reconsidering *Ubuntu*: On the educational potential of a particular ethic of care. *Educational Philosophy and Theory* 44(S2): 6–20.

Watson, Charlotte, Wright, Hannah and Groenewald, Hesta (2018) *Toolkit: Gender Analysis of Conflict*. Available at: www.saferworld.org.uk/resources/publications/1076-gender-analysis-of-conflict (accessed 24 June 2021).

3

Feminist Organising for Peace

Sarai B. Aharoni

This chapter suggests that 'feminist organising for peace' is a feminist response to war and a way to resist violence. In presenting this solution, I engage with research about failed attempts to pursue successful solutions to armed conflict. Despite difficulties in feminist organising to achieve peace arrangements, feminist organising within civil society is a common and necessary reaction to armed violence. Feminist organising offers a practical way for ordinary women to engage in everyday politics and to resist war. Common means for organising include: the physical act of showing up to peace protests, the initiation of street vigils or online activism, and the supply of material aid or emotional support to civilians during war. In long-term conflicts, these acts may transform into local or even international networks, non-governmental organisations (NGOs), or service-oriented institutions. Organising for peace is thus one of the most basic feminist solutions for ending war.

The chapter begins with a brief explanation of feminist peace organising. Next, it explores causes that bring women, mothers and feminists to respond to war. I emphasise the importance of listening to various historical and contemporary narratives of peace activists (Levi-Hazan and Harel-Shalev 2019). These narratives illustrate how women describe personal and collective transformations that are required to resist armed violence and injustice. However, the second part of the chapter complicates peace organising through the concept of 'shadow feminism' and explores the frustration and fatigue expressed by some peace activists. Drawing upon Virginia Woolf's conceptualisation of women's resistance to war as 'outsiders', I demonstrate the fragile wellbeing of activists. Thus, as a feminist solution for ending war, organising for peace not only involves public attempts to resist militarised violence or war, but also requires the creation of feminist spaces where new forms of collective self-care may endure.

WHAT IS DIFFERENT ABOUT FEMINIST PEACE ORGANISING?

Feminist organising against war is both a direct response to violence *and* an attempt to transform deeper social issues that relate to women's rights and wellbeing. In her book, *Maternal Thinking*, first published in 1989, Sara Ruddick (1995) offered an important analytical differentiation between two types of women's political organisations. She identified one type as based on 'women's politics of resistance' and a second type as based on 'feminist politics'. Ruddick's' guidelines for classification are still strikingly relevant for analysing contemporary modes of civil society responses to war.

Ruddick suggested that maternal work and daily tasks of fostering growth in the home and private sphere are relevant for understanding women's responses to global politics, war and injustice. For Ruddick, although mothers 'are not intrinsically peaceful, maternal practice is a "natural resource" for peace politics' (1995, 157). Consequently, *women's politics of resistance* could be identified by three characteristics: 'its participants are women, they explicitly invoke their culture's symbols of femininity, and their purpose is to resist certain practices or policies of their governors' (Ruddick 1995, 222). Indeed, case study research on 20th-century women's grassroots organisations in Argentina, South Africa, Bosnia, Israel, Chechnya, Sri Lanka, Nicaragua and Liberia suggest that Ruddick's observations were correct. In these conflicts, women were politicising their traditional familial roles and using motherhood to mobilise support for peace activism (Kaufman and Williams 2010).

Feminist politics, on the other hand, is used in Ruddick's work to identify 'a politics that is dedicated to transforming those social and domestic arrangements that deliberately or unwittingly penalize women because of their sex' (1995, 234). Although not all women's political movements identify as feminist and not all feminist groups endorse feminine-maternal ideals, these two motivations for action are often interconnected. Feminism, as a movement that aims to change societal perceptions about dominance and inequality, 'shifts the balance within maternal practice from denial to lucid knowledge, from parochialism to awareness of others' suffering, and from compliance to stubborn, decisive capacities to act' (1995, 236).

A decade later, Cynthia Enloe (2000) came to a similar conclusion. Following numerous conversations she had with feminist peace activists around the world, her take was that feminist anti-militarist organising offered local women the possibility to generate knowledge about their own societies as a means to break silence. She writes:

> Feminists from India, Zimbabwe, and Japan to Britain, the United States, Serbia, Chile, South Korea, Palestine, Israel, and Algeria all have found that when they have followed the bread crumbs of privileged masculinity, they have been led time and again not just to the doorstep of the military, but to the threshold of all those social institutions that promote militarization. (2000, 33)

Therefore, while mothers or women may not have an intrinsic drive for activism, the reasons that they often find themselves organising for peace are due to their unique gendered political experiences *as women and mothers*.

Nonetheless, while I appreciate feminist organising as a solution to ending war, I am not uncritical of its actual costs. These concerns echo a postcolonial critique of pragmatic approaches to feminist peace research and the tendency of Western scholars to impose a particular interpretation of 'peace'. The diversity of women's peace initiatives implies that we must pay attention to the 'emic (grounded) understandings of the concept and the everyday negotiations that make life possible within violent torn societies' (Roohi, in Wibben et al. 2018, 91). By listening carefully to the stories of women peace activists, we can learn about the specific institutional choices and the overall challenges of organising and resisting militarism during war.

HOW DO FEMINISTS ORGANISE?

Evidence from various cases suggest that women's activism in times of war often builds on pre-existing contacts, friendships and professional networks. Many times, it starts as a direct response to humanitarian crises and human suffering. This is how Igo Rogova from the Kosovo's Women's Network in Pristina described her group's initial organising process:

> When war started in ex-Yugoslavia, we became part of the regional women's networks that raised their voices against the war and provided help to women and refugees in those very hard times. When the war came to Kosovo, women's rights activists became refugees themselves, but never stopped working with women and for women, this time in refugee camps in Macedonia and Albania. (Barry 2005, 4)

Early phases of organising are often grounded in the material needs and priorities of civilian women and girls. This phase contains a sense of urgency that mobilises women to pursue collective action. As such, women's organisations are on the ground long before international actors arrive and will be there long after they leave, even if their members become victims of the conflict or displaced.

Women's peace organisations, initiatives, dialogue groups or public campaigns vary in their scope, form, size and duration. Some of them are formal institutions while others are grassroots gatherings. Since the 1980s and 1990s, there has been a steady worldwide growth of women's participation in peace activism, which culminated in the formation of transnational network organisations that pushed for and drafted parts of Security Council Resolution 1325 (El-Bushra 2007). Similar to the women who established political parties, international conferences, street rallies and petitions for peace in the early 20th century (Confortini 2012), the surge of these global popular-civic peace movements, many led by women, mothers and feminists, was a form of collective/group organising. Women's organising for peace in this period was related to globalisation and enabled by the growing connections between local women's groups in the decades which followed the signing of the Convention for the Elimination of all forms of Discrimination against Women (CEDAW 1979).

Many women's groups start on the grassroots level and are not part of official state mechanisms. In the early 21st century, NGOs and international non-governmental organisations (INGOs) were the most common institutional forms of women's collective action during and after war (Barry 2005). While initial phases of organisation against war may include flexible and dynamic non-violent resistance through street protests or vigils, over time, NGOs enable more sophisticated structures for communication and build-up. NGOs have often formed when groups become institutionalised and engage in the monitoring and documentation of human rights violations, or when they collaborate to initiate informal dialogue and peace-building efforts, including projects that seek reparations for victims. Peace organising is related to the politics of institutions and the social and economic conditions that enable effective forms of action. As I explain later, these conditions also include emotional attachments that offer possibilities to foster a collective sense of safety and belonging during war.

Advocates of women's transnational organising for peace view it as a pragmatic approach to politics and conflict resolution. Ann Tickner and Jacqui True (2018) argue that women's INGOs and feminist scholars who pushed for the adoption of the Women, Peace and Security (WPS) agenda were followers of the first wave of international feminism in the early 20th century. They identify both periods (post-First World War and post-Cold War) with a liberal-pragmatic position towards the question of women and peace. This pragmatic logic of organising initiatives around WPS perceives the international sphere as a viable alternative to confining gender norms in the national sphere. By supporting local projects that foster dialogue between women from different conflict zones, the logic of transnational feminist solidarity is seen as a way to amplify the voices of political activists, refugees, displaced women and survivors of conflict-related sexual violence (Cockburn 1998; Giles and Hyndman 2004). From this perspective, bringing women's experiences into international policy-making is a liberating path 'to hold states accountable for putting these principles into practice with the ultimate purpose of ending conflict' (Tickner and True 2018, 228).

Transforming women's activism into NGOs may have benefits and limitations that could impact the broader objective of attaining peace. From an institutional perspective, the intense process of transformation from informal groups into formal professional organisations in the fields of peace-building, human rights and women's rights is sometimes referred to as NGOisation (Alvarez 2009). Although NGOs play an important role as transnational normative entrepreneurs (Keck and Sikkink 1999), they have been also criticised for displacing and disciplining grassroots organising and mass social movements (Choudry and Shragge 2011), and for weakening and depoliticising collective struggles for recognition and resources (Jad 2003). Indeed, the effect of global power relations, economic inequality, differences in resources and mobility, as well as the different types of exposure to armed conflict, have influenced the issues and possibilities for local organising (Tripp et al. 2008). The growing access to international funding may result, in certain cases, in a subtle colonial overtone, as international mechanisms to promote the role of women as peace-makers may ignore the long-standing activities of women's organisations working to prevent, assist those affected by and raise awareness of violence against women, torture and rape.

One example of good intentions that have gone wrong is found in the case of Acehnese women's groups in Indonesia that were able to organise two All-Acehnese Women's Peace Forums in 2000 and 2005 with external funding to discuss the ongoing peace talks. Marjaana Jauhola (2016), who followed the history of the Finnish-brokered peace agreement between the Indonesian government and the rebels of the Free Aceh Movement (GAM), argued that 'despite these local peace-building efforts, the results were disappointing, and the peace process legitimated a highly problematic elite-masculinist agenda for the post-conflict reconstruction'. Only one woman, Shadia Marhaban, participated in the actual rounds of negotiations. Marhaban admitted that she was unaware of the importance of including women's rights perspectives at the time and later accused all the negotiating parties of failure to accommodate the concerns of Acehnese women in the post-conflict legal framework, to consider its potential violent consequences for women, or to include redistributive economic measures.

While not all professional NGOs have grassroots origins, these groups have varying degrees of social influence in post-conflict societies (Heideman 2017). In many places, feminist NGOs that work on peace and anti-militarism have managed to promote change by creating spaces for the development of personal and collective capabilities, crafting alternative political visions, and by introducing creative practices to solve conflict-related issues.[1] Indeed, to measure the successes or failures of feminist organising for peace, it is essential to understand the different causes that bring women to publicly resist war and armed conflict.

PERSONAL AND POLITICAL TRANSFORMATIONS OF PEACE ACTIVISTS

Dear Ms. Aharoni,

[...] I am a passionate reader and researcher in matters of conflicts, human rights and women's issues, hence I decided to make these topics the main subject of my Master Thesis entitled: *Women: united in building ties between cultures.* The main goal of my thesis is to put in evidence the bravery of women, their strength and empathy towards one another. [...] I conceive my work as a critic against our patriarchal society, rooted on negative stereotypes regarding women. Naturally I'll be also writing about you in my thesis. (random email sent to author, 2014)

One of the important lessons I have learned as a scholar and activist is that organising for peace often starts with a transformation. Transformation may refer to the personal process of *becoming* a political activist or to the collective build-up of a movement, organisation, project or protest that seeks to resist power, knowledge and political decisions concerning war and peace. Many times, actual experiences or strong emotions about war trigger the imagination of individu-

---

1 For example, the Israeli women's peace movement, which is one of the most documented case studies in this field, has seen the emergence of 25 different groups between 1975 and 2018. Most of them were established by local women (Jewish, Arab and LGBT) during and after violent escalations and became registered NGOs over time. The main types of activity they engaged in are: protest, advocacy, peace education, community work and legal services. Only six of these groups were still active in 2018, the oldest among them is Women in Black, founded in 1988 (Aharoni and Hasson, 2020). For more discussion on the structure and impact of Israeli women's peace organizations see also: Herzog (2008), Hermann (2009) and Lavie (2018).

als in ways that enable new forms of thinking about old problems. Transformation thus appears both as a dramatic signifier in activists' personal life stories and in the histories of social movements.

Reflecting on my life-story, I often think about the introduction to Jean Bethke Elshtain's book *Women and War* (1987) as a good thought exercise. The book, one of the earliest feminist scholarly works about war, was written primarily from the perspective of an American political theorist trying to grapple with questions about politics and motherhood. In the introduction, Elshtain attempts to challenge existing practices of writing about war as a masculine topos and describes her personal transformation from being a girl-child fascinated by stories about Jean d'Arc and heroic combat to an involved adolescent during the 1950s and, later on, to a political theorist and mother. Transformation as a form of political awakening is a key element for peace activism.

The ability to come out in public and share political life stories reflects the 'subjective turn' in Western feminist academic scholarship on peace in the 1980s. Carol Gilligan's (1982) call to listen to women's language and different voice on matters of morality, justice and ethics, had partially inspired Elshtain and many others. Indeed, much of my own 'feminist curiosity' grew out of personal experiences of war, and was later shaped by proximity to feminist organisations. Born in Israel to a father of Jewish Iraqi origin and an American-Jewish mother, I self-identify as a Mizrachi-Jew. Having lived through several armed conflicts (Yom Kippur War, First Lebanon War, First Intifada, First Gulf War, Second Intifada, Second Lebanon War, War(s) on Gaza), I have seen war's three faces. First, as a *civilian* in a shelter, I experienced war at least three times: as a young girl, a high-school student and a young mother of two young boys. Second, as a *woman-soldier*, I served in the Israeli Defense Forces (IDF) during the First Palestinian Intifada and was trained to be part of a military organisation. Finally, unlike most Israeli women, I became involved in a local Israeli feminist organisation, *Isha l'Isha- Haifa Feminist Center* that addresses conflict-related issues, where I became involved in various activities that included protest, education, legal reforms and documentation.

After so many years of living in proximity to a protracted armed conflict, and being part of different feminist activities for peace and against the ongoing military occupation in Palestine together with Jewish and Palestinian women, I am considering the balance of success and failure. Though I acknowledge that feminist organising for peace does not always produce a successful or just resolution of armed conflict, as is the case of Israel-Palestine, I have come to understand that collective actions of coming together have other purposes. In order to demonstrate the historical roots of communal resistance as a practice of survival and care, the remainder of this chapter takes an alternative way of thinking about feminism in hard times – during war, crisis or oppression.

OUTSIDER RESISTANCE

Organising as more than a solution to war: creating a community for peace ...

This new society [...] would have no honorary treasurer, for it would need no funds. It would have no office, no committee, no secretary; it would call no meetings; it would hold no conferences. If name it must have, it could be called the Outsiders Society. (Virginia Woolf, 'Three Guineas', 1938, in Woolf 2007, 860)

Women's collective organising could become an existential means to cope with harmful and violent experiences of war. But collective organising contains tensions about whether women should 'lead from the inside' through the institutionalisation of women's peace groups or whether they should resist war and militarism by organising as 'outsiders'. Drawing upon Virginia Woolf's epistolary essay 'Three Guineas' (1938, in Woolf 2007), I consider if an 'outsider society' may be a radical feminist solution to war.

Woolf, a pacifist, understood war to be a violent and disruptive form of masculine dominance, which created a fraternal bond that excludes women as a group. She theorised that nationalism and its extreme manifestation in Fascist Italy, Spain and Nazi Germany, were interconnected with violent masculinity. As a response, Woolf argued for total refusal and indifference. The 'outsider' should 'refuse in the event of war to make munitions or nurse the wounded' and promise 'not to incite their brothers to fight, or to dissuade them, but to maintain an attitude of complete indifference' (2007 [1938], 860). Most important:

> The outsider will find herself in possession of very good reasons for her indifference. She will find that she has no good reason to ask her brother to fight on her behalf to protect 'our' country. [...] For, the outsider will say, 'in fact, as a woman, I have no country. As a woman I want no country. As a woman my country is the whole world.' (Woolf 2007 [1938], 861)

Woolf's intuition was simultaneously visionary and troubling. While she understood the need for transnational cooperation between (Western, white, educated) women as a way to counter militarised masculinity, *indifference* as an emotional standpoint might seem to reflect a passive and unheroic political plan. Her own suicide in March 1941, when the German invasion of England seemed imminent, reflects an emotional disempowerment to resist extreme forms of violence. Above all, 'Three Guineas' stands out as a reminder of what it means to lose hope and signals the emotional importance of feminist organisations.

Many decades after Woolf's death, feminists and women political activists have learned that creating an organisation is also a way to establish alternative 'homes' in which women can find a shelter from external violence. In the words of Audrey Lorde: 'Caring for myself is not self-indulgence, it is self-preservation, and that is an act of political warfare' (2017 [1988], 130). Consequently, acts of coming together are understood today as deeply political because they enable new forms of collective self-care.

Feminist organising for peace provides community in times when individuals are forced to conform to national, militaristic or other communal values. These benefits of a community are not part of pragmatic objectives linked with the WPS agenda, which include adding women to peace negotiations or including gender-related clauses in peace agreements. Rather, feminist organising as a solution to end war recognises the role of identities and emotions in mobilisation for peace. Feminist organising for peace allows women to use these collective spaces to maintain a sense of belonging. Feminists like Sarah Ahmed (2017) advocate that feminist organisations are spaces in which personal and collective memories and experiences of pain and suffering can resonate. As such, they operate more like fragile shelters than strong, institutional walls: 'It can be painstaking to build a shelter from materials left behind; from histories that make it difficult for some to survive. And yet we need to build such shelters to enable that survival' (Ahmed 2017, 2). As a fellow traveller and long-time documentarist of the Israeli feminist peace movement, my field notes and personal memories contain various references and examples to such spaces. Often referred to as workshops, study groups, dance parties, community events, these fragile gatherings are where friendships grow, personal stories are shared and shared dreams for the future are born.

THE FAILURES OF FEMINIST ORGANISING: SHADOW FEMINISMS

My name is Rawia Lucia Shammas. I am 36 [... once] I believed in feminism as a starting point in changing the world. I was sure that it was my destiny and my mission, being born as a Palestinian in a country called Israel, as a minority, within my homeland, to bring about change. Today I am pessimistic [...] because I think I am unable to change much in my daily life [...] I am stuck here for many reasons; my fate is decided by others. (Loucia Shammas 2008, 109)

Feminist organising for peace does not have a singular script or a clear path towards success. As such, 'getting organised' may summon unwanted opportunities to witness violence, painful encounters and failures. These stories are part of *shadow feminisms* that contrast well-known narrative of success, as they haunt 'the more acceptable forms of feminism that are oriented to positivity, reform and accommodation rather than negativity, rejection and transformation' (Halberstam 2011, 4).

The expectation that women in conflict zones should only speak positively about their efforts to promote peace reflects a general amnesia of past and contemporary suffering. This expectation accords with neoliberal values and a specific United Nations cultural context that favours hopeful and future-oriented 'success stories'. Optimism is viewed by pragmatists as a necessary starting point for peace. Consequently, certain negative emotions – failure, anger, hopelessness – are rarely represented as legitimate responses to armed conflict (Gibbings 2011). Hence, the assumed connection between legitimising women's peace projects by only highlighting successful efforts has become a source of 'cruel optimism' (Berlant 2011) – an attachment to an idea or an object of hope, even after it loses its traction. Given the drive for success stories, the realities of failed efforts to transform and reject militarism and war, and the disappointment and pessimism of those effected, remains in the shadow.

Contrary to the heroic image of women peace-makers as pragmatic visionaries, many women who organise against war encounter negative social responses that range from contempt, disrespect and indifference to bullying, surveillance, direct threats or even physical violence. So, while many activists seek to be public in their resistance to war, peace activism also carries hidden emotional costs: trauma, melancholy, depression and burnout which may lead women to leave politics and engage in more traditional roles of caring for their communities and families. Tova Benski (2007), who documented the public response to a vigil of Women in Black in Haifa, in which I myself was standing every Friday, found that most of the responses from passers-by were characterised by a highly aggressive and emotional language. Responses from bystanders included 'various acts, gestures, slurs, labels, swear words, suggestions, punishments, wishes in the form of "death wish", insults etc.' (2007, 65). I remember standing there and hearing words intended to cast shame, disgust, contempt and hate. We were publicly seen as traitors. But despite this, I continued standing because of the deep and life-changing friendships I made in those vigils.

In 2014, Cynthia Cockburn, an experienced scholar who followed various feminist peace groups for decades, wrote about the nuances of women's failure *and* success to overcome the conditions of inequality and historical injustice in Israel. The opening sentence of the article alludes to the world of fairy tales: 'There was once a dialogue between women of two communities who might have been thought unlikely to have kind words for each other' (Cockburn 2014, 430). This opening suggests that, in order to move forward in feminist organising against war, optimism is needed that does not measure success or institutional change as the 'best practice'. Rather, she also noticed the ability to maintain feminist spaces amidst conflict, war or oppression as an opportunity for these groups to survive, as a political act of resistance.

CONCLUSION: PEACE ACTIVISM AND COLLECTIVE ORGANISATION AS A TOOL AND A SOLUTION

Sometimes women's involvement in peace activism is overlooked or trivialised. In other cases, women's desperate attempt to challenge war is romanticised in ways that hide the possible failures and challenges inherent in such attempts. This chapter offers organising for peace as a feminist solution to ending war and addresses the potential and the pitfalls of organising for peace. I argue that the 'failures' of organising are essential components in the evolution of women's political activism during and after war. Hence, feminist organising in war is not only meant to achieve pragmatic outcomes. Regardless of the ability to transform violent conflict, peace activism can create political, emotional and communal spaces that may counter the dominant masculine-militaristic cultures of war. Consider how women who are active in peace movements often engage in mundane activities: embroidery of peace quilts (Williams 1994); cooking food and camping-out (Cresswell 1994); engaging in poetry, dancing, handicrafts and theatre performances (O'Reilly 2016), and many more ceremonial and artistic activities that are not policy oriented in a strict, pragmatic way. These activities foster peace because they provide a sense of community for those engaged in the emotionally laborious work of peace activism.

Collective organising by local women's groups should not be measured as a solution for war against a liberal political paradigm. In short, collective organising is not simply direct participation in peace negotiations. It is also the relationship-building and communal support that provides peace and solidarity for those resisting war. Feminist organising for peace is not only a solution to war, it is also a solution for personal and communal distress. Self-care can become a *political* reaction to the destructive forces of militarisation, occupation or state violence, especially if it is a collective action (Michaeli 2017). Listening to women's personal stories and emotional narrations about political awakening, transformation, hope, disillusionment and despair is an important reminder that organising for peace has, in fact, many different causes, paths and results.

REFERENCES

Aharoni Sarai B. and Hasson, Yael (2020) *Women's Policy Agencies and State Feminism in Israel 1970-2018 (WPA-IL)*. Dataset version 1.0. [Hebrew]. Ben-Gurion University of the Negev.

Ahmed, Sara (2017) *Living a Feminist Life*. Durham, NC: Duke University Press.

Alvarez, Sonia E. (2009) Beyond NGO-ization? Reflections from Latin America. *Development* 52(2): 175–184.

Barry, Jane (2005) *Rising Up in Response: Women's Rights Activism in Conflict*. Boulder, CO: Urgent Action Fund.

Berlant, Lauren Gail (2011) *Cruel Optimism*. Durham, NC: Duke University Press.

Benski, Tova (2007) Breaching events and the emotional reactions of the public: Women in Black in Israel. In: Helena Flam and Debra King (eds) *Emotions and Social Movements*. Abingdon: Routledge, pp. 67–88.

Choudry, Aziz and Shragge, Eric (2011) Disciplining dissent: NGOs and community organizations. *Globalizations* 8(4): 503–517.

Cockburn, Cynthia (1998) *The Space between Us: Negotiating Gender and National Identities in Conflict*. London: Zed Press.

Cockburn, Cynthia (2014) The dialogue that died: Israeli Jewish and Israeli Palestinian women in hard times. *International Feminist Journal of Politics* 16(3): 430–447.

Confortini, Catia Cecilia (2012) *Intelligent Compassion: Feminist Critical Methodology in the Women's International League for Peace and Freedom*. Oxford: Oxford University Press.

Cresswell, Tim (1994) Putting women in their place: The carnival at Greenham Common. *Antipode* 26(1): 35–58.

El-Bushra, Judy (2007) Feminism, gender, and women's peace activism. *Development and Change* 38(1): 131–147.

Elshtain, Jean Bethke (1987) *Women and War*. Chicago: University of Chicago Press.

Enloe, Cynthia (2000) *Maneuvers: The International Politics of Militarizing Women's Lives*. Berkeley, CA: University of California Press.

Gibbings, Sheri Lynn (2011) No angry women at the United Nations: Political dreams and the cultural politics of United Nations Security Council Resolution 1325. *International Feminist Journal of Politics* 13(4): 522–538.

Giles, Wenona and Hyndman, Jennifer (eds) (2004) *Sites of Violence: Gender and Conflict Zones*. Berkeley, CA: University of California Press.

Gilligan, Carol (1982) *In a Different Voice: Psychological Theory and Women's Development*. Cambridge, MA: Harvard University Press.

Halberstam, Judith (2011) *The Queer Art of Failure*. Durham, NC: Duke University Press.

Heideman, Laura (2017) Cultivating peace: Social movement professionalization and NGOization in Croatia. *Mobilization* 22(3): 345–362.

Hermann, Tamar S. (2009) *The Israeli Peace Movement: A Shattered Dream*. Cambridge: Cambridge University Press.

Herzog, Hanna (2008) Re/visioning the women's movement in Israel. *Citizenship Studies* 12(3): 265–282.

Jad, Islah (2003) The 'NGOization' of the Arab women's movements. *Al-Raida Journal* no vol.: 38–47, https://doi.org/10.32380/alrj.v0i0.442

Jauhola, Marjaana (2016) Decolonizing branded peacebuilding: Abjected women talk back to the Finnish Women, Peace and Security agenda. *International Affairs* 92(2): 333–351.

Kaufman, Joyce P. and Williams, Kristen P. (2010) *Women and War: Gender Identity and Activism in Times of Conflict*. West Hartford, CT: Kumarian Press.

Keck, Margaret E. and Sikkink, Kathryn (1999) Transnational advocacy networks in international and regional politics. *International Social Science Journal* 51(159): 89–101.

Lavie, Smadar (2018) *Wrapped in the Flag of Israel: Mizrahi Single Mothers and Bureaucratic Torture* rev. edn . Lincoln, NE: University of Nebraska Press.

Levi-Hazan, Yael and Harel-Shalev, Ayelet (2019) 'Where am I in this story?' Listening to activist women writers. *Journal of Gender Studies* 28(4): 387–401.

Lorde, Audre (2017 [1988]) *A Burst of Light: And Other Essays*. Mineola, NY: Ixia Press.

Loucia Shammas, Rawia (2008) My identity: Between optimism and pessimism. In: Margot Brown and Jenny Zobel (eds) *Between the Lines: Voice of Women Engendering Peace and Democracy.* A project initiated by Arbeitskries deutscher Bildungsstaetten – AdB. Berlin: AdB, pp. 109–114.

Michaeli, Inna (2017) Self-care: An act of political warfare or a neoliberal trap? *Development* 60(102): 50–56.

O'Reilly, Maria (2016) Peace and justice through a feminist lens: Gender justice and the women's court for the former Yugoslavia. *Journal of Intervention and Statebuilding* 10(3): 419–445.

Ruddick, Sara (1995) *Maternal Thinking: Toward a Politics of Peace,* 2nd edn with a new Preface. Boston, MA: Beacon Press (first published 1989).

Tickner, J. Ann and True, Jacqui (2018) A century of international relations: Feminism from World War I women's peace pragmatism to the Women, Peace and Security agenda. *International Studies Quarterly* 62(2): 221–233.

Tripp, Aili Mari et al. (2008) *African Women's Movements: Transforming Political Landscapes.* Cambridge: Cambridge University Press.

Wibben, Annick T.R. et al. (2018) Collective discussion: Piecing-up feminist peace research. *International Political Sociology* 13(1): 86–107.

Williams, Mary Rose (1994) A reconceptualization of protest rhetoric: Women's quilts as rhetorical forms. *Women's Studies in Communication* 17(2): 20–44.

Woolf, Virginia (2007) *Selected Works of Virginia Woolf.* Ware, Herts: Wordsworth Editions.

4

Piecing-up Peace in Kashmir: Feminist Perspectives on Education for Peace

Shweta Singh and Diksha Poddar

This chapter draws on feminist perspectives from the global South to identify strategic pathways towards transformative and sustainable peace. While we resist the idea of a simplistic and singular feminist solution to ending war, we envision feminist education for peace as a potential pathway. We understand this pathway to include values such as non-violence, compassion, coexistence and empathy.

We begin by introducing two approaches in peace studies. *Education for peace* is grounded in the ethos of equity and value-based learning. When such strategies are developed with attention to the local context and power dynamics, they hold the potential for interrupting patterns of violence and laying the foundations for sustainable peace. The second approach, *critical peace education*, problematises a one-size-fits-all template. This subfield draws from postcolonial theory. It underlines that peace education could become part of the problem that it tries to solve, particularly if it overlooks the Western, Eurocentric assumptions about peace and peace education (Gur-Ze'ev 2001; Zakharia 2017; Zembylas and Bekerman 2013). According to Bajaj and Hantzopoulos (2016, 4), there are three underlying principles to critical peace education: first, critical peace educators pay attention to how unequal social relations and issues of power must inform both peace education and corresponding social action; second, critical peace education pays close attention to local realities and local conceptions of peace that amplify marginalised voices; third, critical peace education draws from social reproductive theory and critical pedagogy (as advocated by Freire 1970) to view schools as potential sites of both marginalisation and/or transformation.

While critical peace education has re-centred the gaze to issues of voice, agency and situated knowledge, this work has long been studied by feminist scholars writing on peace in the global South. Yet despite the important contributions made, feminist peace research from the global South has been marginalised within both peace studies and the subfield of critical peace education. Feminist education for peace, as distinct from both *education for peace* and *critical peace education* approaches, not only foregrounds an alternative vocabulary for examining peace, but also draws attention to issues of universality, difference and politicisation of experience (for more details see Singh 2021).

Feminist education for peace provides pathways to build long-term transformative peace, piece-by-piece. Situations of protracted conflicts, like Kashmir, are complex. Just as a singular narrative of conflict is problematic, a universalising notion of solutions for peace is problematic. Thus, this chapter resists identifying a singular solution to ending war. Instead, drawing upon perspectives of feminist education for peace in the global South (Singh 2021), our chapter offers a collaborative approach to building peace based upon our experiences as academics and practitioners.

Global North scholarship can be trapped in a 'one-size-fits-all' analytical frame that tends to 'know what politics must be, because we know where politics is, because we know the sites of politics, and/or how politics takes place – we know the processes called "political"' (Walker 2010). We re-centre our analysis in 'everyday' stories on youth and violence to offer an alternative perspective. We draw on our field experiences from Kashmir to examine key challenges for peace and youth education and build upon feminist education for peace. We address two key questions: first, what are the key tenets of a feminist education for peace from the global South, and why is it significant for long-term transformative peace? Second, how can we identify strategic pathways for building transformative peace, particularly at the level of the everyday? The everyday in Kashmir is marked by stories of militarisation, dehumanisation, alienation, pain, 'betrayal' and, most importantly, a discourse of 'us' and the 'other'. While feminist education for peace is not a complete 'solution' to ending war or creating peace, we advocate these approaches as a starting point from which a multiplicity of contextual pathways to peace may follow. When developing feminist solutions for ending war, context matters.

This chapter proceeds in three parts. The first part introduces the readers to the distinctions in peace research between 'education for peace', and 'critical peace education' as theoretical models for developing peace. The second part describes the nuances of conflict in Kashmir and outlines why Kashmir is a valuable context to explore feminist peace education's potential to build transformative peace in the Kashmir Valley. The third part identifies two strategic pathways for building long-term transformative peace and offers insights on how feminist peace education translates peace from a normative goal to a transformative lived reality.

FEMINIST PERSPECTIVES ON PEACE EDUCATION

The field of peace research has problematised the assertion that the absence of direct violence means peace. In other words, peace means more than merely the absence of war. Peace research aims to expand the meaning and scope of categories of war, violence and peace. Writing in the 1960s, Johan Galtung put forth the argument that if the absence of violence means peace, we need to redefine the category of violence to include physical, cultural and structural violence. He explained the distinction between *negative peace*, which he defined as absence of visible/direct violence and *positive peace*, which meant the absence of not just physical, but also cultural and structural violence. This conceptualisation of peace was not new, as both Mahatma Gandhi and Frantz Fanon had previously written and spoken about notions of structural, cultural and psychological violence in their writings on colonialism, freedom, violence and non-violence. However, Galtung's work was part of a chorus of work that established the field of peace research and brought these categories of violence and peace onto the agenda of peace research, peace education and activism.

For feminists, these categorisations of violence and peace were inherently problematic. Feminists argued that war, violence and peace impact men and women differently (Brock-Utne 1985; Chenoy

2002; Enloe 2004, 2005; Jayawardena 1986; Reardon 1985). More importantly, they underlined the continuities between different forms of violence in and outside war – including domestic violence and sexual violence – and thus argued for a continuum approach to violence (Confortini 2006; El-Bushra 2007). The evolution of the field of feminist peace research is significant as it provides 'insights on not only what can be termed "spectacular" instances of violence or peace but also sharpens our analysis of the everydayness of reconciliatory measures and the mundaneness of both violence and peace' (Wibben et al. 2019).

Evolution in the field of feminist peace research was marked by a growing recognition of education both as a site for violence and as a site that could facilitate pathways towards peace. Feminist peace research scholars highlight that since continuities exist between different forms of violence, peace education should critically look at cognitive learning with an emphasis on personal and relational change, which can lead to structural change (Brock-Utne 2009; Reardon 1985). Within the broader ambit of peace research, Reardon (1999, 7) defines *peace education* as the transmission of knowledge about the requirements of, obstacles to, and possibilities for achieving and maintaining peace, training in skills for interpreting the knowledge, and the development of reflective and participatory capacities for applying the knowledge to overcoming problems and achieving possibilities. Education for peace, as a subfield of thought, involves an integrative and holistic approach with an emphasis on cognitive learning that deals with attitudes and changes in behaviour (Brock-Utne 2009, 213).

Feminist scholars writing on gender perspectives on peace education draw attention to the following three points: first, education and socialisation are conditioned by social values, which in many cases produce a predisposition to war (Reardon 1985). Second, education can legitimise militarism and sexism, and perpetuate a predisposition towards war; feminists critique values like militarism and sexism (Brock-Utne 1989, 2009; Reardon 1985). Scholars like Patricia Molloy (1995, 235–6) argue that a feminist reconceptualisation of peace requires a cultural critique of militarism and a deconstruction of the type of strategic thinking that informs the discourse within which we live, act and form our subjectivities. Molloy (1995) argues that any hope for peace entails the creation of new discourses, thus moving into the realm of desire and the imaginary. She states that it is within this realm that 'peace, politics and pedagogy meet' (1995, 3). Third, feminist scholars argue for a need to understand peace education as an act of freedom that hinges on an 'engaged pedagogy' that pays attention to emotion and feeling, which, bell hooks argues, is mediated by lived experiences, and in this case of being black or white (hooks 1994).

In addition to these three points, feminists in the global South problematise a universal, or hegemonic, conception of peace, noting that the experiences of violence/peace cannot be separated from struggles of colonialism, imperialism and liberation struggles (Jayawardena 1986). For feminists in South Asia, questions of war and violence are intimately connected to the conceptualisation of the 'political' itself. For instance, Menon (2004, 217) speaks of the 'political' in reference to potentialities 'to subvert, to destabilise, not just dominant values and structures, but ourselves'. So, for feminists in the global South, education is also a site for resistance through 'politicisation of experience' (Mohanty 1989). Scholars like Mohanty (1989), writing on intersectionality and difference, underline how pedagogical practices need to focus on the 'politicisation of experience' to translate normative goals into lived transformative experiences. We agree, and argue that both the content and process of this pedagogical practice cannot be scripted in a universalising language of transformative peace. Educational interventions need to be attentive to complex power relations that are embedded in situations of protracted conflict, and thus any 'technocratic' or universalising approach to peace education can itself be an act of hegemonic violence (Gur-Ze'ev 2001). Singular 'solutions' to ending war can be counter to critical-feminist peace education, which prioritises paying attention to local dynamics, community voices, and histories of colonisation.

For the purpose of this chapter, we draw on feminist perspectives to education for peace from the global South to demonstrate strategic pathways towards transformative peace. Drawing on the case of Kashmir, we highlight two key challenges: first, the narrative of 'us' and the 'other', which creates differentiation and distancing and thus poses a challenge to transformative peace; second, the need to pay attention to issues of voice, agency, history/histories, and power in situations of protracted conflict. The case of Kashmir is significant as it highlights how protracted conflicts impact youth and education, as well as providing insights into why many young people pick up the gun, or walk the path of violence rather than peace. Drawing on our field experiences, we can state that the case of Kashmir elucidates how there is never a singular narrative on conflict, and thus a universalising approach to peace can itself be an act of hegemonic violence. The following section highlights some of the key challenges for youth and education, and how a feminist education for peace can address some of these challenges.

PERSPECTIVES ON FEMINIST PEACE EDUCATION, TRANSFORMATIVE PEACE AND KASHMIR

> 'I am a stone pelter.'
> 'I am too, you can arrest me,'
> 'I was not, but now I will be.'
> Seema Mustafa (2011)

Insecurity in Kashmir is often represented in a narrative that centres Kashmir as a factor in state-centric India–Pakistan relations (Jammu-Ladakh and Valley of Kashmir). In scholarship on Kashmir, the primary referents of analysis have been state, power, military capabilities and jingoistic national security discourse. However, the story of political conflict in Kashmir is more complex. The contemporary conflict has its roots in a militancy movement of the late 1980s, which shaped a protracted mobilisation for *azaadi* (freedom). State-centric approaches to Kashmir that focus on national security discourse are incomplete. If we are to understand the connections between the militancy movement and contemporary conflict we must draw attention to the 'everyday' in Kashmir, with particular attention to youth and education. The everyday in Kashmir is marked by stories of militarisation, de-humanisation, alienation, pain, 'betrayal' and, most importantly, a discourse of 'us' and the 'other' (Singh 2021). The context of 'the everyday' is a site of analysis for considering pathways to transformative peace.

We draw upon extensive fieldwork that identifies three defining features of the conflict in Kashmir: first, the collective identity of Kashmiri Muslims, and their experiences of pain, alienation, dehumanisation and 'othering'; second, militarisation in the Valley; and, third, the asymmetrical relationship between the state and its people (Singh 2018). We proceed with a brief discussion of post-2008 experiences of youth in Kashmir – particularly in the Valley – to highlight the importance of education as a critical site for transformative everyday peace in Kashmir.

Since 2008, Kashmir has seen increased involvement of youth in incidents of stone pelting and other violent resistance against the militarisation of the Valley. A series of high-profile violent events, such as the Amarnath land transfer row (in 2008), the Shopian rape case (2009), and the accidental death of a young schoolboy, Tufail Mattoo in the summer of 2010, triggered mass protests led by Kashmiri youth. Our fieldwork mapped the increasing sense of anger, frustration and alienation that young Kashmiri people experience, given the state of militarisation, and the use of coercive apparatus by the state. In response to the militarisation of the Valley and heavy-handed military force by the state, youth in Kashmir engage in stone pelting (throwing stones at armed personnel) as an act of resistance. These are subversive acts as space(s) for democratic dissent are limited in the Valley.

In 2016, these previous events inspired a watershed moment for the youth protest movement. Burhan Wani, a 22-year-old, tech-savvy militant and school dropout was killed by state security forces on 8 July 2016. He had joined the ranks of militant activists six years earlier and was the commander of Hizbul Mujahideen, a militant organisation in Kashmir. He was a 'poster boy' for a large number of Kashmiri youths. Many argue that Wani joined the militant ranks after he and his brother were stopped and beaten up by security forces when they went out for a picnic one day years earlier (Dasgupta 2016). The narratives about Wani reflect the connection between youth frustration with militarisation and excessive state police violence, and youth resistance movements and activities like stone pelting. The response to state militarisation in the Valley was one of counter-militarisation. Wani soon became a popular face of the movement that glorified violence and militancy, and had become infamous through social media where he promoted anti-state rhetoric.

Wani's death came at a time when young students were increasingly picking up guns and using force to express themselves to the state. Less than a year later, in 2017, 15-year-old Faizan Ahmad Bhat from Tral, a young Kashmiri militant, died in a gunfight. Motta (2016), states that many educated young minds, who picked up stones as an act of resistance shared a 'common thread of experience: all have been witness to, or have experienced first-hand, beatings, torture, harassment and humiliation at the hands of the security forces'. Anthropologists like Haley Duschinski (2009) show how intensive militarisation and a coercive state apparatus identify segments of the Kashmiri population as 'threats to national order'. This characterisation brings in sense of alienation, dehumanisation and 'othering', and more often than not young people take recourse to acts of stone pelting (and in many cases join the ranks of the militants) as resistance against militarisation.

STRATEGIC PATHWAYS FOR BUILDING LONG-TERM TRANSFORMATIVE PEACE

The story of Burhan Wani and many others from our fieldwork led us to wonder whether children's experiences would have been different if educational spaces and critical pedagogy provided space to address issues of 'lived experiences' of youth in situations of protracted conflict. Perhaps if Wani had had the opportunity to engage in peace education – through pedagogies of empathy, understanding, and contextualising difference – he might have taken alternative actions to joining a militarised resistance. If so, can feminist education for peace from the global South provide insights on how to actualise this? In the case of Kashmir, limited study indicates that school curricula and pedagogical practice are not designed to take cognisance of the 'lived experiences' of young people. Yet education holds great potential for transformative peace. We argue that, in situations of protracted conflict like Kashmir, education must account for the various experiences of insecurity in order to create space for innovative thinking about peace. We argue that a feminist education for peace is key to addressing the limitations of current gaps in education in places like Kashmir. Education for peace and feminist pedagogy are two strategic pillars that could provide pathways to transformative peace. Through this type of education, issues of distancing and differentiation could be addressed in a pedagogical narrative that legitimises these experiences and acknowledges different voices and agency in Kashmir.

But what exactly might feminist education for peace look like in terms of normative commitments and pedagogical tools? In this section we outline what feminist pedagogy can mean and how it can contribute to lasting peace. In the previous section, drawing on our field experiences, we highlighted how in situations of protracted conflict like Kashmir, experiences of humiliation and alienation create constant distancing and differentiation, and many young people like Burhan Wani may chose violence as a means of expression, and reject peace. Esther Yogev (2008; in the context of Israel) argues that, 'One's identity motivates attitudes of constant distancing and differentiation.' The types of 'constant distancing and differentiation' (Yogev 2010; see also Singh 2018) that can take place in insecure contexts and war zones leads to a trust deficit, a security dilemma which poses a significant challenge to long-term transformative peace.

We advocate for a normative, feminist approach to education for peace grounded in the ethos of equity and value-based learning. This pedagogy would include values such as non-violence, compassion, coexistence and empathy. These pedagogical values can play a significant role in shifting the lens of distancing and differentiation, and, in turn, facilitate a process of re-humanisation of the 'other' (Sewak 2002).

In her path-breaking work *Teaching to Transgress*, bell hooks writes:

I came to theory because I was hurting – the pain within me was so intense that I could not go on living. I came to theory desperate, wanting to comprehend – to grasp what was happening around and within me. Most importantly, I wanted to make the hurt go away. I saw in theory then a location for healing. (hooks 1994, 59)

For feminist scholars in the global South, hooks' work is particularly important as it foregrounds that 'lived experiences' are different and dependent on multiple factors, including class, race, religion, sexuality, and geography. Thus, transformative peace cannot be scripted in a language that does not acknowledge difference, voice and agency. hooks asserts that education cannot be hinged on a mind/body split, that 'education as an act of freedom' hinges on an 'engaged pedagogy'. We must, therefore, pay attention to emotion and feeling, which is mediated by experiences of being black or white (hooks 1994). We advocate a need to reconceptualise difference and voice in methods of education within contexts of protracted conflict. We must provide the educational tools for youth to make sense of their experiences and recognise that difference has led to their diverse experiences in conflict. Drawing on Mohanty (1989, 181), we define difference as 'asymmetrical and incommensurate cultural spheres situated within hierarchies of domination and resistance'. Thus, any 'thrust to universalize or homogenize concepts or approaches may be counter-productive by masking power relations embedded in complex historical relations and undermining local understandings of how participants might cultivate their sense of transformative agency' (e.g. Bajaj 2008; Hantzopoulos 2010; Zembylas and Bekerman 2013). We must, especially in education, pay attention to local voice(s) in order to cultivate a sense of transformative agency (Bajaj 2008, 135).

Education can be a pathway for peace. We align with feminist scholars like Betty Reardon, who explains that education can socialise for war and peace, and thus we must pay attention to militarism and sexism embedded in teaching-learning processes. While we pay attention to questions of violence and militarism, we also need to pay attention to questions of historical injustice, power, agency and voice when we design peace education interventions in situations of protracted conflict.

While schools can do this by employing critical pedagogy, informal spaces can also be a site for social change. These informal spaces impinge on the everyday experiences of youth, as we demonstrated through the case analysis of Burhan Wani. In addressing complex conflict like that in Kashmir, 'resistance lies in self-conscious engagement with dominant, normative discourses and representations and in the active creation of oppositional analytic and cultural spaces' (Mohanty 1989). It is with the goal of providing tools and helping youth make sense of dominant discourses in the Valley that we advance feminist education for peace for its emancipatory potential to address these challenges.

CONCLUSION

We wish to conclude by emphasising that a singular narrative of peace, or conflict, is problematic, and thus there is a need to pay attention to the continuum of violence. Situations of protracted conflict are characterised by distance, differentiation and a narrative of 'us' and the other. Youths, in many instances, pick up guns because of their lived experiences of dehumanisation and alienation that underlie this complex narrative of us and the 'other'. In order to provide tools and the space to make sense of these experiences, we advocate a feminist education for peace as a pathway to shift narratives, through pedagogy, from dehumanisation to re-humanisation of the other. While the practices must be context specific, we see critical-feminist pedagogy, such as bell hooks' 'engaged pedagogy' as foundational for building a feminist education for peace in Kashmir.

REFERENCES

Note: All URLs checked on 24 June 2021.

Bajaj, M. (2008) Critical peace education. In: M. Bajaj (ed.) *Encyclopedia of Peace Education*. Charlotte, NC: Information Age Publishing, pp.135–146.

Bajaj, M. and Hantzopoulos, M. (2016) Introduction. In: M. Bajaj and M. Hantzopoulos (eds) *Peace Education: International Perspectives*. New York: Bloomsbury.

Brock-Utne, B. (1989) *Feminist Perspectives on Peace and Peace Education*. New York: Pergamon Press.

Brock-Utne, B. (2009) A gender perspective on peace education and the work for peace. *International Review of Education* 55: 205–220.

Chenoy, A.M. (2002) *Militarism and Women in South Asia*. New Delhi: Kali for Women.

Confortini, C.C. (2006) Galtung, violence, and gender: The case for a peace studies/ feminism alliance. *Peace and Change* 31(3): 333–367.

Dasgupta, P. (2016) Who was Burhan Wani and why is Kashmir mourning him? *Huffpost*, 11 July. Available at: www.huffingtonpost.in/2016/07/11/who-was-burhan-wani-and-why-is-kashmir-mourning-him_a_21429499/

Duschinski, H. (2009) Destiny effects: Militarization, state power, and punitive containment in Kashmir Valley. *Anthropological Quarterly* 82(3): 691–717.

El-Bushra, J. (2007) Feminism, gender, and women's peace activism. *Development and Change* 38(1): 131–147.

Enloe, C.H. (2004) *The Curious Feminist: Searching for Women in a New Age of Empire*. Berkeley: University of California Press.

Enloe, C.H. (2005) What if patriarchy is the big picture? An afterword. In: D.E. Mazurana, A. Raven-Roberts and J.L. Parpart (eds) *Gender, Conflict, and Peacekeeping*. Lanham, MD: Rowman and Littlefield.

Freire, P. (1970) *Pedagogy of the Oppressed*. New York: Herder and Herder.

Gur-Ze'ev, I. (2001) Philosophy of peace education in a postmodern era. *Educational Theory* 51(3): 315–336.

Hantzopoulos, M. (2011) Institutionalizing critical peace education in public schools: A case for comprehensive implementation. *Journal of Peace Education* 8(3): 225–242, doi: 10.1080/17400201.2011.621364.

hooks, b. (1994) *Teaching to Transgress: Education as a Practice of Freedom*. New York: Routledge.

Jayawardena, K. (1986) *Feminism and Nationalism in the Third World*. London: Zed Books.

Menon, N. (2004) *Recovering Subversion: Feminist Politics beyond the Law*. Delhi: Permanent Black; Urbana and Chicago: University of Illinois Press.

Mohanty, Chandra T. (1989) On race and voice: Challenges for liberal education in the 1990s. *Cultural Critique* 14.

Molloy, P. (1995) Subversive strategies or subverting strategy: Towards a feminist pedagogy for peace. *Alternatives* 20(2): 225–242.

Motta, S.A. (2016) Armed with the original weapon. *Outlook Magazine*, 12 September. Available at: www.outlookindia.com/magazine/story/armed-with-the-original-weapon/297804

Mustafa, S. (2011) Driven into a corner, youth in Kashmir look back in anger. *Sunday Guardian*, 10 April.

Reardon, B. (1985) *Sexism and the War System*. New York: Teachers College Press.

Reardon, B.A. (1999) *Peace Education: A Review and Projection*. Peace Education Report. Malmo: School of Education, Department of Educational and Psychological Research. Available at: https://peacelearner.files.wordpress.com/2010/01/betty-reardon-peaceeducation-a-review-and-projection1.pdf

Sewak, M. (2002) *Re-humanizing the Other*. New Delhi; WISCOMP.

Singh, S. (2018) Education for peace through transformative dialogue: Perspectives from Kashmir. *International Review of Education* 64(1).

Singh, S. (2021) Gendering education for peace: Critical perspectives. In P. Confortini and F. Väyrynen (eds) *Handbook of Feminist Peace Research*. Abingdon: Routledge.

Walker R.B.J. (2010) *After the Globe, Before the World*. Abingdon: Routledge.

Wibben, A.T.R. et al. (2019) Collective discussion: Piecing-up feminist peace research. *International Political Sociology* 13(1): 86–107.

Yogev, E. (2010) A crossroads: History textbooks and curricula in Israel. *Journal of Peace Education* 7(1).

Zakharia, Zeena (2017) 'Getting to "no"': Locating critical peace education within resistance and anti-oppression pedagogy at a Shi'a Islamic school in Lebanon. *Research in Comparative & International Education* 12(1): 46–63.

Zembylas, Michalinos and Bekerman, Zvi (2013) Peace education in the present: Dismantling and reconstructing some fundamental theoretical premises. *Journal of Peace Education* 10(2).

5

Learn from Kurdish Women's Liberation Movements to Imagine the Dissolution of the Nation-state System

Eda Gunaydin

This chapter focuses on the Kurdish women's liberation movements of Rojava, an autonomous administration region in north-east Syria (NES). These women theorise that ending war requires a dissolution of the nation-state system. There are three key elements to the solution to ending war offered by Kurdish women's liberation movements. First, the solution is grounded in jineology, a woman-centred theory, that makes explicit critiques of Western feminism and the nation-state model. Second, the solution relies on the self-governance model of democratic confederalism, which is a non-state, municipal form of governing. Finally, the solution draws on two connected understandings of self-sustainability, which help articulate a clear and potent view of women's autonomy. This radical solution to the enduring conflict in the Middle East requires placing the legitimacy of use of violence into the hands of the people, including women, rather than into the hands of the state. If communities are trained and organised to defend themselves and to engage in collective self-defence, it is argued, peace becomes more attainable, because it is the current system of states that perpetuates violence.

In exploring this solution, the chapter adopts a postcolonial feminist approach. This approach requires paying attention to the ways of knowing that are subjugated by our current political ordering (Milliken 1999), which tends to see Middle Eastern women as passive, silent victims in need of saving (Spivak 1988). The chapter focuses on Kurdish women's activism in NES, and uses original translations of these female militants' work. Kurdish women's *self-representa-tions* – that is, what they themselves say about their values, beliefs and goals – show that these women are political actors in their own right, possess their own political theories, and have formed their own women's rights movements (Bell 2014; Yegenoglu 1998). In other words, it is important to be attentive not just to what these women 'do' as part of building peace, but also how they theorise about it. The chapter therefore explores both the practical and theoretical implications of the jineological solution to ending war through the dissolution of the nation-state system.

In the first part of this chapter, I provide a description of the Rojava region and a brief history of the groups operating in the region. Next, I explore *jineology*, the theoretical approach used by Kurdish women to address long-standing conflict in the Rojava region. The 'solutions' to war offered by jineology – rejection of the nation-state system, governance in a system of *democractic confederalism*, and the promotion of *self-sustainability* through ecological awareness and collective armament – have been embraced by Kurdish women. Rather than seeing this as an explicitly feminist solution, Kurdish women view many of these jineological principles in contrast to Western feminism, as they associate Western feminism with capitalism and statism. Nonetheless, the jineological principles endorsed by Kurdish women are concerned with challenging patriarchy and they view patriarchy as intersecting with these other forms of hegemony.

I first illustrate how Kurdish women's access to education and knowledge production is an empowering mechanism used to challenge patriarchy. I proceed to explain the tenets of democratic confederalism, a model of non-state governance implemented in Rojava that has been envisioned as a means to bring peace to the Mesopotamian region. A key element of democratic confederalism is women's involvement in governance and engagement in political life, another element of *jineology* that challenges patriarchy and statism. Finally, I examine how principles of self-sustainability are key to ending war, as these principles enable women to fend for and defend themselves rather than relying on the state. In sum, this chapter offers a feminist solution to ending war that moves beyond state-centric feminist imaginings and is inspired by the knowledge of Kurdish women.

THE 'KURDISH QUESTION'

The Kurds are a large, stateless ethnic group, numbering up to 25 million, and living in northern Syria, south-east Turkey, northern Iraq and western Iran. Within these nation-states, the Kurds are an ethnic minority who have at times wished to form a nation-state of their own. The 'Kurdish question' has therefore long been a contentious issue. In 1978, inspired by global decolonisation movements, the Kurdistan Workers' Party (PKK), initially a Marxist-Leninist political party, was formed, and it fought for an independent state of Kurds in Turkey (Öcalan 2015, 1). States' attempted 'solutions' to the 'problem' have historically involved policies such as assimilation, banning Kurdish language and culture, and mass incarceration or even genocide. For example, in Syria, before the outbreak of the civil war in 2011, Kurdish political activity was banned (Yildiz 2005, 106); Syrian Kurds were systematically stripped of citizenship rights (Human Rights Watch 1991, 88); members of the Democratic Union (PYD) political party, which maintains the paramilitary forces discussed in this chapter, were often detained en masse and kept as political prisoners (Human Rights Watch 2009). In Iraqi Kurdistan in the 1980s, the Ba'athist government used chemical and neurological weapons against Kurdish populations to displace over 1 million and kill over 100,000 (Yesiltas 2014, 51).

The Kurdistan Communities Union (KCK) is an umbrella organisation of which the PYD and PKK are members. In 2005, the KCK abandoned separatism and sought to establish democratic confederalism, eschewing the pursuit of a separate state for Kurds (Öcalan 2005). Since 2012, the landscape of Kurdish politics has altered after the PYD took control over a large swath of northern Syria. This was made possible by the PYD's practice of maintaining a paramilitary force, which allowed the group to meet the security needs of the region after Assad's forces withdrew from the area. In 2013, the PYD, in coalition with other political parties, declared autonomy and started self-governing. Rojava, or the Autonomous Administration of North and East Syria, is the name given to the region of northern Syria administered under the model of democratic confederalism. Prior to the Turkish invasion of the region (2016–present), Rojava comprised around one fifth of the Syrian landmass. The PYD paramilitary force has two main arms – the People's Protection Units (YPG), and its female counterpart, the Women's Protection Units (YPJ). The YPG grew rapidly out of a core of mobile, PKK-trained elite fighters, with the addition of civilian volunteers (Arango 2012; Knapp et al. 2016, 137–8; VICE Media 2013). Taken together, the YPJ/YPG is the armed wing of the PYD, who, from 2016 onwards, formed the majority of the Syrian Democratic Forces (SDF). The group was seen as responsible for the defeat of the Islamic State (ISIS) in Syria and is the most significant ally to the West in the conflict with ISIS.

The Kurdish women's liberation movement draws heavily upon the theory of Abdullah Öcalan, founder of the PKK. Öcalan coined the term 'jineology' and invented democratic confederalism, the system of government implemented in Rojava. Other Öcalan (or 'Apoist') influences in Rojava include fighters and politicians wearing Öcalan's likeness on their uniforms; the use of Apoist slogans and songs; and swearing an oath on Apoist principles (ecology, self-defence, democratic autonomy) when they join the YPG and YPJ (Dirik 2015a; *RT* 2015). In addition, the general education system in Rojava is based upon these Apoist principles. With an absence of universities in northern Syria, Rojava created a system of women's and *asayish* academies. At academies, trainees in the military or in the political movement, as well as any interested parties, are required to receive revolutionary education in 'women's and people's freedom', which involves studying Öcalan's work (Kendal and Oak 2016; Üstündağ 2016, 204). We can look to both the Rojava movement's written works and their direct political activities to learn more about their post-state solution to war.

'JINEOLOGY' INSTEAD OF FEMINISM

This section details the origins and rationale of jineology and how it makes an essential part of a Kurdish feminist solution to ending war. Since it is not possible to provide an exhaustive account of jineology, this section will focus specifically on the ways Kurdish women articulate their critiques of Western feminism and their own vision of liberation. The section begins with a discussion of the ways that jineology emphasises the interlinkages of all forms of hegemony, including patriarchy, with the states system and the devaluation of women's knowledges, before moving to explicit critiques of Western feminism offered by jineology.

Jineology is a philosophy that consists of the Kurdish word for woman, '*jin*', and the suffix -*ology*, as a 'science of'. Jineology advocates a rejection of multiple, intersecting forms of hegemony, not only patriarchy. Jineology identifies other forms of hegemonic power, including the nation-state and capitalism as contributors to women's oppression (JA 2015, 19). Therefore, the Kurdish women's liberation movement has directed its struggle simultaneously against both nationalist oppression and gender oppression. This makes sense when considering that Kurdish women have been oppressed both by patriarchy and the Syrian state. To that end, jineology espouses an awareness that nation-statism has been fundamentally imbricated with patriarchy; the nation-state reproduces patriarchy because the nation-state is intrinsically hegemonic and masculinist (Dirik 2014). Jineologists therefore use the formulation 'statism-sexism-powerism' to capture the indivisibility of these hegemonies (JA 2015, 103).

Jineology's project is to 'de-other' women, giving them access both to learning and to knowledge production. According to this approach, positivism is viewed as an approach to knowledge cultivated in the West, primarily by men, that leads to a science which is 'confined to the appearance of things, which it equates with reality itself' (Öcalan 2015, 15). This understanding of positivism sees that whatever is not the (male) self is designated as 'other', and whatever the self cannot observe of the other is deemed unknowable. This critique runs through works of jineology, which attempt to recover the 'unknowable': knowledge about women. It calls itself a corrective science of women, studying their lives to produce knowledge that ameliorates the assumption that she is merely a 'defective' version of a man and compensates for her absence throughout intellectual history. Its goal, then, is to rehabilitate aspects of female existence, such as 'women's work', that are traditionally belittled (JA 2015, 44).

In September 2014, northern Syria's first ever university, the Mesopotamian Social Sciences Academy, opened in Qamishlo (*Rojava Report* 2014). An example of re-centring women's knowledges at the university is the delivery of classes on folklore by older women (Dirik 2015b). Folklore has been a way of knowing about the world that is particular to Kurdish women, who historically have only been able to pass on these stories outside of formal institutions. In addition, women in Rojava have also established over twenty Women's Education and Research Centres, where women can access classes on practical skills, as well as 'culture and art' (Knapp et al. 2016, 70). Women in Rojava have also started their own radio show; a press association called the Kurdish Women's Press Association (RAJIN); a newspaper called *Dengê Jiyan* (Voice of Life); and opened women's centres such as one in Qamishlo, which 'investigates and documents cases of domestic violence' (Knapp et al. 2016, 66, 67, 70, 74). These initiatives reflect the jineologist project of making women visible in the history of thought, art, media, and politics in Rojava. These projects are a core means of creating both a gender-equal as well as a self-organised society, because they provide alternatives to traditionally patriarchal institutions. In Kurdish women's liberationists' view, dismantling positivism and patriarchy contributes to dismantling all other forms of power too.

While these initiatives may reflect elements of Western feminism, jineologists are clear that their philosophy is distinct. I will outline three specific critiques jineologists make of Western feminism before linking these to the feminist solution offered in this chapter. First, for female participants of the reconstruction in northern Syria, jineology actually surpasses Western feminism because rejecting each of these forms of hegemony – that is patriarchy and positivism – rather than patriarchy alone, leads to the establishment of a more sustainable peace. This is because, in their view, jineology is more holistic, incorporating all of society. For example, at the height of the Rojava revolution, both men and women were required to take classes on jineology and ecology, and jineology is embedded in the area's governance model rather than being treated as a 'rights-based side issue that puts the burden on women' (Dirik 2015a, 4).

Second, to jineologists, Western feminism has become co-opted by capitalism and liberalism, or what Kurdish women's liberationists dub 'capitalist modernity'. As jineologists state in *Introduction to Jineology* (JA 2015, 94): 'we have to salvage the female sex from [both] religious, feudal backwardness and the objectifying, commodifying approach of capitalism'. This is because:

> liberalism, which replaced the sexist society [a previous stage of history], was not satisfied with only exploiting women for profit in the home. In addition, liberalism has achieved ... the sale of woman in the marketplace as a commodity. Men only turn their labour into commodities, whereas women's bodies and souls are commodified too. [...] This is the trap that modernity has sprung for women. From turning women into fodder for advertisements, to sex and pornography, these are tools of exploitation. (JA 2015, 139)

A practical example can help illustrate this quotation. YPJ fighters have often criticised the tendency in the West to commodify their activities. In October 2014, for example, H&M launched a line of khaki jumpsuits resembling, and inspired by, the YPJ's uniforms. After widespread criticism, the company was forced to issue an apology and recall the clothing (Taylor 2014). YPJ fighters, such as Zilan Diyar (2014), criticised the transformation of the women's political struggle into a 'fashion trend'. A month prior, twelve young YPJ fighters, including a 12- and 14-year-old, were featured in an editorial for the fashion magazine *Marie Claire*. In photographic portraits, the women appeared posing in their uniforms, holding their Kalashnikovs in their arms (Griffin 2014). Fighter Dilan gave the following statement about this phenomenon: 'Isn't it odd that a capitalist consumerist magazine that objectifies women appropriates us in this way? It's ridiculous' (quoted in Letsch 2015).

In critiquing liberalism, capitalism and, finally, the state, jineologists advocate for a movement that focuses on holistic anti-system principles (JA 2015, 85). They write:

> Because feminism has not overcome the dominant masculine system; continues with a statist mentality; and has not surpassed a Eurocentric positivist-orientalist point of view, feminism offers few solutions to women's realities in the Middle East and other regions of the world. (JA 2015, 88)

It is to the principle of anti-statism that I turn in the next section.

DEMOCRATIC CONFEDERALISM

This section explores the theory of anti-statism embedded in jineology in more detail, showing how it underpins the solutions implemented during the Rojava revolution, including the rise of militancy. Öcalan's book *Democratic Confederalism* (2015) explains that the KCK abandoned nationalism and separatism a decade ago. He argues that it is the idea of the nation-state that created the 'Kurdish problem' in the first place. In his view, states use violence to force citizens to take on a single identity (one nation), rather than allowing for ethnic, religious and national plurality. This valuing of plurality can be observed in Rojava, for example in the dropping of the name 'Western Kurdistan' (in favour of Rojava, and now NES) in order to include other religious and ethnic minorities in its territory. Furthermore, the first lines of Rojava's Social Contract (2014) are:

We, the people of the Democratic Autonomous Regions of Afrîn, Cizîre, and Kobanê, a confederation of Kurds, Arabs, Assyrians, Chaldeans, Arameans, Turkmen, Armenians, and Chechens …

Öcalan also views nation-states as irreparably undemocratic due to their connection with capitalism. Nation-states are viewed as inherently serving the ruling class, and therefore are an enemy of the people. Moreover, on this view, war occurs because states are seeking to redistribute capital (Öcalan 2015, 13). This state-capitalism formation is one perspective on history that Apoist Kurds dub 'capitalist modernity'.

By contrast, the Rojava movement considers itself to be building 'democratic modernity'. Democratic modernity requires a non-state polity, which its adherents argue is the sole pathway to democracy and peace. While states are seen as sites of power and coercion, democratic modernity relies on voluntary participation, collective consensus and direct democracy. What can be observed here is a radical untethering of democracy and peace from the need to establish a nation-state. Members of the Rojava movement see themselves as operationalising an entirely new type of non-state polity in democratic confederalism. This system of self-governance has been described as the 'most radical experiment in democracy and gender equality in the world' (Gupta 2016).

Administratively, democratic confederalism refers to the goal of establishing a series of linked but self-governing democratic autonomous regions, that is, the cantons of Rojava (Güneser 2015). At its largest, Rojava was composed of three cantons: Afrin, Kobane and Cizre.

In Rojava, the smallest possible autonomous unit was theorised as the commune, which brought together up to 350 families or households. By contrast, the nuclear family was viewed as capitalist modernity's smallest collective unit, which democratic confederalism views as a site of women's oppression and which communes are envisaged as eventually replacing (Omrani 2015). The commune is supposed to restore politics and the process of democracy to the everyday and to replace the abstract and static nation-state. Communes hold weekly gatherings, and members attend general meetings as well as any relevant autonomous meetings (for example, of the Women's Committee).

The commune model was represented as a means of restoring the people's natural sense of morality, or 'social ethics', which they had been alienated from, and which had been replaced by externally imposed law (Dirik 2016). This could also be called direct democracy, instead of representative democracy. Most disputes were to be resolved at the communal level without involving any institutional bureaucracy. In 2016, many, though not all, inhabitants of the region had joined a commune (B. 2016). By their own account, over 75 per cent of Kurdish women became politically active in the wake of the Rojava revolution (Bengio 2014). All the way up the administrative chain, from the commune to the city to the canton level, there is a quota for one male and one female co-president, and a minimum requirement of 40 per cent representation of women. The principle of dual leadership is also referred to as *hevserok* (Knapp et al. 2016, 69).

On the ground, during the peak of its stable governance (2014–18), Rojava resisted implementing state-like or top-down structures, albeit with varying levels of success (Schmidinger 2018, 134). Although not always successful, principles of democratic confederalism include: communes should not *submit* to higher governance structures, but rather maintain autonomy despite them; and communes should continually appropriate state functions, with the objective of eventually making them redundant (Üstündağ 2016, 203).

Understanding the logics governing democratic confederalism clarifies why supporters of the Rojava movement have represented democratic confederalism as a solution to the Kurdish conflict. For example, it may appear puzzling that the Rojava Social Contract (2014) 'recognises Syria's territorial integrity', while its militant activities, which have involved repelling both Syrian and Turkish state forces, are suggestive of a desire to secede. However, these non-state democratic autonomies do not require the state to be overthrown first; instead, individuals self-govern at the radically local level despite, and regardless of, the state (Dirik 2014). Democratic confederalism is seen as a feasible solution to the 'Kurdish problem' not only in Syria, but also Turkey, Iran and Iraq (Öcalan 2015, 34–41), and therefore as a means of securing lasting peace in the region. This is because the proposed solution does not require secession to occur, nor therefore the replacement of one patriarchal nation-state with another.

SELF-SUFFICIENCY: ECOLOGY AND COLLECTIVE SELF-DEFENCE

The third element of the solution of dissolving the state system proposed in this chapter is the principle of self-sufficiency, which has two components. The first is the idea of ecology, which says that we must find new, less masculinist ways of viewing our relationship with our environment. To Hawzhin Azeez (2016), member of the Kobani Reconstruction Board, ecology refers to the idea that societies must consider:

[t]he limitations we experience as a community and the resources we have access to. […] To be ecological on our own terms means to preserve the cultural, traditional values within the community. Ensuring that communities are organic, natural, and traditional as they have always been – not mega-malls, structures and buildings that are not natural to the way the community lives here.

Ecology therefore differentiates itself from patriarchal capitalism, which sees nature as something to be exploited. Returning to 'traditional' practices, such as cooperative greenhouses and animal husbandry (B. 2016), has allowed Rojava to combat the wheat monoculture previously imposed on the region. It has also granted women improved economic self-sufficiency. One way in which women have implemented the notion of ecology is by establishing a women- and girls-only village called Jinwar, where residents live communally, grow their own food, and even run their own school (Alesali and Zdanowicz 2019).

The second component of self-sufficiency relates to the idea of collective self-defence, including women's armament. The core aim of this concept is to redistribute the means of violence as widely as possible (Üstündağ 2016, 199). Women's militias are a mainstay of KCK organisations, and women arming themselves is viewed as key to equality in the movement. Self-defence reduces war by taking the means of force away from the state, which is believed to be the core perpetrator of violence. Üstündağ (2016) points out that the idea of women's wings as a means of achieving peace also evolved from Öcalan's experiences in the PKK, which helped inform the practices of the YPJ. Throughout the 1980s, the PKK's leftist goals risked co-option by guerrilla leaders who monopolised arms and information, and the party nearly devolved into paramilitary forces without political aims. As a result, in 1993, Öcalan encouraged the formation of an independent women's army and other autonomous institutions, which 'not only guaranteed women's protection against men … but also disrupted channels of secrecy, transformed relations with locals, and effectively developed an opposition to the abuse of power' (Üstündağ 2016, 200). The ethos of women's militias is therefore part of a long-existing practice of democratising the means of force. Because much of the fighting that the YPJ engage in is defensive in nature, it has also been likened to a rose: a flower defending itself from attack (Knapp et al. 2016, 139).

Women comprise between 20 and 45 per cent of the YPG (similarly to the PKK) (Cousins 2014; *Sputnik* 2016; Terrorism Research and Analysis Consortium 2016). In Rojava, any woman over the age of 18 can enlist at a YPG/YPJ centre. Following this, they attend and receive training at one of the military academies located in each municipality, before they are assigned to handling security on access roads or defending their home cities (Knapp et al. 2016, 151–2). A recent development in Rojava has been the proliferation of additional self-defence groups beyond the YPG/YPJ and the police force (*asayish*). Other non-Kurdish militias include the Yezidi women's militia, Êzîdxan Women's Units, and the Bethnahrain Women's Protection Forces for Assyrian women. In addition to these Yezidi and Assyrian women's groups, further examples include Sutoro, a self-defence militia for Syriac Christians, as well as the Hêza Parastina Cewherî (HPC) (B. 2016; Quinn 2015). They exist to further devolve and decentralise military power to the commune level, and for each religious and ethnic group to acquire self-sufficiency. To be clear, this solution is not simply about 'arming women', but about promoting self-defence and shifting force away from the state because of the state's historic use of violence. It therefore counters the conventional monopolisation of force observed in state systems.

Despite containing a diverse population, including multiple different ethnic groups who have now been armed, Rojava remains relatively peaceful internally. In their view, this is because of their emphasis on plurality, decentralisation and autonomy. Kurds see themselves as having the right to defend themselves only against hegemonic forces. In the case of ISIS, the YPG/YPJ fought against the group's virulent misogyny. In the case of the Turkish invasion of the region, YPG/YPJ has intermittently engaged in battle against these state attacks. Self-defence also extends into the ideological realm, discussed above, where Rojava participants claim the right to defend themselves from epistemological or 'symbolic' attacks by making decisions, and producing knowledge, about themselves. It is for this reason that Women's and Youth Committees were put in place, as they retained veto power over decisions that affected them; it is also for this reason that women's and asayish academies exist, and that jineology was created.

CONCLUSION

This chapter has considered the activities of the YPG and YPJ in northern Syria. Their solution to ending war is to dissolve military power at the state level and empower individuals to be self-sufficient, militarily, ecologically and economically. The chapter has shown that nation-states cannot solve the problems created by nation-states, and therefore suggests that one arm of the fight against oppression must involve critiquing and dismantling the state system, understood as fundamentally imbricated with patriarchy. One of the most effective means of dismantling the state system, in these Kurdish women's view, is to implement democratic confederalism. A core part of this requires reclaiming the means of violence from the state and placing it into the hands of the people, including women.

REFERENCES

Note: All URLs last accessed on 24 June 2021.

Alesali, L. and Zdanowicz, C. (2019) These Syrian women built a female-only village to escape from ISIS and war. *CNN*, 4 May. Available at: www.cnn.com/2019/05/04/middleeast/jinwar-syria-female-only-village-trnd/index.html

Arango, T. (2012) Syrian opposition gets key sources of support: EU urges new coalition to develop a 'credible alternative' to Assad. *International Herald Tribune*, 21 November.

Azeez, H. (2016) The Rojava revolution: A beacon of hope. Talk delivered as part of the Socialism for the 21st Century conference, 14 May, University of Sydney.

B., A. (2016) Eroding the state in Rojava. *Theory & Event* 19. Available at: https://muse.jhu.edu/article/610227

Bell, A. (2014) *Relating Indigenous and Settler Identities: Beyond Domination*. London: Palgrave Macmillan.

Bengio, O. (2014) The Kurdish women's revolution. *Jerusalem Post*, 10 March. Available at: www.jpost.com/Opinion/Op-Ed-Contributors/The-Kurdish-womens-revolution-344927

Cousins, S. (2014) Thousands of Syrian women are signing up to fight ISIS. *New Republic*, 9 October. Available at: https://newrepublic.com/article/119741/ypgs-womens-wing-ypj-battles-islamic-state-syrias-kurdish-land

Dirik, D. (2014) Stateless state. Talk delivered as part of the New World Summit conference, 2 September, Brussels. Available at: https://vimeo.com/107639261

Dirik, D. (2015a) Why Kobanî did not fall. *Kurdish Question*. Available at: www.kurdishquestion.com/oldsite/index.php/kurdistan/west-kurdistan/why-kobani-did-not-fall/570-why-kobani-did-not-fall.html (accessed 18 August 2019).

Dirik, D. (2015b) Feminism and the Kurdish liberation movement. Talk delivered at the Dissecting Capitalist Modernity: Building Democratic Confederalism conference, Hamburg, April.

Dirik, D. (2016) Building democracy without the state. *ROAR Magazine*, 18 March. Available at: https://roarmag.org/magazine/building-democracy-without-a-state/

Diyar, Z. (2014) Vakti geldi [It's time]. *Yeni Ozgur Politika*, 13 November. Available at: www.yeniozgurpolitika.org/index.php?rupel=nuce&id=36153

Griffin, E. (2014) These remarkable women are fighting ISIS. It's time you know who they are. *Marie Claire*, 1 October. Available at: www.marieclaire.com/world-reports/inspirational-women/these-are-the-women-battling-isis

Güneser, H. (2015) The Rojava revolution. Talk delivered on 23 January, Helsinki. Available at: www.youtube.com/watch?v=yf36jHu8wOA (accessed 24 June 2021).

Gupta, R. (2016) Military fatigues and floral scarves. *New Internationalist*, 1 May. Available at: http://newint.org/features/2016/05/01/rojava-women-syria/

Human Rights Watch (1991) Human Rights Watch World Report 1990 – Syria and Syrian-occupied Lebanon. Available at: www.refworld.org/docid/467fca3ec.html

Human Rights Watch (2009) Group denial: Repression of Kurdish political and cultural rights in Syria. Available at: www.hrw.org/report/2009/11/26/group-denial/repression-kurdish-political-and-cultural-rights-syria

JA (Jineology Academy) (2015) *Jineolojiye giriş [Introduction to Jineology]*. Neuss: Mesopotamia Press.

Kendal, C. and Oak, G. (2016) Interview with YPG Commander Cihan Kendal – by a British YPG International fighter. *Revolutionary Women*, 1 August. Available at: https://internationalrevolutionarywomen.wordpress.com/2016/08/01/interview-with-ypg-commander-cihan-kendal/

Knapp, M., Flach, A. and Ayboğa, E. (2016) *Revolution in Rojava: Democratic Autonomy and Women's Liberation in Syrian Kurdistan*. London: Pluto Press.

Letsch, C. (2015) Kurdish women pray for peace as fears of civil war in Turkey mount. *The Guardian*, 16 August. Available at: www.theguardian.com/world/2015/aug/16/women-join-kurdish-rebel-ranks

Milliken, J. (1999) The study of discourse in International Relations: A critique of research and methods. *European Journal of International Relations* 5(2): 225–254.

Öcalan, A. (2005) KCK Sözleşmesi [Contract of the KCK]. Available at: https://tr.wikisource.org/wiki/KCK_S%C3%B6zle%C5%9Fmesi (accessed 24 June 2021).

Öcalan, A. (2015) *Democratic Confederalism*. London: Transmedia Publishing.

Omrani, Z. (2015) Introduction to the political and social structures of democratic autonomy in Rojava. *Kurdish Question*, 4 October. Available at: https://mesopotamia.coop/introduction-to-the-political-and-social-structures-of-democratic-autonomy-in-rojava/

Quinn, J. (2015) Rojava dispatch six: Innovations, the formation of the Hêza Parastina Cewherî (HPC). *Modern Slavery: A journal for the abolition of all forms of enslavement*, 31 October. Available at: http://modernslavery.calpress.org/?p=949

Rojava Report (2014) First new university to open in Rojava. *The Rojava Report*, 31 August. Available at: https://rojavareport.wordpress.com/2014/08/31/first-new-university-to-open-in-rojava/

Rojava Social Contract (2014) Charter of the Social Contract. Available at: https://peaceinkurdistancampaign.com/charter-of-the-social-contract/

RT (2015) *Her war: Women vs. ISIS*. Documentary. 15 June. Available at: www.youtube.com/watch?v=2EnWzbQ-qok

Schmidinger, T. (2018) *Rojava: Revolution, War, and the Future of Syria's Kurds*, trans. M. Schiffmann. London: Pluto Press.

Spivak, G.C. (1988) Can the subaltern speak? In: C. Nelson (ed.) *Marxism and the Interpretation of Culture*. Chicago: University of Illinois Press, pp. 271–313.

Sputnik (2016) Meet the head of Syrian Kurds' women fighters, who kill and humiliate Daesh. *Sputnik News*, 2 April. Available at: https://sputniknews.com/middleeast/20160204/1034243327/kurdish-ypj-leader-interview.html

Taylor, V. (2014) H&M denies jumpsuit was inspired by Kurdish fighter uniforms. *NY Daily News*, 7 October. Available at: www.nydailynews.com/life-style/fashion/h-m-denies-jumpsuit-inspired-kurdish-fighter-uniforms-article-1.1966181

Terrorism Research and Analysis Consortium (2016) Terrorist groups – YPJ (Women's Protection Unit). Available at: www.trackingterrorism.org/group/ypj-womens-protection-unit

Üstündağ, N. (2016) Self-defense as a revolutionary practice in Rojava, or How to unmake the state. *South Atlantic Quarterly* 115: 197–210.

VICE Media (2013) *Rojava: Syria's Unknown War*. Documentary, 36 mins. September. Available at: www.youtube.com/watch?v=p2zxlFQxkQ4

Yegenoglu, M. (1998) *Colonial Fantasies: Towards a Feminist Reading of Orientalism*. Cambridge: Cambridge University Press.

Yesiltas, O. (2014) Iraq, Arab nationalism, and obstacles to democratic transition. In: D. Romano and M. Gurses (eds) *Conflict, Democratisation, and the Kurds in the Middle East: Turkey, Iran, Iraq, and Syria*. New York: Palgrave Macmillan, pp. 41–58.

Yildiz, K. (2005) *The Kurds in Syria: The Forgotten People*. London: Pluto Press.

6

Queer Our Vision of Security

Cai Wilkinson

THE TRUTH IS:
Security is a lie.
Your genes will not protect you.
Liberal leaders will not protect you.
The military will not protect you.
Marriage will not protect you.
The government will not protect you.
LGBT organizations will not protect you.
Money will not protect you.
The closet will not protect you.
Assimilation will not protect you.

(Pink Tank 2005, 23)

To be *queer* – that is, to *not* be gender conforming and/or heterosexual – is to know that security is a lie. It is to know that one's personal safety is always precarious, and that institutions that are supposed to help often harm. It is to experience how definitions of security exclude and erase queer bodies and lives, with the assumption of protection replaced by experiences of gender/ed policing and punishment for 'failing' to be the 'right' kind of man or woman. It is to understand just how deeply gender is woven into systems of power and violence at every level, from the international to the intimate. It is to know that because of how your gender identity and/or sexuality are perceived, *because of who you are*, you are inevitably and unavoidably insecure, and that your body and being is a battleground in an everyday war.

This chapter will explore queering 'security' as a feminist solution to ending war. The erasure and othering of queer bodies and lives directly contributes to the perpetuation of war and everyday violence through the (re)enforcement of binary and essentialist norms of gender and sexuality. Drawing on queer experiences of insecurity at borders, in bathrooms and in bedrooms, this chapter uses a queer feminist lens to show how queering our definitions of security is an important feminist solution to ending war. Queering 'security' enables us to transcend existing logics of security and imagine and practise security for all people, regardless of their gender and/or sexual orientation. Queering 'security' also allows us to challenge what constitutes war, and the spaces and places in which institutionalised violence occurs.

WHAT IS A QUEER SOLUTION?

While queer is often used as a synonym for lesbian, gay, bisexual and transgender (LGBT), or to describe people who are not heterosexual, in this chapter it is used as the antonym of *straight*. Straight is a term that brings together sexuality and gender and highlights how heterosexuality requires the 'correct' performance of gender in order to be recognisable to others. Queer, in contrast, is used here to denote people who do not conform to the norms and ideals of the heteropatriarchal gender order of man/woman due to their sexuality and/or gender identity and/or presentation. Especially given its long history of being used as a pejorative term – a weapon of everyday warfare – against LGBT people and the inevitable contentiousness of reclaiming words (Rocheleau 2019) it should not be assumed that queer is a word that people will use to describe themselves.

As a verb, queer works to denaturalise and destabilise the categories of gender and sexuality that are built into our societies, challenging assumptions that heterosexuality and binary gender(ed) identities are 'normal', rather than just 'common'. This process of *queering* enables us to see how existing norms of gender and sexuality contribute to insecurity and legitimise gender policing, making it possible to blame queers for the structural and physical violences that they experience. In this sense, queering aligns with, and extends, the work that feminists have done – and continue to do – in showing how women's experiences of in/security and violence differ from those of men due to the ways heteropatriarchical structures and institutions perpetuate masculinism, a 'totalising worldview that implicitly universalises and privileges the qualities of masculinity, and in doing so subordinates and "others" alternative ways of understanding, knowing and being' (Nicholas and Agius 2018, 5). Just as feminists have argued that women's voices and bodies must be explicitly included in our accounts, analyses and (re)actions, so queer activists and academics argue that the voices and bodies of non-heterosexual and gender non-conforming voices and bodies must be included if we are to successfully challenge heteropatriarchal norms that continue to position anyone who is not a heterosexual cisgender straight-acting (that is, *not queer*) male as less worthy of a secure existence.

This is not to say that there are not tensions between feminist and queer agendas. While both are committed to advancing the inclusion of groups of people who are marginalised on account of their gender, there is considerable diversity within and across feminist and queer communities in how gender is defined and how it is understood to structure experiences of exclusion (Pearce et al. 2020). Darcy Leigh (2017, 355) explores the differences between the two approaches directly in her examination of the 'uneasy alliance' between Feminist International Relations (IR) and Queer IR. Leigh explains that the central reason for the unsettled relationship between the two approaches is the 'many different strands of feminist and queer politics' that they contain, raising challenging questions about each others' commitments and understandings of structures of power and marginalisation within their own communities as well as beyond them.

Despite these differences, which reflect those of feminist and queer politics more widely, Leigh argues persuasively that these tensions can be productive and outlines what a commitment to both perspectives looks like for IR:

Queer Feminist International Relations must operate within/from these tensions: expanding analysis far beyond 'where are the [white, cis, heterosexual] women?' even while continuing to ask 'where are the women and femmes?'; making sex, sexuality and sexual deviance central without losing sight of gender; disrupting binaries and fixed identities without losing the political leverage that sometimes comes with them; and acknowledging entanglements with the institutions Feminist and Queer IR seek to transform while also resisting being neutralized by assimilation. (Leigh 2017, 355)

A queer feminist analysis of security, therefore, means making explicit the connections and overlaps between the experiences of queers and other groups that experience marginalisation and insecurity, and highlighting how subjugation of the female/feminine/femme and corresponding veneration of the (able-bodied, white, normatively masculine) male re/produce existing dynamics and configurations of in/security.

WHY QUEER[ING] SECURITY?

It's hard to quantify and pin down. It's not just bathrooms. It is locker rooms. It is getting misgendered by your professor. It's all sorts of little worries you have throughout the day that have this cumulative effect of dampening your zeal or making you more tired. It cramps your potential when you have to spend so much time thinking about how other people might or might not hurt you. We will never know, right now, the full potential of trans people in our society because we have to spend so much time living, just trying to survive. (Mitch Kellaway, 27, He/him, cited in Lang 2016)

The process of queering our definitions of security begins from the premise that queer 'lives are lived, hence liveable' (Scheman 2011, 210). This statement may seem obvious, but as Mitch's reflection above demonstrates, the insecurity of being queer means that it cannot be taken for granted. Queer lives are frequently endangered by hetero- and cis-normative assumptions about relationships, identities and bodies, to say nothing of deliberate denials of queer existence and attempts to eliminate us politically and physically. Consensual same-sex sexual conduct between adults continues to be criminalised in 62 countries, including 6 in which the death penalty is possible. A further 55 offer no specific legal protections to same-sex attracted people, with just 66 countries providing broad or constitutional protections against discrimination based on sexual orientation (ILGA World: Mendos 2019, 178). Trans and gender-diverse people, meanwhile, are even more vulnerable: according to the 2017 F&M Global Barometer of Trans Rights, just 3 per cent of countries offered legal protections for transgender people sufficient to be classed as 'protecting', whereas 76 per cent of countries had so few – if any – provisions that they are most accurately described as 'persecuting' (Dicklitch-Nelson et al. 2019).

These statistics – and many, many more like them – point to the fact that for queer people, a multitude of everyday insecurities creates a state of *everyday war* that requires constant vigilance and preparedness lest one get caught in a skirmish with either those who deliberately oppose LGBTQ human rights or those who have simply never considered the realities of queer lives. In either case, lives are put at risk, and, for some, made unliveable. As Catherine Baker poignantly describes, the filter between security and insecurity is 'so much more fragile when you are queer':

> Something about your body and how you live in it – your queerness – and where on the planet you are doing whatever you are doing means that you at least think about in/security, sometimes, in the everyday, in a way that a straight white man living somewhere as a citizen has under normal, peacetime circumstances never considered that he would have to do. (Baker 2017, 110)

Given this, queering security not only challenges mainstream approaches to security, which often erase queer lives and bodies, but also challenges mainstream understandings of war as a contained and finite activity. In fact, a queer approach to war asks us to reverse Clausewitz's dictum, and consider that politics is a continuation of war by other means, touching all aspects of life from the bathroom to the bedroom and everywhere in between.

Moving beyond our initial premise, therefore, queering security requires that we ask *what everyday conditions make queer lives im/ possible?* In order to explore the solution of queering security and to answer this question about everyday insecurity, this chapter visits three sites of queer insecurity: borders, bathrooms and bedrooms.

Although the experience of queer insecurity is ontological, its intensity and impact on an individual's everyday life varies significantly, especially within the wider societal dynamics of marginalisation generated by racism, ablism, classism, poverty, criminalisation, xenophobia and colonialism. Yet while privilege undoubtedly protects, the fierce significance of gender and sexuality for both individuals and collectives means that privilege is always precarious and liable to be undone. Being queer in the contested territory of society means that it is always possible that one's efforts to keep the gender(ed) peace are not enough. Everyday security can always be eroded or even completely washed away. The consequences of being queer transform from abstract risk to calculating immediate probabilities of violence in real time. These calculations require that queer individuals continually ask: *How will this person react? How vulnerable am I? How can I stay safe, or at least limit harm?*

SITES OF EVERYDAY WAR: BORDERS,
BATHROOMS AND BEDROOMS

While insecurity may be experienced anywhere, there are particular everyday spaces and situations in which queer people are vulnerable. These are often in gendered spaces that reproduce binary hetero logics and therefore influence how others respond to their own and others' sexuality and/or gender identity. At borders, in bathrooms and in bedrooms (that is, when dating or having sex), queer people are disproportionately likely to experience violent reactions as their non-conformity with societal norms of gender and sexuality provoke confusion, consternation, disapproval, denial and disgust. It is no coincidence that these locations are all ones in which security is deemed to be of particular importance, and perceived threats are responded to with particular potency.

In the rest of this section, I consider queer experiences at borders, in bathrooms and in bedrooms (that is, navigating potentially intimate encounters) and how the gendered and/or sexualised security logics of these spaces (re)produce insecurity for queer people. All three sites are ones in which the ongoing positioning of queer people's non-conformity with norms of gender and sexuality as a constant Other is particularly tangible. The realities of travelling, peeing and dating while queer clash violently with the gendered boundaries that encircle and structure individual, societal and state imaginaries of security.

At best, queer people and their bodies are highlighted as an anomaly, a deviation from the (binary, straight, gendered norm) that is justifiably treated with suspicion, facing questions like: *Why can't you just act normal? What sort of freak would want to look like that?* At worst, queers are a threat that cannot be tolerated, their alleged transgressions of the masculinist and heterosexist binary gender order provoking consternation, panic and even violence, meeting questions and abuse such as: *You know this is the ladies' room, right? But you don't look like a woman! You're disgusting! You don't belong here! There's a man in women's restroom! Get out! I'll call security! If you won't show ID, you'll need to leave the restroom and come with us, sir* (see Lopez 2016).

Borders

> Every time I have to go through the Gender Tube [airport body scanners] there's always a moment of hesitation that I can feel from the TSA [Transport Security Administration] agents when they have to decide whether to scan my body as a man's or a woman's. Sometimes, I can hear them quietly talking among themselves as they speculate on my genitals. Sometimes they'll ask me if I have anything in my pockets or some other random inquiry presumably in an attempt to parse my voice, which is equally as androgynous. The worst times are when my chest is flagged as an anomaly and a male TSA agent feels me up. (James Factora, 21, they/them, cited in Ettachfini 2019)

As the above quote highlights, for queer people, going through security screening at an airport is often to find oneself caught in a clash between 'different epistemic sources of knowledge about gender – individual narrative or gender presentation, the classification as M (male) or F (female) on the document one carries, and one's body'

(Currah and Mulqueen 2011, 558). Put more simply, with the push of a (pink or blue) button, who you are becomes a potential cause for alarm and the liveability of your queer life becomes suspicious and a target for heightened scrutiny. *Are you a man or a woman? Are you one of those freaks? What are you really?*

The 2015 US Transgender Survey reported that 'Forty-three percent (43%) of transgender identifying individuals who went through airport security in the past year experienced at least one issue related to their gender identity or expression', including incorrect pronoun or title use, being patted down or having their luggage searched for gender-related reasons, or having the name or gender on their identity documents questioned (James et al. 2016, 222). People whose bodies do not correspond to that expected of their perceived gender are particularly prone to encounter 'gender trouble', to borrow the title of Judith Butler's 1990 book. Even if the TSA agent presses the button that reflects your gender identity (assuming that there is one), the presumed correspondence of identity and body must still be navigated. Trans men report being flagged for pat-downs due to the scanner reading the absence of normatively male genitalia as incongruent with their gender presentation, although others report that their prosthetic genitalia also triggered the alarm (Capener 2019; Stafford 2015). Similarly, transgender women have found themselves flagged for having 'anomalous' groin areas (Rogers 2015), while some intersex people have reported that they trigger alarms regardless of which button is pushed (Viloria 2017).

'Border security' practices, including airport security practices and biometric scanners, perpetuate and compound insecurities for those whom Puar (2010, 2, cited in Quinan 2017, 156) calls 'other others': Black women have repeatedly reported being subjected to intrusive 'hair pat-downs' following false positive readings caused by their hair (Medina et al. 2019), and there have been instances of women using breast prosthetics after mastectomies as part of cancer treatment being ordered to undergo additional pat-downs or searches (Holstege 2013). Muslim women wearing hijabs have complained of harassment from TSA agents (Rojas 2018), and the Sikh Coalition (2019) has noted that Sikhs of all genders 'continue to face disproportionately higher rates of secondary screening by TSA in comparison to the average traveler' – something that they have in common with people with disabilities, who have long reported multiple instances of inequitable treatment at checkpoints (Morris 2018).

All of these examples point to the dangers of being 'not average' according to societal norms. Deviation from the racialised, ablist, embodied norms of gender that are programmed into the scanner and reinforced by TSA agents' protocols results in intensifications of othering that punish, police and securitise difference. *You don't present as a woman/man should, therefore you are wrong, different, aberrant, abnormal, dangerous, threatening.*

Few would argue that the experience of being flagged for additional investigation during security screening is not unpleasant and intrusive. Yet too often the response is to justify the practice as being necessary 'for the greater good', rather than recognise the uncomfortable reality that the othering of those who do not conform to society's norms is a deliberate part of the theatre of security that is performed at airports. After all, without their insecurity – that is, without their humiliation and dehumanisation – how could we possibly know that the system is working and that we are protected from ever-stealthy and devious enemies that threaten our way of life? *It's unfortunate and I really feel for them, but the policies are there for a reason, you know.*

Bathrooms

> There's always in the back of my mind that anything I do, especially if I'm in someplace where people know I'm trans, if I even blink wrong, if I look the wrong way, if I spend too much time in the bathroom, [or] if I do anything besides get in and get out, that somebody is going to accuse me of something. My bathroom visits are surgical strikes ... you do one thing without collateral damage. (Brynn Tannehill, 41, She/her, cited in Lang 2016)

Public bathrooms continue the logic of national borders, with gender policing central to ensuring that only the 'right' people enter.[1] Rather

---

1   At least in locations where public bathrooms are commonly designated as either male or female. While all-gender bathrooms are gradually becoming more common, it remains the case that gender segregation of public bathrooms is the global norm.

than relying on formal processes and documentation, however, the first line of defence for men's or women's bathrooms is fellow bathroom users' perceptions of your conformity with the relevant gender norms. One must be recognisable as a 'normal' man or a woman if one wishes to be confident they can pee in peace. Bathrooms are powerfully gendered and sexed spaces. Should someone decide that you don't look sufficiently like a woman or a man for their liking, the onus is on the now-questionable queer to prove that they are not, in fact, in the 'wrong' bathroom or face the consequences. *Think fast: how are you going to prove you're in the 'right' bathroom? Can you? Is there time to leave before the first fist hits or security arrives? You can't blame them for it; if you'd just do something about how you look, this wouldn't happen.*[2]

In the intimate spaces of bathrooms and bedrooms, we can see the fragile logics and violent consequences of masculinism writ large. Masculinism is an underlying ethos and worldview that universalises and privileges the qualities of masculinity while subordinating alternative ways of being (Nicholas and Agius 2018, 5). Public bathrooms are spaces that exemplify masculinism. Public bathrooms have become a battleground for gendered heteronormative standards that 'marginalize people whose bodies deviate from normative male embodiment, such as people who are unable to urinate at urinals for medical, anatomical, or social reasons' (Davis 2017, 200–1).

As Heath Fogg Davis goes on to argue, this reductionist and absolutist sex segregation perpetuates insecurities at both individual and systemic levels. It 'harms everyone because it constricts our individual freedom to say who we are in relation to the categories of male and female, regardless of how we appear to others and who is in our care while we are in public' (Davis 2017, 201), thereby reinforcing normative assumptions about gender identities and roles. More widely, sex-segregated public bathrooms generate 'sex-based disadvantage' by hindering women and others who do not conform to ableist and masculinist norms from freely accessing public spaces (Davis 2017, 210). The idea of 'peeing in peace' seems more aspira-

---

2 A comment made to me when I was a graduate student and had been asked to leave a bathroom on campus.

tional (and unattainable) than ever when there may not be any toilets provided in the first place, or when what is available is unusable due to poor maintenance, inconvenient locations, long wait times, and/or insufficient consideration that caregiving frequently crosses sex and gender categories.

Yet gendered imaginaries of security continue to dictate the organisation, design and use of public bathrooms. Facilities for women are 'positioned as both especially safe and (potentially) especially dangerous', a framing that has led some to argue vehemently that permitting trans and queer people to use the bathroom aligned with their gender identity is a violation of women's rights and safety (Jones and Slater 2020: 838–9). Underpinning this claim is a rigid understanding of sex and gender as binary and essential, with queer and trans lives the price that must be paid to maintain existing logics of security even as they perpetuate insecurity for all.

Bedrooms

> I happened to cross the street, thinking that two other people were female, which they weren't. And we engaged in conversation and I guess a friend of mine must have realised you know, that was a guy instead of a girl and he yelled out, you know, what it was. And as I pushed away, you know, trying to leave, I guess he – he must have pushed back. You know, I was drunk so I got enraged, you know. And then I attacked. (James Dixon, cited in Maigne 2019)

The victim of the attack described above was Islan Nettles, a 21-year-old transgender woman. In statements to the police, Dixon said he was flirting with Islan, but then turned on her when friends made him aware that she was transgender and mocked his apparent interest in her. Dixon's punch knocked her to the ground, and Dixon hit her again while she lay on the ground. Five days later, having never regained consciousness, Islan died of the head injuries that she had sustained. In 2016, Dixon pleaded guilty to her manslaughter and was sentenced to 12 years in prison (McKinley Jr 2016).

The circumstances of Islan's death were far from uncommon. Between 1 January 2008 and 30 September 2019, Transgender

Europe's Trans Murder Monitoring (TMM) project registered the murder of 3,314 trans and gender-diverse people around the world. The vast majority of those killed were transwomen, and more than 60 per cent were sex workers (TGEU 2019). These figures point to the fact that for queer people, especially (but not exclusively) transgender women, safer sex begins with not getting killed or attacked by one's prospective intimate partner before even getting to the bedroom.

In bathrooms, at borders and in bedrooms, the violence faced by queer people is not coincidental. Rather, it reflects the systematic and institutionalised dehumanisation of those deemed to threaten the heteropatriarchal gender order. One of the clearest manifestations of this is the persistence of the so-called gay or trans panic defence, 'a legal strategy which asks a jury to find that a victim's sexual orientation or gender identity is to blame for the defendant's violent reaction, including murder' and downgrade the severity of the charges (Holden 2019). This defence remains permissible in all but nine US states (Fitsimons 2020), as well as in South Australia (Nielsen 2020), a tangible indication of how male violence continues to be condoned in the everyday war to secure masculinity against the queer enemy. *It's either them or us!*

QUEER VISIONS OF SECURITY FOR ALL

Ending war, defined strictly as military violence, is insufficient. We must end both structural violence and physical and psychological violences if everyday war is to end. Ending war and violence requires both a queer vision of what security means and also a commitment to de-centring masculinism, cis-heterosexism, ableism, racism and other forms of domination in processes of securitisation/militarisation. By way of illustration, consider queer activist Mattilda Bernstein's (2017) surprisingly positive response to President Trump's announcement that he would reinstate the ban on trans people serving in the US military. She writes:

At last, here was step one in a three-point plan for dramatic structural change, handed right to us: Step 1: Ban trans people from serving in the military. Step 2: Ban everyone from serving in the military. Step 3: Ban the military. (Bernstein 2017)

Bernstein continues that in these three simple steps:

> we could free up the resources to fund everything we've ever dreamed of in this country – universal housing and health care, a guaranteed minimum income, safe houses for queer and trans kids to escape abusive homes – you name it. With redistribution of the hundreds of billions of dollars allocated to the military every year (nearly half the entire federal budget), surely the slogan 'A better world is possible' could become more than an aspirational refrain. (Bernstein 2017)

By destabilising and denaturalising our understandings of how security is both gendered and sexualised, and the ways in which this perpetuates violence, processes of queering open up space for us to imagine alternative definitions and practices of security that are more inclusive of all genders and sexualities, and for all 'other others'. To queer security, therefore, is not simply to seek emancipation (helping people survive the current system through reforms), but to foster liberation (revolutionary change and dismantling of patriarchy). Ending war cannot just be about a rejection of militarism, but rather must involve challenging all forms of violence so that queer bodies and lives cease to be battlegrounds in an everyday war.

REFERENCES

Note: The URLs were last accessed on 24 June 2021.

Baker, Catherine (2017) The filter is so much more fragile when you are queer. *Critical Studies on Security* 5(1): 109–112.

Bernstein Sycamore, Mattilda (2017) Swords into marketshare, *The Baffler*, 21 September. Available at: https://thebaffler.com/latest/swords-into-marketshare

Capener, Aaron (2019) FTM packing and airport security | Avoid airport mishaps. Transguy Supply, blog post, 24 July. Available at: https://transguysupply.com/blogs/news/ftm-packing-and-airport-security

Currah, Paisley and Mulqueen, Tara (2011) Securitizing gender: Identity, biometrics, and transgender bodies at airports. *Social Research* 78(2): 557–582.

Davis, Heath Fogg (2017) Why the 'transgender' bathroom controversy should make us rethink sex-segregated public bathrooms. *Politics, Groups, and Identities* 6(2): 199–216.

Dicklitch-Nelson, Susan, Buckland, Scottie Thompson, Yost, Berwood and Rahman, Indira (2019) *Global LGBT Human Rights Trends: 2011– 2017 Data for 197 Countries.* Lancaster, PA: Franklin & Marshall College. Available at: www.fandmglobalbarometers.org/results/

Ettachfini, Leila (2019) The horrible things that happen to trans people going through airport security. *Vice*, 28 August. Available at: www.vice.com/en_au/article/qvgbv5/transgender-airport-security-harassment-experiences-tsa

Fitsimons, Tim (2020) N.J. bans gay and transgender 'panic defenses'. *NBC News*, 23 January. Available at: www.nbcnews.com/feature/nbc-out/n-j-bans-gay-transgender-panic-defenses-n1120416

Holden, Alexandra (2019) The gay/trans panic defense: What it is, and how to end it. Member Op-Ed, American Bar Association, 1 April. Available at: www.americanbar.org/groups/crsj/publications/member-features/gay-trans-panic-defense/

Holstege, Sean (2013) Phoenix airport screening draws angry complaints. *USA Today*, 12 October. Available at: www.usatoday.com/story/news/nation/2013/10/11/phoenix-airport-screening-draws-angry-complaints/2970589/

ILGA World: Lucas Ramón Mendos (2019) *State-sponsored Homophobia 2019: Global Legislation Overview Update.* Geneva: ILGA. Available at: https://ilga.org/downloads/ILGA_World_State_Sponsored_Homophobia_report_global_legislation_overview_update_December_2019.pdf

James, S.E., Herman, J.L., Rankin, S., Keisling, M., Mottet, L. and Anafi, M. (2016) *The Report of the 2015 U.S. Transgender Survey.* Washington, DC: National Center for Transgender Equality. Available at: https://transequality.org/sites/default/files/docs/usts/USTS-Full-Report-Dec17.pdf

Jones, Charlotte and Slater, Jen (2020) The toilet debate: Stalling trans possibilities and defending 'women's protected spaces'. *Sociological Review* 68(4): 834–851.

Lang, Nico (2016) What it's like to use a public bathroom while trans. *Rolling Stone*, 31 March. Available at: www.rollingstone.com/culture/culture-news/what-its-like-to-use-a-public-bathroom-while-trans-65793/

Leigh, Darcy (2017) Queer Feminist International Relations: Uneasy alliances, productive tensions. *Alternatif Politika* 9(3): 343–360.

Ley, Heather (2019) Team Minot Wonder Women. *Minot Air Force Base News*, 12 March. Available: www.minot.af.mil/News/Article-Display/Article/1782779/team-minot-wonder-women/

Lopez, German (2016) Women are getting harassed in bathrooms because of anti-transgender hysteria. *Vox News*, 19 May. Available at: www.vox.com/2016/5/18/11690234/women-bathrooms-harassment

MacKenzie, Megan (2009) Securitization and desecuritization: Female soldiers and the reconstruction of women in post-conflict Sierra Leone. *Security Studies* 2(18): 241–246.

Maigne, Juliette (2019) Trans woman's killer used the 'gay panic defence': It's still legal in 42 states. *Vice News*, 21 July.

McKinley Jr, James C. (2016) Man sentenced to 12 years in beating death of transgender woman. *The New York Times*, 19 April. Available at: www.nytimes.com/2016/04/20/nyregion/man-sentenced-to-12-years-in-beating-death-of-transgender-woman.html

Medina, Brenda, *ProPublica* and Frank, Thomas (2019) TSA agents say they're not discriminating against black women, but their body scanners might be. *ProPublica*, 17 April. Available at: www.propublica.org/article/tsa-not-discriminating-against-black-women-but-their-body-scanners-might-be

Morris, John (2018) What we learned at the 2018 TSA Disability Meeting. *Wheelchair Travel*, 13 August. Available at: https://wheelchairtravel.org/takeaways-2018-tsa-disability-conference/

Nicholas, Lucy and Agius, Christine (2018) *The Persistence of Global Masculinism: Discourse, Gender and Neo-colonial Re-articulations of Violence.* Cham, Switzerland: Palgrave Macmillan.

Nielsen, Ben (2020) SA led the way for many reforms, so why is 'gay panic' still a defence? *ABC News*, 3 June. Available at: www.abc.net.au/news/2020-06-03/proposal-to-abolish-gay-panic-defence-in-sa/12311350

Pearce, Ruth, Erikainen, Sonja and Vincent, Ben (2020) TERF wars: An introduction. *Sociological Review* 68(4): 677–698.

Pink Tank (2005) We will not protect you. Available at: www.againstequality.org/files/we_will_not_protect_you_2005.pdf

Quinan, Christine L. (2017) Gender (in)securities: Surveillance and transgender bodies in a post-9/11 era of neoliberalism. In: Matthias Leese and Stef Wittendorp (eds) *Security/Mobility*. Manchester: Manchester University Press, pp. 153–169.

Rocheleau, Julie (2019) A former slur is reclaimed, and listeners have mixed feelings. *NPR Public Editor*, 21 August. Available at: www.npr.org/sections/publiceditor/2019/08/21/752330316/a-former-slur-is-reclaimed-and-listeners-have-mixed-feelings

Rogers, Katie (2015) T.S.A. defends treatment of transgender air traveler. *The New York Times*, 22 September. Available at: www.nytimes.com/2015/09/23/us/shadi-petosky-tsa-transgender.html

Rojas, Nicole (2018) Fourteen women claim TSA harassed them for wearing hijabs at Newark Airport. *Newsweek*, 8 June. Available at: www.newsweek.com/fourteen-women-claim-tsa-harassed-them-wearing-hijabs-newark-airport-967771

Scheman, Naomi (2011) Queering the center by centring the queer: Reflections on transsexuals and secular Jews. In *Shifting Ground: Knowledge and Reality, Transgression and Trustworthiness.* Oxford: Oxford University Press, pp. 111–144.

Sikh Coalition (2019) Statement of Sim J. Singh, Senior Manager of Advocacy and Policy, at Hearing on 'Perspectives on TSA's policies to prevent unlawful profiling', Committee on Homeland Security, 4 June. Available at: www.sikhcoalition.org/wp-content/uploads/2019/06/TSA-Hearing-6.4.19.pdf

Stafford, Zach (2015) TSA agents who flag trans people cause trauma and don't make us safer. *The Guardian*, 24 September. Available at: www.theguardian.com/commentisfree/2015/sep/23/tsa-agents-transgender-people-trauma

TGEU (2019) TMM update Trans Day of Remembrance 2019. Available: https://tgeu.org/tmm-update-trans-day-of-remembrance-2019/

Viloria, Hida (2017) Fear of flying – or at least the TSA – while intersex. *Daily Beast*, 18 March. Available at: www.thedailybeast.com/fear-of-flyingor-at-least-the-tsawhile-intersex

7

Abolish Nuclear Weapons: Feminist, Queer, and Indigenous Knowledge for Ending Nuclear Weapons

Ray Acheson

This chapter will explore nuclear abolition as a feminist objective to ending war. It explores the role of intersectional feminism in shaping activism against the bomb. The bomb itself is the most extreme expression of violence and control of the patriarchal, racist and capitalist world order. Those who possess or desire nuclear weapons argue that the mere possession of the bomb prevents conflict and deters attack. Nuclear weapons are discussed in the abstract, as magical tools that keep us safe and maintain stability in the world. But nuclear weapons are not abstract. They are made of radioactive materials. They are made to destroy flesh and bone. To melt the skin from our bodies. To reduce entire cities to ashes.

To the majority of people struggling daily under this oppressive order, the abolition of nuclear weapons may not seem like a priority. When confronting settler colonialism, imperial intervention, war, mass incarceration, poverty, displacement, environmental devastation, and violence in our homes and communities, nuclear weapons may seem like an abstraction indeed. But these weapons are part of the spectrum of institutionalised violence. They are the pinnacle of a state's monopoly on violence, the ultimate signifier of domination. These weapons can manifest extraordinary violence in a single moment – extreme death, destruction, and despair.

Thus, to resist injustice requires attention to the role nuclear weapons play in our world order, at the intersection of patriarchal, racist, colonial and capitalist oppressions. We must privilege voices and perspectives of those who are historically overlooked, ignored or ridiculed. Doing so means changing the conversation, changing the location of conversations, and diversifying the participation in conversations about nuclear weapons.

This chapter is grounded in the belief that nuclear weapons abolition work must contribute to broader struggles for social justice. I seek to engage with feminist, queer and Indigenous writing, not to distract from other structural and physical oppressions these activists target. Rather, I believe that nuclear abolitionists can learn from other activists working against systems of patriarchy, racism and colonialism. It is useful to recognise various perspectives and experiences that revolt against hegemonic normative structures and systems of thought; nuclear abolition requires us to challenge social ordering and logics of knowledge production that give 'social and political difference their discursive power' (Eng 2013, 4). This chapter proceeds with an overview of the history of nuclear weapons and feminist efforts to abolish them, before engaging with a range of scholars to learn how to continue to resist and craft efforts to abolish nuclear weapons.

NUCLEAR WEAPONS, INTERSECTIONAL OPPRESSIONS AND MYTHS OF SECURITY

The history of nuclear weapons is a history of colonial exploitation. Nuclear-armed states have tested bombs outside of their territories, often in colonies or lands they deemed inferior (Hawkins 2018). When nuclear-armed governments have conducted tests on their own territories, it has primarily been on Indigenous lands. For example, the Western Shoshone Nation in the south-western United States is the most bombed nation on Earth (Johnson 2018). In a statement to the negotiations of the United Nations (UN) Treaty on the Prohibition of Nuclear Weapons (TPNW) in July 2017, 35 Indigenous groups declared, 'Governments and colonial forces exploded nuclear bombs on our sacred lands – upon which we depend for our lives and livelihoods, and which contain places of critical cultural and spiritual significance – believing they were worthless' (Indigenous Statement 2017). Delivered by Karina Lester, a Yankunytjatjara-Anangu woman from South Australia, the statement highlighted that Indigenous people 'never asked for, and never gave permission to poison our soil, food, rivers and oceans. We continue to resist inhumane acts of radioactive racism.'

Activists in the United States have long recognised the racism inherent in the practice of nuclear weapon policy: 'The atomic bombings of Hiroshima and Nagasaki were inextricably linked to colonialism and racial equality' (Intondi 2015, 22). Coretta Scott King, Dr Martin Luther King Jr, W.E.B. Du Bois and others elaborated the inseparability of nuclear disarmament, the end of colonial empires and civil rights (Intondi 2015).

Similarly, feminist scholars have mapped the connections between militarised masculinities, the quest for dominance in international relations, and nuclear weapons. Carol Cohn's (1987a, 1987b) examination of the gendered discourse on nuclear weapons provided the foundations for a feminist analysis of nuclear war, nuclear strategy and nuclear weapons themselves. Drawing upon a Hindu nationalist leader who, after India's 1998 nuclear weapon tests, explained, 'we had to prove that we are not eunuchs', Cohn et al. (2006) argued that statements like this are meant to 'elicit admiration for the wrathful manliness of the speaker' and to imply that being willing to employ nuclear weapons is to be 'man enough' to 'defend' your country. They also examined how disarmament is 'feminised' and linked to disempowerment, weakness and irrationality, while militarism and attaining nuclear weapons are celebrated as signs of strength, power and rationality (Cohn et al. 2006).

Feminists also observe how masculinised expectations for political leaders may be coupled with anxieties about sexual performance and reproduction, emphasising that 'technostrategic speak' is enforced to signal elite 'expertise' (Eschle 2012). In discourses that defend nuclear weapons as necessary for security, 'the protector' is coded as masculine and 'the protected' as feminine. These discourses reinforce, and play into, fantasies of 'real men' and masculinity as defined by 'invulnerability, invincibility, and impregnability' (Eschle 2012). Feminists criticise a masculinised approach to security, specifically in realist International Relations theory that accords status to nuclear weapons as both markers of masculine domination (capable of inflicting violence) and masculine protector (capable of deterring violence) (Duncanson and Eschle 2008).

Nuclear-armed states seek to discredit those who demand the abolition of nuclear weapons. Proponents of nuclear weapons seek to use a logic of rationalism and power to defend their possession of these weapons while seeking to 'feminise' opponents of nuclear weapons by claiming they are emotional and irrational. In the development of the UN Treaty on the Prohibition of Nuclear Weapons negotiations, the representatives from nuclear-armed states berated governments and activists pushing to ban the bomb. In one case, a Russian ambassador suggested that those wanting to prohibit nuclear weapons are 'radical dreamers' who have 'shot off to some other planet or outer space'. In another, a UK ambassador said the security interests of ban-proponents were either irrelevant or non-existent. A US ambassador asserted that banning nuclear weapons might undermine international security so much it could even result in the use of nuclear weapons (Acheson 2019a). These assertions exemplify patriarchal techniques – including victim-blaming and gaslighting. The message is clear: if you try to take away our toys of massive nuclear violence, we will have no choice but to use them, and it will be your fault. This discourse that presents anti-bomb activists as 'emotional', ignores the effects that nuclear weapons inflict on people and denies individuals the space to express their concerns about these genocidal tools. This is a form of gaslighting – insisting that these weapons are a source of security and accusing anyone who thinks otherwise of being emotional, overwrought, irrational, or impractical (Acheson 2018).

Those who determine what is considered realistic, practical and feasible are men and women of incredible privilege; elites of their own societies and in the global community – such as politicians, government personnel, military commanders, and 'national security' practitioners and academics. This field often ignores people affected by nuclear weapons development, testing, stockpiling, use, or threatened use. The common narrative is that nuclear weapons are required in a world where there will always be those who want to retain or develop the capacity to wield massive, unfathomable levels of violence over others. Elites who possess nuclear weapons argue they are 'rational' actors who must retain nuclear weapons for protection against irrational others.

For example, in 2018, the US government asserted that past commitments to nuclear disarmament were out of date and out of step with today's 'international security environment' – ignoring that the international security environment is heavily affected by the US government's own actions, including its build-up of its nuclear arsenal. The Trump administration articulated a new approach to nuclear weapons policy, focused not on what the US can do for nuclear disarmament but what the rest of the world can do so the US – the most heavily militarised country in the world – can feel 'safer' (Acheson 2019b).

This logic insists upon the notion that states are always at odds with one another, rather than collectively pursuing a world in which mutual interdependence and cooperation could guide behaviour through an integrated set of common interests, needs and obligations (Acheson 2019a). Feminists dispute that security can be 'possessed or guaranteed by the state ... It is a process, immanent in our relationships with others and always partial, elusive, and contested' (Duncanson and Eschle 2008, 15). Security is not an object or an achievement, it is a process that depends on the interactions of many moving parts. Security cannot be reached through weaponisation but through our relationships to one another and with our environment – and these are always changing, as are we. '*How* we live, *how* we organize, *how* we engage in the world – the process – not only frames the outcome, it is the transformation', writes Michi Saagiig Nishnaabeg scholar and activist Leanne Betasamosake Simpson (Simpson 2017, 19).

DECONSTRUCTING AND RECONSTRUCTING NORMATIVITY

To abolish nuclear weapons, we must devalue them. Feminism, along with queer and Indigenous experience and activism, is essential to the process of deconstructing and reconstructing what is considered normative about nuclear weapon acquisition. We must privilege voices and perspectives of those who are usually overlooked, must change perspectives about what is realistic and rational, and must offer alternative ways to organise and engage in relationship in inter-national society.

Feminist, queer, and Indigenous writing attempts to disrupt the status quo and build something in its place by challenging what is considered normative and credible. These approaches provide three tangible tools useful for resisting and abolishing nuclear weapons: changing the conversations that are happening; changing the location of these conversations, and diversifying the participation in these conversations.

Changing the conversation helps us deconstruct, disrupt and change normative frameworks of thought and action. In her ground-break-ing study of gender, queer feminist scholar Judith Butler (1999, xxiii) argues: 'The naturalized knowledge of gender operates as a preemp-tive and violent circumscription of reality.' Power is not static; it operates in the production of frameworks of thought. In challenging power, Butler suggests we need not just to critique the *effects* of insti-tutions, practices and discourses that the powerful create – we need to ask what possibilities emerge when we challenge the assertions of what is normative, and challenge what is taken in mainstream under-standings to be common ground or absolute reality. 'No political revolution is possible without a radical shift in one's notion of the possible and the real,' says Butler (1999, xxiii).

A feminist, queer, and anti-racist analysis of nuclear discourse helps to deconstruct nuclear weapons as symbols of power and tools of empire. The association between nuclear weapons and emblems of power is not inevitable and unchangeable but a gendered social construction that upholds a patriarchal, racist and capitalist order. Nuclear disarmament begins by highlighting how the value of nuclear weapons is socially constructed (Acheson 2016).

Challenging normative discourse is also helped by *changing the location* within which these discussions take place. Queer and Indigenous activists have articulated challenges to the dominant understandings and social orderings of sexuality, gender, rights, race and citizenship, not just through courts and other social institutions of the powerful but also through outright challenges to those insti-tutions. For example, for some queer activists it is not sufficient for LGBT rights to be 'recognised' or 'tolerated' by heterosexist societies when queer lives are being destroyed and diminished in multifaceted ways. Assimilation risks allowing privileged members of marginal groups to access the status quo, while vulnerable members of these communities continue to be stigmatised and oppressed (Cohen 1997). 'Queer struggles aim not just at toleration or equal status but at challenging those institutions and accounts' (Warner 1993, xiii). This may offer an approach based not on integrating into dominant structures but on transforming 'the basic fabric and hierarchies that allow systems of oppression to persist and operate efficiently' (Cohen 1997, 437).

Similarly, some Indigenous activists maintain that it is not sufficient for Indigenous communities to be granted certain rights on certain land by the very settler colonial governments that conducted campaigns of genocide against them. They fight for environmental protections and rights as citizens of First Nations, not of the states that continue to steal, rape, murder and destroy their bodies, land and water with which they live (Driskill et al. 2011; Estes 2019). Indigenous activists and scholars recognise that systems set up by the heteropatriarchal settler colonial state are not systems in which those seeking protection from the violence inherent to those systems will receive it. Within these parameters and spaces, the settler colonial state will always dominate interactions with Indigenous populations. As Simpson (2017, 45) writes:

> The state sets up different controlled points of interaction through its practices ... and uses its asymmetric power to ensure it always controls the processes as a mechanism for managing Indigenous sorrow, anger, and resistance, and this ensures the outcome remains consistent with its goal of maintaining dispossession.

Nuclear-armed states utilise similar processes in order to maintain control of and dominance over issues related to nuclear weapons. Diplomats and activists alike get excited about a rare UN Security Council meeting on nuclear weapons, but the traditional spaces in which international interactions on nuclear weapons occur – such as within Non-proliferation Treaty meetings and the Conference on Disarmament – are regulated by and do not challenge the power of those that possess the bomb. Similarly, the ways that a settler colonial state may try to promote Indigenous culture in a narrative about the 'multicultural mosaic' of the country, without challenging the dispossession upon which the state is based, is reminiscent of how the nuclear-armed states and their allies call for 'bridge building' and 'dialogue', fundamentally arguing that the radicals opposed to nuclear weapons need to calm down and get back in line.

Thus, opposing these systems requires creativity about how and where change is made. Consider how nuclear activists turned to the UN General Assembly to prohibit nuclear weapons. The international diplomatic forum in which nuclear disarmament negotiations are 'supposed' to take place – the Conference on Disarmament, based at the UN in Geneva – is closed to activists and to the majority of UN member states. It has only 65 states as members, and each is given an absolute veto over every decision the forum can take, including the establishment of its agenda. No substantive work has taken place in this forum since 1996, yet the nuclear-armed governments maintain that it is the only forum in which questions of nuclear weapons can be credibly discussed. By taking the issue to the General Assembly, the rest of the world's governments rejected the structure of oppression imposed upon them by the nuclear-armed, forging a new path outside of 'credible' channels in order to allow the voices and interests of those not in control of massive world-destroying arsenals not only to be heard, but to hold court.

This change in location was also imperative in terms of how diplomats worked to change their own government's policies. In the early years of working towards the nuclear ban treaty, diplomats and activists gathered outside of established institutions to discuss, think, and learn. In these small-group discussions at various sites in the world, the individuals involved could work with each other to develop arguments and strategies to take back to their own national institutions in order to bring their government on board with pursuing and even leading the way for a new treaty. If this initial work had taken place within pre-existing processes or institutions, the objective to ban nuclear weapons might have been shut down before it had a chance to crystallise into a credible policy goal. It allowed people to come together to discuss 'radical' or 'unrealistic' ideas in novel spaces, and resulted in a solution to a seemingly intractable problem. Consciously or not, the decision to turn to alternative forums allowed marginal positions on nuclear weapons to inform progressive change by queering the process. These alternative spaces permitted 'a political agenda that seeks to change values, definitions, and laws which make these institutions and relationships oppressive' (Cohen 1997, 444–5).

Essential to the task of challenging *what* is considered normative and from *where* challenges can be mounted is to consider *who* is included in the conversation – by *diversifying participation*. In dissenting from normative frameworks of heteropatriarchy and colonialism, for example, some Indigenous queer and feminist scholars and activists work to interrogate and challenge what or who is a subject, what or who is considered credible and legitimate, what or who can be a source of knowledge and intellectualism. In this work, they critique the intellectual frameworks colonial regimes employ in order to suppress identities and opposition, and 'hold heteropatriarchal legacies accountable to change' (Driskill et al. 2011, 19).

In the context of nuclear weapons, the dominant voices are men representing government or academic institutions in nuclear-armed states – people who directly benefit from the production of theories and perspectives that justify the possession and continued development and modernisation of nuclear arsenals. These 'authorities' often deny and dismiss anti-nuclear activists, often ignoring those who have suffered from the development, testing, and use of these bombs.

Presently, there has been a concerted push to include women in nuclear weapons-related dialogue and negotiations. The Treaty on the Prohibition of Nuclear Weapons, for example, recognises that the 'equal, full and effective participation of both women and men is an essential factor for the promotion and attainment of sustainable peace and security', and expresses the commitment of its states parties to 'supporting and strengthening the effective participation of women in nuclear disarmament'. Such calls for 'women's participation' in the fields of nuclear weapon policy and other militaristic pursuits are often premised on a legitimate concern at the lack of gender diversity in these discussions or institutions. But 'adding women' is not only insufficient, it also risks further legitimising the institutions, practices, and policies that many seeking 'gender equality' would arguably like to change.

The nuclear policy field is dominated by cisgender heterosexual white men who compose a self-described 'nuclear priesthood' that espouses normative masculinised perspectives on security and weapons. A recent study published by *New America* (Hurlburt et al. 2019) paints a portrait of the sexism and gendered stereotypes, and noted that there were high levels of attrition of women in the field. Women (mostly white, cisgender women) who did successfully participate in nuclear policy institutions were often forced to prove their competency by 'mastering the orthodoxy' and having to 'master the technical details before you could have an opinion' (Hurlburt et al. 2019). The very few women who succeed in this sector are celebrated as crossing the divide from 'feminine' arms control to 'masculine' nuclear war planning. Former Deputy Assistant Secretary of Defense for Nuclear and Missile Defense Policy Elaine Bunn explained, 'There was the soft, fuzzy arms control side and then there was the real military side, the deployment side, and I felt like I had to prove my bonafides on the other side.' She remembered a mentor telling her if she was going to stay in the Defense Department, she needed to 'do the targeting, the hard side of this, not just the arms control side', or she would not be taken seriously.

One interviewee, a graduate fellow at the National Nuclear Security Administration, argued that, as a woman of colour, she wanted to interrogate the impacts of nuclear policies not just on women but also on Indigenous communities and communities of colour:

> We detonated some of our strongest weapons in Bikini Atoll and in Micronesia and the Marshall Islands. It wasn't the suburbs of Montana that we were doing that in … Whether it's criminal justice policy or national security policy, when we talk about who is a valuable life, black and brown people are the last in the line of that list. (Hurlburt et al. 2019)

However, other women interviewed in the study expressed they did not consider civilian impacts to be important or useful. One interviewee suggested that nuclear weapons have had a positive impact on women and others because of the number of women that they have saved through nuclear deterrence.

These women policy-makers' statements demonstrate that 'adding women' to nuclear policy discussions is not enough to ensure that meaningful change can be achieved. This is further amplified by the fact that, as of January 2019, the chief executive officers of four of the United States' biggest weapons-producing companies – Northrup Grumman, Lockheed Martin, General Dynamics, and the weapons-wing of Boeing – were women. The Pentagon's top weapons purchaser – the Undersecretary of State for Arms Control and International Security Affairs – as well as the Undersecretary for Nuclear Security are also women (Brown 2019). These women are not challenging the patriarchal structures and systems that have created the militarised world order – they are actively maintaining it and profiting from it. In March 2019, the Minot Air Force Base celebrated an 'all-women missile alert', during which only women were responsible for launching nuclear missiles at the site for 24 hours. For the occasion, they donned a special patch with Wonder Woman emblazoned on it. One of the women who took part in the mission said, 'There's a lot of beauty in an all-female crew standing together as a part of history to accomplish the mission for the three ICBM [inter-continental ballistic missiles] wings' (Ley 2019).

As feminist scholar Cynthia Enloe says, 'You can militarise anything, including equality' (in Hayda 2019). Women have been advocates for nuclear weapons, at times leveraging their position as mothers and wives to justify this support. Former US Ambassador to the UN, Niki Haley, appealed to her status as a mother to justify her defence of nuclear weapons. 'First and foremost, I'm a mom, I'm a wife, I'm a daughter', she said at a press conference where she opposed the negotiation of an international treaty prohibiting nuclear weapons (*Democracy Now!* 2017). 'And as a mom, as a daughter, there's nothing I want more for my family than a world without nuclear weapons. But we have to be realistic.' She identified the desire for disarmament with her womanhood but connects her desire to 'protect' her family to the 'necessity' of retaining nuclear weapons.

This idea that nuclear weapons possession is a *realistic* credible policy is inherent to the normative security discourse deployed in nuclear-armed states. Adding women to the discussion does not, on its own, challenge the normativity of these claims. Women gaining access to these discussions are primarily from the same class, background, perspective and identity as the men that are already there. The vast majority of women who hold any positions within the nuclear or broader 'security establishment' in the United States are white, heterosexual, cisgender, middle- or upper-class women. They are primarily interested in climbing the ladder and 'breaking the glass ceiling', not in challenging or reconfiguring the instructions or structures to which they have been granted acceptance. Adding women to discussions of nuclear policy, particularly in 'traditional' spaces, does not guarantee a different perspective. Women are as socialised into militarised ideas of security, and can support politics infused with the notion of threat. Presenting militarised solutions to 'threats and enemies' is legitimised when decision-making sites are perceived to provide 'equal opportunity' for participants of different identities.

In an effort to establish their legitimacy, state actors sometimes even embrace the language of their critics – describing themselves or their foreign policy as feminist. Assertions of 'feminist foreign policy' by governments is a means to legitimise their leadership despite these states' continuation of arms transfers, their participation in wars or military interventions, and their refusal to come to terms with their status as settler colonial states. The use of the label 'feminist' reflects what Duriesmith (2019) calls the 'cynical use of gender programming to legitimise other forms of violence'.

The Women's International League for Peace and Freedom (WILPF) has always stood in solidarity with the bombed over the bombers. WILPF works for peace and disarmament and against the arms industry, capitalism, racism and environmental destruction. WILPF was a member of the International Campaign to Abolish Nuclear Weapons (ICAN), which led the efforts to achieve the Treaty on the Prohibition of Nuclear Weapons. During this period of work, ICAN included many women, queer-identified folks, activists of the global South, representatives of affected Indigenous communities, atomic bomb survivors, and others who had experienced the impacts of nuclear weapons. This was part of a concerted effort to diversify the participation in conversations about these weapons. The participants in policy-making about nuclear weapons matter: it matters who is at the table, because diversity of participation is the only way to help ensure diversity of perspectives.

It is also vital to take an intersectional approach to issues of equality, justice and security within our work for nuclear abolition. Drawing from feminist, queer and Indigenous activism, it is in the recognition of the complementarity of our struggles that we can find resilient strategies to change it. Water Protectors at Standing Rock identified the oppressor not just as the US government, the military or capitalist corporate interests. They understood that heteropatriarchy, racism and imperialist pursuit of empire are at the core of the challenges they face in trying to protect land and water from the violence of pipelines (Estes 2019). Queer activists see political promise in a 'broad critique of multiple social antagonisms, including race, gender, class, nationality, and religion, in addition to sexuality' and in 'a broadened consideration of the late-twentieth-century global crises that have configured historical relations among political economies, the geopolitics of war and terror, and national manifestations of sexual, racial, and gendered hierarchies' (Eng et al. 2013, 1).

In the context of nuclear weapons, this means recognising that campaigning for nuclear disarmament without understanding the racist, patriarchal and capitalist injustice these weapons represent in international relations and local experiences does a disservice both to fighting for disarmament and for justice. Our critique of nuclear weapons needs to also be a critique of the settler colonial state, which believes that it can conduct nuclear tests or store nuclear waste on stolen lands. It needs to be a critique of racism, with attention to the bodies and lands upon which nuclear weapons are tested and used. It needs to critique patriarchy, with a mind to how nuclear weapons involve gendered norms, and how they are used to reinforce social hierarchies, control and domination.

An intersectional approach to nuclear disarmament also means ensuring that the voices and perspectives of those who experience the violence of nuclear weapons and of the intersection of these oppressions are leading our critiques and our work. This includes looking to the lessons of others who have struggled to make change from non-normative and marginalised positions, learning from them and being led by them.

It means not simply relying on established institutions to 'allow' us to participate, or to settle for minor accommodations within those institutions. A critique of nuclear weapons in the locations and with the language of nuclear weapons proponents will not work. At best it may help achieve slight reductions in numbers of warheads or missiles, or the establishment of arms control regulations and non-proliferation initiatives. It does not get us to abolition. Only by situating our critique in the struggles of Indigenous, queer, feminist and anti-racist activists can we honestly account for nuclear weapons, what they do, and who they are really 'for'. Only by rethinking our relationship to existing institutions, which tend to co-opt participants into the status quo rather than providing opportunities for participants to change things 'from the inside', can we start to think about alternative spaces and relationships to engage in meaningful processes. Much more work remains to be done, and the more we can learn from each other's theories and practices of action and participation, the better impact we will have across a range of social justice struggles.

REFERENCES

Note: All URLs last accessed 24 June 2021.

Acheson, Ray (2016) Foregrounding justice in nuclear disarmament: A practitioner's commentary. *Global Policy* 7(3): 405–407.

Acheson, Ray (2018) The nuclear ban and the patriarchy: A feminist analysis of opposition to prohibiting nuclear weapons. *Critical Studies on Security*, 30 April: 1–5.

Acheson, Ray (2019a) Patriarchy and the bomb: Banning nuclear weapons against the opposition of militarist masculinities. In: Betty A. Reardon and Asha Hans (eds) *The Gender Imperative: Human Security vs State Security*. New York: Routledge, pp. 392–409.

Acheson, Ray (2019b) Moving the nuclear football, from 1946 to 2019. *NPT News in Review* 16(2): 1–2. Available at: http://reachingcriticalwill.org/images/documents/Disarmament-fora/npt/NIR2019/NIR16.2.pdf

Brown, David (2019) How women took over the military-industrial complex. *Politico*, 2 January. Available at: www.politico.com/story/2019/01/02/how-women-took-over-the-military-industrial-complex-1049860

Butler, Judith (1999) *Gender Trouble: Feminism and the Subversion of Identity*. New York: Routledge.

Cohen, Cathy J. (1997) Punks, bulldaggers, and welfare queens: The radical potential of queer politics? *GLQ* 3: 437–465.

Cohn, Carol (1987a) Sex and death in the rational world of defense intellectuals, within and without: Women, gender, and theory, *Signs* 12(4): 687–718.

Cohn, Carol (1987b) Slick 'ems, glick 'ems, christmas trees, and cookie cutters: Nuclear language and how we learned to pat the bomb. *Bulletin of the Atomic Scientists* June: 17–24.

Cohn, Carol, Hill, Felicity and Ruddick, Sara (2006) The relevance of gender for eliminating weapons of mass destruction. *Weapons of Mass Destruction Commission* 38.

Democracy Now! (2017) U.N. considers a historic ban on nuclear weapons, but U.S. leads boycott of the talks. 30 March. Available at: www.democracynow.org/2017/3/30/un_considers_a_historic_ban_on

Driskill, Qwo-Li, Finley, Chris, Gilley, Brian Joseph and Morgensen, Scott Lauria (eds) (2011) *Queer Indigenous Studies: Critical Interventions in Theory, Politics, and Literature*. Tuscon, AZ: University of Arizona Press, pp. 1–28.

Duncanson, Clare and Eschle, Catherine (2008) Gender and the nuclear weapons state: A feminist critique of the UK government's White Paper on Trident. *New Political Scientist* 30(4): 545–563.

Duriesmith, David (2019) Promoting ally politics in the liberal state during the age of paleo-masculinism. *The Disorder of Things*, 17 April. Available at: https://thedisorderofthings.com/2019/04/17/promoting-ally-politics-in-the-liberal-state-during-the-age-of-paleo-masculinism

Eschle, Catherine (2012) Gender and valuing nuclear weapons. Working Paper for Devaluing Nuclear Weapons: Concepts and Challenges conference, University of York, Department of Politics, 20–21 March.

Eng, David L., Halberstam, Judith and Muñoz, José Esteban (2013) Introduction: What's queer about queer studies now? Special issue, *Social Text* 23(3–4): 2–17.

Estes, Nick (2019) *Our History is the Future: Standing Rock versus the Dakota Access Pipeline, and the Long Tradition of Indigenous Resistance*. New York: Verso.

Hawkins, Dimity (2018) Nuclear weapons testing in the Pacific: Lessons for the Treaty on the Prohibition of Nuclear Weapons. Unpublished paper, Swinburne University of Technology, Melbourne, Australia, draft as of 21 May.

Hayda, Julian (2019) Women now at top of military-industrial complex: A feminist reaction. *WBEZ 91.5 Chicago*, 8 January. Available at: www.wbez.org/shows/worldview/women-now-at-top-of-militaryindustrial-complex-a-feminist-reaction/900b5028-9f25-4fe0-b778-24b04f4a6115

Hurlburt, Heather, Weingarten, Elizabeth, Stark, Alexandra and Souris, Elena (2019) The 'consensual straitjacket': Four decades of women in nuclear security. *New America*, 5 March. Available at: www.newamerica.org/political-reform/reports/the-consensual-straitjacket-four-decades-of-women-in-nuclear-security

Indigenous Statement to the UN Nuclear Weapons Ban Treaty Negotiations (2017) Available at: www.icanw.org/wp-content/uploads/2017/05/Indigenous-Statement-June-2017.pdf

Intondi, Vincent (2015) *African Americans Against the Bomb*. Stanford, CA: Stanford University Press.

Johnson, Taylor N. (2018) 'The most bombed nation on Earth': Western Shoshone resistance to the Nevada National Security Site. *Atlantic Journal of Communication* 26(4): 224–239.

Simpson, Leanne Betasamosake (2017) *As We Have Always Done: Indigenous Freedom through Radical Resistance*. Minneapolis, MN: University of Minnesota Press.

Warner, Michael (1993) Introduction. In M. Warner (ed.) *Fear of a Queer Planet: Queer Politics and Social Theory*. Minneapolis, MN: University of Minnesota Press, pp. vii–xxxi.

8

Make Foreign Policies as if Black and Brown Lives Mattered

Yolande Bouka

So make no mistake, because we acted quickly, a humanitarian catastrophe has been avoided and the lives of countless civilians – innocent men, women and children – have been saved.

President Barack Obama on the military
intervention in Syria (2011 weekly radio address)

This chapter argues that to end wars, we need to reimagine the world as one where Black and Brown people's lives matter. In this vision, racialised groups' vulnerabilities to, and experiences with, physical and structural violence would inform foreign policies when evaluating cost and benefits of war and military interventions. Reimagining this world is not a project of science fiction. It is a necessary endeavour for which Black feminist thought, anti-colonial scholarship, and Feminist International Relations scholars have laid the foundations. Grounding foreign policy in these theoretical traditions has the potential to help us rethink war, promote peace, and preserve human dignity.

There are multiple ways to reimagine a world in which Black and Brown lives matter. This chapter imagines such a world by asking readers to challenge current justifications for war. Too often, military interventions are waged in the name of civilian protection and promotion of democracy. These claims obscure the underlying foreign policy priorities of political and military elites. Military interventions place racialised and vulnerable groups at a disproportionate risk of extreme and long-term violence. This chapter argues that in order to end war, we must not only pay attention to the circumstances in which militarised interventions are deployed but must also interrogate the gendered and racialised implications of moral justifications of war. We must critically assess the reasons for intervening, the rules of engagement on the ground, and the type of peace-building strategies used for, on, and against Black, Brown, or otherwise racialised people.

This chapter foregrounds feminist and anti-colonial approaches to examine contemporary military interventions as a continuation of masculine, colonial and imperial projects. First, it seeks to demonstrate the global hierarchy where human lives are valued based on where they are situated along the colour line. I ask why and how powerful states choose to intervene in the name of the 'responsibility to protect' (R2P) when, for the most part, civilians in zones of interventions end up suffering disproportionately from the direct and indirect impacts of war. Second, this chapter seeks to illustrate how gendered protection discourses and practices used to legitimate war and interventions obscure how women and girls are disproportionately burdened by militarised responses to threats. Ending war requires us to see the connection between war, colonial logic, and masculine logics of militarisation.

In this chapter, I use W.E.B. Du Bois' conceptualisation of racism as a root of war and echo Sojourner Truth's provocation that Black women (and other women of colour) do not benefit from the same level of protection as their white counterparts in military interventions. I also draw on Black feminist theory, including Kimberlé Crenshaw's concept of intersectionality. Black feminist thought has helped illuminate the deep and layered forms of insecurity that Black and Brown men, women and children face before, during and after war. In this chapter I draw on intersectionality to examine and rethink the cost of war. I argue that intervening actors often measure the cost and utility of war in ways that ignores the impact on Black and Brown bodies.

When we apply Crenshaw's analytical tool of intersectionality to understanding war, we see that, ultimately, Black women face overlapping and interdependent systems of vulnerabilities. In militarised conflict, the 'personal is political': violence increasingly blurs the lines between home front and battlefront. As such, an intersectional approach is necessary to disentangle the racist and sexist logics of war and their gendered and racialised consequences. This chapter invites the reader to unequivocally accept the equal worth of racialised civilians and consider using Black feminist epistemologies in understanding war and oppression. In short, to end wars, we must think about how to cease exploitative conditions that lead to political violence.

In laying out this feminist solution to ending war, and the reimagining of a world in which Black and Brown lives matter, I begin by explaining how modern-day military interventions follow a long tradition of colonial and imperial projects. I draw on feminist and anti-colonial thought to critique the logics of humanitarian intervention and activities that ignore and erase racialised individuals. The chapter will then use the 2011 intervention in Libya to illustrate that, despite 'women and children' being used as a justification for humanitarian intervention, the militarised response increased the insecurity of civilians in Libya and the surrounding region. The case study will be analysed to show how racial dynamics influenced the decision to intervene and the selected modes of engagement. Finally, the chapter offers its solution by putting forth the types of data and criteria that should be taken into consideration when deciding to engage in military solutions and reflections on the conditions necessary to prevent their use.

RETHINKING INTERVENTION AND WAR AS EXTENSIONS OF MASCULINE COLONIAL RULE

The end of the Cold War prompted new ideas about the world order, war, and the role of women in global politics. Indeed, the 1990s saw the collapse of the Soviet Union, the end of the Namibian War of Independence, and the diversity of Third Wave Feminism. This global feminist movement cemented its principles during the Nairobi and Beijing conferences on women (1989 and 1995). There was a great deal of optimism about broader conceptualisations of collective security and neoliberalism as foundations for peace and security. Similarly, international feminist coalitions pushed for the inclusion of women in all aspects of political life, including peace and security. By 2005, both the Responsibility to Protect (R2P) and the Women, Peace and Security agenda had emerged as part of a United Nations (UN)-endorsed discourse and practices on civilian protection, international intervention, and women and security. Yet, the 1990s, also hailed as the 'long peace' because of the reduction in direct wars between so-called superpowers, erased the experiences of many communities around the world that continued to face war and insecurity. While the number of inter-state wars decreased, the West engaged in a series of interventions, directly or by proxy, in the name of the promotion of democracy and security in the global South. These interventions were often violent, steeped in colonial framings of security, and put women of colour at great risk of structural and physical violence.

Instead of unlocking more peaceful conditions for women around the world, many of the post-Cold War interventions not only deepened gendered vulnerabilities but also pushed a 'New World Order': a global agenda of Western saviourism and dominance. In most cases, public and international discourses about the impetus for intervention revolved around civilian and gendered protections norms. However, these norms also became tools to reframe political goals along the colour line without fully considering the short- and long-term consequences of militarised responses on those they claimed to protect.

One of the first post-Cold War interventions was the Gulf War (1990–91), where the United States led an offensive in response to Iraq's invasion and annexation of Kuwait. While President George H.W. Bush focused his arguments on Saddam Hussein's violation of human rights at home and abroad, the war and the sanctions that were later imposed resulted in civilian deaths during and follow-ing combat operations, crippled the economy, and restricted access to basic services, all while furthering US interests in the region. Similarly, when the UN intervened in Somalia (1993), the multidi-mensional mission assumed a complete take-over of the state in the name of humanitarian imperatives. However, by 1995, the mission had failed, and reports emerged detailing abuse of civilians by peace-keepers. While other less militarised interventions such as in East Timor fared better, UN missions in Rwanda, Bosnia, and Haiti were marred by neocolonial and racist power struggles between powerful states, and were disastrous for women. Three decades later, despite a sustained UN presence in global conflicts, thousands of African Union (AU) troops, and the intensification of the use of unmanned combat aerial vehicles (combat drones), civilians – particularly women – are more exposed to violence than ever.

FEMINIST AND ANTI-COLONIAL CRITIQUE OF INTERVENTIONS

Feminist and anti-colonial analyses of military interventions help us to understand how gender and race shape the design and implementation of violent militarised responses in a way that sustains white supremacist capitalist patriarchy (hooks 2000). African American sociologist W.E.B. Du Bois proposed the colour line as analytical tool to understand the 'relations of the darker to the lighter races of men in Asia and Africa, in America and the islands of the sea' (1903, 19). He saw racism as an organising principle of global power relations and ultimately as one the root causes of the First World War (Du Bois 1915). Du Bois' concept of colour line is key to understanding the history and trajectory of humanitarian intervention (Vitalis 2000, 342).

Kimberlé Crenshaw's (1989) concept of intersectionality helps us take stock of layered forms of insecurity, and the overlapping and interdependent systems of vulnerabilities to masculine violence of the international system. Rooted in Black feminist thought, intersectionality refers to the ways in which multiple systems of power intersect and create specific types of compounded oppression. Intersectionality operationalises the concept of 'simultaneity' developed by the Combahee River Collective (1977), identifying that issues of race, class, gender and sexuality intersect and operate simultaneously. Intersectionality is a prism that allows us to examine how these intersecting identities result in specific types of power matrixes based on one's position.

Like Third World and transnational critical feminisms, I advocate a transnational understanding of intersectionality that 'places importance on the intersections among gender, ethnicity, sexuality, economic exploitation, and other social hierarchies in the context of empire building or imperialist policies characterised by historical and emergent global capitalism' (Grabe and Else-Quest 2012, 159). As such, not only nationality but also its position along Du Bois' global colour line matter. Black and other racialised women, and their vulnerabilities, enter into conversation with local, national and international determinants of peace and security; intersectionality helps us to conceptualise women's relation to war in the international system.

An anti-colonial analysis of the global world order sheds light on how interventions sustain neocolonialism and coloniality. While colonialism operates in specific locations and is bounded in time, 'coloniality refers to a specific matrix of power, in which political, economic, cultural, racial, gender, and epistemic hierarchies that were established or emerged as part of the colonial administration remain ingrained in current power relations' (Azarmandi 2018, 72). For example, most African states gained their independence in the 1960s, thereby officially and legally ending colonial rule. However, in addition to the neocolonial economic structures that tethered them to Western imperialism, neocolonialism is reproduced in the production of knowledge about what Africa is and should be, a conversation that disproportionately takes place from a Western perspective. One of the most insidious manifestations of the continuity between colonialism and coloniality is the persistent way in which imperialism aims to cast doubt on the inalienability of African sovereignty. From the 1890 Brussels Conference Act, which legitimised European control of African territories under the guise of improving 'the moral and material conditions of existence of the native races', to the economic policies imposed by the World Bank and the International Monetary Fund through the structural adjustment programmes that devasted African economies, to the language of 'state failure', which became a catch-all term that created an ahistorical hierarchy of governance capacity along the colour line, there has been an uninterrupted project calling into question African countries' full membership in the community of states (Niang 2018; Wai 2014 2018).

Coloniality and white supremacy in the international order reproduce themselves through military interventions. Some scholars have argued that colonial norms are no longer legitimate and that intervention practices have moved away from the 'might is right' approach to organisation of violence towards a conceptualisation of state interest that embraces the normative inclusion of non-white Western people into the global community of people deserving humanitarian interventions (Finnemore 2003). However, critical scholars disagree with this assessment (Owens 2004). Instead, they point to the durability of colonial logic of 'civilizing interventions' that have shaped humanitarian interventions and the Global War on Terror (Anghie 2004; Knox 2013; Wai 2014).

The colonial logic of intervention maintains stereotypical and racialised discourses of non-European cultures as deficient and in need of humanitarian intervention to rescue passive and powerless victims (Owens 2004, 360). Labelling non-Western states as 'failed' or 'rogue' mimics 19th-century colonial international law, where rogue states – which are a source of instability within the international order – require intervention and transformation into liberal, democratic and stable states (Anghie 2005). Democracy then simply becomes the face of imperialism (Du Bois 1925). Within this colonial logic, those who make decisions about interventions and are permitted to intervene are sitting in Western capitals. Ultimately, these states claim for themselves the right to what Mbembe argues to be the ultimate expression of sovereignty: 'the power and the capacity to dictate who may live and who must die' on a global scale (Mbembe and Meintjes 2003, 17). For powerful Western states, sovereignty trumps human rights, yet these states also use human rights selectively to justify interventions when it suits their foreign policy goals (Okpotor 2017, 76–7). Moreover, it is on the frontier of the colour line that new war technologies, such as combat drones, are deployed in the name of minimising causalities among foreign Western fighters, all the while ignoring Black and Brown casualties incurred from this technology. Ultimately, military interventions are means to promote and protect the continuation of hegemony rather than create an alternative world order (Owens 2004).

While leaders often use the protection of civilians, and particularly that of women and children, as a moral justification to go to war, feminist scholars point to the nefarious effects of the logic of masculinist protection on which discourses and practices of international interventions rely (Young 2003). The masculinist logic operates in a Hobbesian understanding of the world where disorder and violence characterise human behaviour. Relying on a benign conceptualisation of masculinity that focuses on chivalry and virtue, the masculine actor sees himself as entitled to deploy his protective shield to protect those under his dominion (Young 2003, 4). This logic is binary in nature, where there are those doing the protection and those in need of protection. One of the central features of the masculinist logic is that persons who are being 'protected' are in a subordinate position and therefore concede a critical distance from how and where decisions about military interventions are made (Young 2003, 4). In the international system, masculinist protection logic uses the language of civilian 'woman and children' protection, that produces a narrative that feminises entire populations. These (often racialised) populations are cast as weak and in need of protection through the deployment of masculine violence via military intervention (Ling 2002). Along the colour line, this logic also pathologises Black and Brown men, reproducing stories of white Western saviours needing to protect Brown women from Brown men (Mohanty 1984). When taken together, anti-colonial and feminist critique clearly illustrate white supremacy within the masculinist protection logic. Logics of masculinist protection erase the experiences and lives of those the intervention is purported to 'save'.

Feminists have challenged human rights and civilian protection framing in military interventions, noting that these militarised responses to security threats often do not contain feminist sensitivity. Despite UN Security Council Resolution 1325 and the Women, Peace and Security agenda, the lack of feminist consciousness in the UN Security Council has devastating consequences for women's security. The diversity of women's experiences before and during a humanitarian intervention is not adequately attended to in the collective security process (Heathcote 2018, 205). Women on the other side of the colour line are not only marginalised by patriarchy when it comes to issues of security, but also by gender, nationality and race. Their voices and concerns are often ignored in the design and implementation of humanitarian intervention. Despite claims of protection, many of these interventions have brought disproportionate and unbearable costs to the people (often gendered and racialised) who were supposed to be protected. For example, after decades of US and allied intervention, Afghanistan has been deemed one of worst places in the world to be a woman. It is therefore essential to interrogate the protectionist claims of interventions, when the evidence suggests that such interventions can be harmful.

THE CASE OF LIBYA

The 2011 military intervention in Libya illustrates how coloniality and the masculinist protectionism logic permeates international interventions. It also highlights the contradictions between the stated objectives of civilian protection and the actual outcomes and impacts of military interventions. The Libyan case points to how powerful Western countries legitimise their foreign policy objectives through the UN Security Council and dismiss interested parties on the other side of the colour line in favour of Western-led militaristic approaches. Of equal importance is the way in which decision processes were marked by the near-absence of concrete engagement with women and civilian groups about the nature of the intervention. The North Atlantic Treaty Organization (NATO) leadership chose to focus its engagement with men-led military actors on the ground, which unsurprisingly had devastating consequences for Black and Brown civilians in Libya and the region.

On 19 March 2011, NATO, under US leadership, launched a military intervention against Libyan forces. The intervention took place shortly after the beginning of the Libyan Civil War, where rebel forces took up arms against forces loyal to Colonel Muammar Gaddafi following mass protests to oust the regime. When violence escalated during the Benghazi protests, human rights organisations reported that government forces targeted an increasing number of civilians. Without consulting women's groups in Libya or the region, (Heathcote 2018, 6) the UN Security Council passed Resolution 1973 to demand an immediate ceasefire, impose a no-fly zone, and authorise the international community to protect civilians. Libyan forces violated these provisions and Resolution 1973 became the basis for military intervention.

The United States, the United Kingdom, and France drove the efforts to authorise military intervention in Libya. Washington, DC, London and Paris framed their rationale in civilian protection, which gave them the legal basis to successfully advance their military objectives, while working intensely within and between their governments to end the Gaddafi regime. Their unilateral recognition of rebel forces as a legitimate government blatantly violated basic principles of state sovereignty. Meanwhile, at the AU in Addis Ababa, debates raged about how to handle the Libyan Civil War. For many, the AU's mediation-based response was simply inadequate and seemed to prove the alleged incompetence of the regional organisation. Influenced by the revolutionary nature of the Arab Spring in Tunisia and Egypt, its constitutive opposition to unconstitutional changes in government, and its own civilian protection norm, the AU struggled to be militarily decisive and offered, instead, a weak mediated solution (Abass 2014). Ultimately, NATO, well in charge of the situation, dismissed the AU's mediation efforts by cutting safe passage for AU representatives attempting to go to Libya. NATO's casual dismissal of the AU's mediation should be seen not only as evidence of their lack of faith in the AU's capacity, but also as an indication of the hierarchy of who gets to decide the meaning of 'all means necessary' to protect civilians and what the 'legitimate order' in Libya should look like. Ultimately, military intervention prevailed.

The immediate goals of the military intervention – to depose Gaddafi and stop his government from killing civilians – were achieved without protecting Libyan and other African women. The bombings, the intensification of confrontations between factions, and the ensuing collapse of the regime resulted in tens of thousands of dead and wounded, and exposed civilians to mass displacement and significant gender-based violence. NATO countries that participated in the interventions, such as France, the UK, the US and Canada, did not send troops on the ground, but instead bombarded Libyan installations and forces while providing overt support to rebel forces. The seven months of aerial operations may have limited the risks to NATO forces and cost of the interventions, but this approach, combined with the lack of long-term policy following the fall and death of Gaddafi, left Libyan civilians and women in particularly vulnerable positions, caught between the loyalist forces, rebels and the international community.

REIMAGINING FOREIGN POLICY AND INTERVENTION AS IF BLACK AND BROWN LIVES MATTER

What would the world look like if we reimagined foreign policy and intervention as if Black and Brown people, and particularly women, mattered? What would the world look like if we dismantled the hierarchies that differentiate the value of lives based on where they are located along the colour line and replaced them instead with a system where human dignity was equally afforded to all? How transformative would it be if, to assess the potential benefits of an intervention, decision-makers developed security policies that took a long view approach that acknowledged that wars are not time bound: that is, that the violence often starts before the first explosion and its consequences are felt well beyond the silencing of the guns? This requires a broad framework that looks at the cost of intervention and war in terms of the impact on those we aim to protect and at what it would take to eliminate the need for militarised interventions. Drawing on radical critical thought, we need to push for foreign policy rooted in the abolition of systems of oppression that create conditions ripe for violent conflict.

A first step towards this would be to draw on epistemologies that centre human experiences to understand war, which can give us a different understanding of war from the perspective of those who live in and through it. In foreign policy, wars are often defined in terms of military objectives, battle-related fatalities of troops in combat, equipment deployed, and military manoeuvres. Decision-makers should follow in the footsteps of critical scholars and rectify the traditional exclusion of the perspectives of women, people of colour, and other marginalised communities by making their lived experiences of war central to their analysis (Enloe 2010; Harding 2015; Schwartz-Shea and Yanow 2012; Sylvester 2013). A cost–benefit analysis of the interventions should pay attention to the special modes of oppression, discrimination and victimisation faced by people of colour, and particularly women of colour, in the international system to understand who really pays the price of war and how (Du Bois1903; Fanon 1991; Mama and Okazawa-Rey 2012). By looking at how civilians on the other side of the colour line from hegemony experience war, decision-makers will be able to account for the activities, mundane and extraordinary, that shape how conflicts unfold. This will enable them to pay attention to individuals and their bodies as sources of analysis of the content of war and its violence (Scarry 1985; Sylvester 2013).

Such an approach would enable decision-makers to truly assess civilians' needs, and also to understand how the means and consequences of interventions often run counter to such needs. Making sense of war and intervention in this way enables decision-makers to truly assess not only what civilians stand to gain from intervention but also what they stand to lose from it. An assessment matrix that considers how racialised and vulnerable civilians experience international military interventions offers clarity on how said interventions can make large groups of people unsafe. How actors make war and deploy interventions matters. Each mode of intervention and weaponry decision comes with their own strategic advantages and drawbacks, but also varying degree of impact on civilians. From permanent militarisation of society, devastation of the environment and infrastructure, to high levels of civilian casualties, these tools deployed to bring peace maim, kill and devastate.

The geography of intervention is also relevant. Increasingly, the blurred lines between home front and battlefront disrupt civilian lives and bring violence uncomfortably close to communities. It may mean that fighters return home to their families after long days of fighting and violently impose their militarised authority in their homes and neighbourhoods. People's livelihoods and ability to sustain themselves and their families can be threatened by the violence. When the disruptions become too much to bear, people in affected countries who have the means and opportunity may leave their communities or countries in search of safety. Displacement upends lives, reduces access to basic services, and increases people's vulnerabilities to violence, malnutrition and infectious diseases. Moreover, displacement's corollaries are gendered as women become more vulnerable to sexual and gender-based violence and negative health outcomes on the road or in camps. Finally, instead of calculating tolerance thresholds for casualties based on the number of foreign soldiers' lives lost during interventions, decision-makers should focus on the potential loss of Black and Brown civilians' lives and humanise the victims from affected countries.

Designing foreign policy that values Black and Brown lives would account for the long-term impacts of war on affected societies. It would account for the entire neighbourhoods devasted by the violent death of loved ones (Enloe 2010). It would account for the large number of people with disabilities and long-term injuries as a result of the war (Hermansson et al. 1996). It would account for the complexities of reintegrating communities after months or years of displacement (Baines and Gauvin 2014). It would account for the months and years of schooling and training lost by children and young adults, and vanished employment opportunities (Verwimp and Muñoz-Mora 2018). It would account for increased domestic violence in homes (Østby et al. 2019). It would account for the time and resources necessary to rebuild roads, schools and sanitation systems, and how this impacts the day-to-day of survivors (Le and Nguyen 2020). It would account for emotional trauma and how it can potentially be passed down from one generation to the next. Interestingly, the physical and emotional scars of war and intervention also affect foreign soldiers who are deployed in affected countries. And the costs for them and their families are too often ignored as well (Enloe 2010). The idea here is not to ignore civilian protection because interventions are deadly. Instead, it calls for the radical acceptance that, in many cases, the full cost of militarised responses often runs counter to stated objectives. We must interrogate the normalisation of the use of force in the name of human rights and push for more sophisticated alternatives. If this reimagined assessment of the cost of war and intervention results in a tally that is prohibitively high in terms of Black and Brown lives, then we need to put our energies towards reducing the need for intervention.

CONCLUSION

Despite the discursive centring of civilian protection as a justification for military interventions, critical scholarship points to the neocolonial foundations of such deployments. An anti-racist and intersectional approach to understanding war interventions demonstrates that not only are these Western-led missions often based on racist tropes that infantilise and subordinate societies on the other side of the colour line, but that they are also a step into the logic of masculine protection and thus reinforce the patriarchal structures of the current world order. To end war, or at the very least reduce the need for these types of wars, we need to develop foreign policies that centre those who disproportionately suffer from the immediate and long-term consequences of oppression, war and interventions. As such, we need to put the experiences of Black and Brown people, and women of colour in particular, at the centre of our assessments and discussions about the utility of interventions as a means to address security and human rights concerns. To dismantle systems of oppression internationally, there must be a commitment to dismantle them domestically. After all, how societies treat racialised citizens at home will often inform their foreign policy towards people of colour abroad (Du Bois 1925; Pailey and Niang 2020). Finally, valuing Black and Brown lives in foreign policy and international relations for the promotion of peace means engaging in the radical dismantling of all forms of exploitation. For it is by abolishing neocolonialism, capitalism, white supremacy and patriarchy that we will find freedom for one and for all.

REFERENCES

Abass, Ademola (2014) The African Union's response to the Libyan crisis: A plea for objectivity. *African Journal of Legal Studies* 7(1): 123–147.

Anghie, Antony (2004) The Bush administration preemption doctrine and the United Nations. *American Society of International Law Proceedings* 98: 326–329.

Anghie, Antony (2005) The War on Terror and Iraq in historical perspective. *Osgoode Hall Law Journal* 43(1): 45–66.

Anievas, Alexander, Manchanda, Nivi and Shilliam, Robbie (2015) *Race and Racism in International Relations: Confronting the Global Colour Line.* New York: Routledge.

Azarmandi, Mahdis (2018) The racial silence within Peace Studies. *Peace Review* 30(1): 69–77.

Baines, Erin and Gauvin, Lara Rosenoff (2014) Motherhood and social repair after war and displacement in northern Uganda. *Journal of Refugee Studies* 27(2): 282–300.

Combahee River Collective (1977) *The Combahee River Collective Statement.* Available at: https://americanstudies.yale.edu/sites/default/files/files/Keyword%20Coalition_Readings.pdf

Crenshaw, Kimberlé (1989) Demarginalizing the intersection of race and sex: A Black Feminist critique of antidiscrimination doctrine, feminist theory and antiracist politics. *University of Chicago Legal Forum* 1989(1): article 8, 139–168.

Du Bois, W.E.B. (1903) *The Souls of Black Folk.* New York: New American Library Inc.

Du Bois, W.E.B. (1915) The African roots of war. *Atlantic Monthly*, May: 707–714.

Du Bois, W.E.B. (1925) Worlds of color. *Foreign Affairs* 3(3): 423–444.

Enloe, Cynthia (2010) *Nimo's War, Emma's War: Making Feminist Sense of the Iraq War*, 1st edn. Berkeley, CA: University of California Press.

Fanon, Frantz (1991) *Black Skin, White Masks.* New York: Grove Weidenfeld.

Grabe, Shelly and Else-Quest, Nicole M. (2012) The role of transnational feminism in psychology: Complementary visions. *Psychology of Women Quarterly* 36: 158–161.

Haastrup, Toni (n.d.) 'Silencing the guns' as militarisation: A feminist perspective on African security practices.

Harding, Sandra (2015) *Objectivity and Diversity.* Chicago, IL: University of Chicago Press.

Heathcote, Gina (2018) Humanitarian intervention and gender dynamics. In: Fionnuala Ní Aoláin, Naomi Cahn, Dina Francesca Haynes and Nahla Valji (eds) *The Oxford Handbook on Gender and Conflict.* Oxford: Oxford University Press, pp. 199–210.

Hermansson, Ann-Charlotte, Thyberg, Mikael and Timpka, Toomas (1996) War-wounded refugees: The types of injury and influence of disability on well-being and social integration. *Medicine and War* 12(4): 284–302.

Hill Collins, Patricia (1990) *Black Feminist Thought: Knowledge, Consciousness, and the Politics of Empowerment.* Boston, MA: Unwin Hyman.

hooks, bell (2000) *Feminist Theory: From Margin to Center*. London: Pluto Press.

Jabri, Vivienne (2006) War, security and the liberal state. *Security Dialogue* 37(1): 47–64.

Knox, Robert (2013) Civilizing interventions? Race, war and international law. *Cambridge Review of International Affairs* 26(1): 111–132.

Le, Kien and Nguyen, My (2020) Aerial bombardment and educational attainment. *International Review of Applied Economics* 34(3): 361–383.

Ling, L.H.M (2002) Cultural chauvinism and the liberal international order: 'West versus rest' in Asia's financial crisis. In: Geeta Chowdhry and Sheila Nair (eds) *Power, Postcolonialism, and International Relations: Reading Race, Gender, and Class*. London: Routledge.

Mama, Amina (2007) Is it ethical to study Africa? Preliminary thoughts on scholarship and freedom. *African Studies Review* 50(1): 1–26.

Mama, Amina and Okazawa-Rey, Margo (2012) Militarism, conflict and women's activism in the global era: Challenges and prospects for women in three West African contexts. *Feminist Review* 101(1): 97–123.

Mbembe, J.-A. and Meintjes, Libby (2003) Necropolitics. *Public Culture* 15(1): 11–40.

Melamed, Jodi (2015) Racial capitalism. *Critical Ethnic Studies* 1(1): 76–85.

Mohanty, Chandra Talpade (1984) Under Western eyes: Feminist scholarship and colonial discourses. *Feminist Review* 30(1): 61–88.

Niang, Amy (2018) Rehistoricizing the sovereignty principle: Stature, decline, and anxieties about a foundational norm. In: M. Iñiguez de Heredia and Z. Wai (eds) *Recentering Africa in International Relations: Beyond Lack, Peripherality, and Failure*. London: Palgrave Macmillan, pp. 121–144.

Okpotor, Faith I. (2017) Human rights, humanitarian intervention, international politics and, US foreign policy: A feminist normative analysis of the Libyan intervention. *Air & Space Power Journal – Africa and Francophonie*, Fall: 74–92.

Østby, Gudrun, Leiby, Michele and Nordås, Ragnhild (2019) The legacy of wartime violence on intimate-partner abuse: Microlevel evidence from Peru, 1980–2009. *International Studies Quarterly* 63(1): 1–14.

Owens, Patricia (2004) Theorizing military intervention. *International Affairs* 80(2): 355–365.

Pailey, Robtel Neajai and Niang, Amy (2020) The US government kills Black people with impunity both at home and abroad. *The Nation*, 16 June. Available at: www.thenation.com/article/world/antiblack-racism-africa-us/ (accessed 7 August 2020).

Scarry, Elaine (1985) *The Body in Pain: The Making and Unmaking of the World*. New York: Oxford University Press.

Schwartz-Shea, Peregrine and Yanow, Dvora (2012) *Interpretive Research Design*. New York: Routledge.

Sylvester, Christine (2013) *War as Experience: Contributions from International Relations and Feminist Analysis*. New York: Routledge.

Verwimp, Philip and Muñoz-Mora, Juan Carlos (2018) Returning home after civil war: Food security and nutrition among Burundian households. *Journal of Development Studies* 54(6): 1019–1040.

Vitalis, Robert (2000) The graceful and generous liberal gesture: Making racism invisible in American international relations. *Millennium: Journal of International Studies* 29(2): 331–356, https://doi.org/10.1177/0305829 8000290020701.

Wai, Zubairu (2014) Empire's new clothes: Africa, liberal interventionism, and contemporary world order. *Review of African Political Economy* 41(142): 483–499.

Wai, Zubairu (2018) International Relations and the discourse of state failure in Africa. In: Marta Iñiguez de Heredia and Zubairu Wai (eds) *Recentering Africa in International Relations: Beyond Lack, Peripherality, and Failure*, New York: Palgrave Macmillan, pp. 31–58.

Young, Iris Marion (2003) The logic of masculinist protection: Reflections on the current security state. *Signs* 29(1): 1–25.

9

Draw on Ecofeminist and Indigenous Scholarship to Reimagine the Ways We Memorialise War

Sertan Saral

In this chapter, I propose reimagining the ways we memorialise war – particularly in state-sponsored national war memorials – as a feminist solution to ending war. I do this in three steps. First, I establish the cultural and economic significance of these public spaces. Second, I problematise the ways that national war memorials, specifically the Australian War Memorial (Canberra) and the National Mall World War II Memorial (Washington DC), ask us to remember war. Specifically, I dispute the assumption that the purpose of these state-sponsored projects is to educate the population or reflect solemn national remembrance of the lives lost in war. Instead, I show how war memorials idealise the figure of the soldier (mostly embodied by neurotypical unmaimed white heterosexual cis men) and abstract accounts of war. I argue that the effect of this idealisation and abstraction is to reproduce attachments to nation, and through these attachments, deflect accountability for the enactment of violence.

Crucially, while reflection and mourning are possible in war memorials, the reproduction of attachments to nation forecloses any thought that might be given to questioning the basic assumption – that war is necessary and inevitable – eliciting a follow-on assumption that there will always be more war. In the third section of this chapter, I outline the potential of feminist reimagining of war memorialisation; reimagining that resists current models of memorialisation by standing with a coalition of anti-war movements, expanding on campaigns like the Make It Right Project in the United States, and refusing the settler state's authority to tell or recognise war stories through its processes of war memorialisation. This intervention in memorials is important as a feminist project as it highlights one way that patriarchy and militarism permeate the everyday and entangle us in war's machinery (Terry 2017, 4). A feminist solution to ending war requires challenging war memorials as neutral public spaces and instead making visible the patriarchal, colonial and militarist myths reproduced in these spaces.

WAR MEMORIALS AS SITES OF STUDY: WHY THEY ARE IMPORTANT

War memorials are iconic. The language and look of Western war memorials share common characteristics. Generally speaking, they are immaculately landscaped spaces made by commissioned artists and designers, their aesthetic starkly contrasting with the subject they represent. They can include statues depicting key figures (almost exclusively white men) of history, names of dead soldiers or a symbol to represent them, inscriptions by famous world leaders commemorating the deaths of soldiers, dates of key events (usually battles) in the war being represented, and many other shared features. The stated function of war memorials can be taken for granted, assuming that they are strictly objects and sites of edification, remembrance and mourning, an outlet for national grief. Some memorials are iconic, such as the Lincoln Memorial and Washington Monument, which appear in innumerable television shows and movies. There are public holidays dedicated to commemorating soldiers who died in war, such as Anzac Day in Australia, where these sites are utilised for public gatherings to underscore the day's meaning. War memorials are spaces that are held in exceptionally high regard by the public and the state. They are often perceived as inviolable, sacred sites.

The Australian War Memorial is situated in close proximity to the state's centre of power and attracts over 1 million visitors per year (Australian War Memorial 2018). The National Mall in Washington DC is similarly located and popular (accounting for scale and the US's position as global superpower), with over 25 million visitors per year, more than Yellowstone National Park, Yosemite National

Park and the Grand Canyon combined (Braxton and Line n.d., 1). The Australian War Memorial, built in 1941, has grown into a site that commemorates Australian soldiers who died while in service throughout the history of the forces. It is described on its government website as 'a *shrine*, a world-class museum, and an extensive archive' (Australian War Memorial n.d. a). Consider how, in 2014 when protesters against the Australian government's 'terror raids' against Muslim citizens held their demonstration on the grounds of the Lakemba War Memorial in a suburb of Sydney, the media and public reaction was one of revulsion against what was perceived to be a violation of 'sacred' ground (Godfrey 2014). Echoing these narratives, the US National Parks official website describes the Washington DC World War II Memorial in terms with religious connotations, such as 'sacrifice', 'ritual' and 'tribute' (National Parks Service 2015). War memorials hold widespread popular appeal and are often viewed as sacred sites and yet this only represents one way in which they are important sites of study for ending war.

National war memorials attract large-scale funding. The government of Australia, between 2014 to 2028, will have committed or spent at least AUD 1.1 bn on new commemoration projects (Daley 2018). As of 2015, Australia spent over AUD 8,800 in commemorative spending for each digger (soldier) killed in the First World War. This investment is significantly more than Britain's and Germany's per soldier figure of AUD 109 and AUD 2 respectively (McPhedran 2015). The Australian War Memorial's corporate partners include military contractors like Boeing and Thales (Australian War Memorial n.d. b). In his support for an AUD 500 million redevelopment proposal, then Australian War Memorial director Brendan Nelson justified the cost stating: 'Whatever the cost, as one man said to me: "We've already paid. We've paid in blood ..."' (Greene 2018). Here we see a direct connection between the type of language used in war memorials ('paid in blood') to justify the large taxpayer and private investment in them.

In the Women In Military Service For America Memorial in Arlington Cemetery you can find a list of benefactors near the entrance, ranging from veterans' organisations like the American Legion, corporations like Boeing, and states like Kuwait and Saudi Arabia, all of whom made donations in the hundreds of thousands (USD). The extreme investments and varied sources of funding muddy the assumption that war memorials are sites of commemoration and education. Instead, the investments in war memorials demonstrate that they are strategically designed to reaffirm the bonds between actors (states, corporations, organisations and individuals) invested in war making, not war ending.

War memorials are iconic, often considered sacred, essential sites of annual national activities. They are well-recognised and well-attended national sites. There are political choices in how war is memorialised – what is featured and not featured at these sites – which have significant implications for how war is understood and remembered. Memorials impact public support for war and legitimise the institutions who wage it. Memorials deflect accountability for war's horrors. War memorials curate national memory and stir patriotic sentiment. They reproduce attachments to war and the figure at the centre of it, the (predominantly cis, male, heterosexed, white) soldier.

PROBLEMATISING THE WAYS NATIONAL WAR MEMORIALS ASK US TO REMEMBER WAR

Val Plumwood's (2008) ecofeminist work highlights the problem with forming attachments to an idealised 'homeplace' without looking to the contingent relationships they have to other, discarded, 'shadow' places. Briefly, our attachments to homeplace or idealised places come from imbuing them with the qualities and principles we associate with our sense of self. For example, a national war memorial may stir patriotic pride and thereby reaffirm an attachment to both the place (for example, the memorial and its surrounding locale) and the principles and qualities associated with that place (such as patriotism and the willingness to serve one's country). However, these idealised places have a contingent relationship to what Plumwood refers to as 'shadow places'. Shadow places are locales in our environment that, in the context of a global market of ideas, commodities and nationalisms, are by design hidden from view. Shadow places provide essential material and ecological support to idealised places; they make idealised places possible.

The reverse is also true: idealised places make shadow places possible. The Second World War left devastation in its wake; however, in the World War II Memorial in the National Mall in Washington DC, almost all of this is relegated to the shadows or muted because it does not comfortably sit foregrounded within this idealised place. Even further, the materials procured to construct the memorial and its ongoing maintenance are also dependent on unseen labour and global supply chains that are maintained by military power. A patriot who visits the World War II Memorial in the National Mall is not encouraged to think of these things. Plumwood's work became an animating concept that allowed me to view war memorials as sites of contest which 'do' much more than just educate visitors about war and allow for reflection.

States which sponsor war memorials, these idealised places, are engaging in cultural work that reinforces existing power structures. In the context of settler colonialism, patriarchy, militarism, national-ism and capitalism, war memorials are a projection of power. They are sites where deep reflection about war is possible. They are also sites where mourning can take place. However, they are not designed to educate or provide a universal understanding of particular wars they represent, even though some designers and artists of war memo-rials boldly make this claim (Boeschenstein and Mennel 2012). They can make this problematic claim and disregard the possibility of personal interpretation, perhaps, because war memorials are state sponsored. We must be critical of the state's self-ordained authority to tell war stories and be wary of proposals for war memorials that, for instance, demand recognition of previously unacknowledged service. In her work on the Mohawks of Kahnawà:ke, Audra Simpson (2014) argues that recognition reinforces the state's authority to conduct its business.

Instead, Simpson (2014, 11) argues for refusal, a stance which rejects the assumption that state authority is a given. Such forms of resistance and refusals of state sovereignty exist in Australia as well, such as in the Aboriginal Tent Embassy in Canberra (Foley 2007; Nicoll 2013). While the context of refusal in Simpson's work is specif-ically located in the urgent tensions between the sovereignties of the Mohawks of Kahnawà:ke and the settler state, its provocations may be a necessary baseline from which to reimagine war memorialising. A refusal of the state's authority to give any account of war in the form of a war memorial is also a refusal of the state's authority to mark out land used for such memorials as sacred. It is, very directly, a refusal of the state's authority to consecrate military service, and the kinds of bodies who embody it, as the highest ideal of citizenship.

War memorials reproduce abstract and reductive knowledges. It is not in the interest of any state's military to focus on the scars on bodies and landscapes if that state wishes to continue pursuing its interests unencumbered. The 1946 documentary film *Let There Be Light*, directed by John Huston, drew intimate portraits of returning GIs suffering from what is now understood to be post-traumatic stress disorder (PTSD). It was commissioned by the US Army but the War Department suppressed its release for 35 years. When asked why he thought the department had suppressed the film, Huston pointed to the necessity of the myth of the American soldier to maintain recruitment:

> I think it boils down to the fact that they wanted to maintain the 'warrior' myth, which said that our American soldiers went to war and came back all the stronger for the experience, standing tall and proud for having served their country well. Only a few weaklings fell by the wayside. (Simmon 2012, 6)

In perhaps a moment of lapsed vigilance against the deflation of this myth, the US Army, in advance of Memorial Day weekend in 2019, asked the following question via their Twitter account to veterans and service members: 'How has serving impacted you?' It received thousands of responses detailing traumatic experiences such as sexual assault and combat and the ongoing effects of them (Samuel et al. 2019). These are not the sort of experiences that are commonly represented in war memorials.

Instead, war memorials abstract war and reduce its memories to platitudes to present the goodness of power exercised. They reinforce the dangerous notion that power, especially military power, can be good if wielded by actors who, we are urged to presume, are 'innately good', such as the United States and Australia. Through these abstractions, war memorials direct our attention away from the horrors caused by military and governmental institutions which wage war. They maintain our focus on words like 'sacrifice', 'spirit' and 'the fallen'. These focus words do not conjure images of the horrors of war so much as they summon affective tethers to one's own country (Daley 2018). They preserve the scope of the state as a war-making institution, instilling trust it will act in good faith in the interests of the public. War memorials reproduce attachments to nationhood and war within the public by underscoring the perceived necessity of war for security and for enacting the ideal principles of nation.

These attachments are unevenly distributed. War memorials typically celebrate the exploits of men, elevating their status as embodying the ideal of the state at the expense of those who embody other (often intersecting) markers of identity, such as women and persons with disability. Consider the *Yininmadyemi Thou didst let fall* Memorial in Hyde Park, Sydney, by Aboriginal artist Tony Albert, an atypical example of a war memorial. It was constructed to foreground the service of Aboriginal and Torres Strait Islander people in Australia's military and it shares park ground with the more prominent Anzac Memorial (Perkins n.d.).

The service of Aboriginal and Torres Strait Islander soldiers was previously unacknowledged and unlike conventional war memorials, *Yininmadyemi* does not display a statue or sculpture designed to represent men (or a specific *man*) who served. Instead, the memorial is made up of four large bullets, standing upright, and three fallen shells. What is foregrounded here is not the figure of the soldier, but the object (the bullet) designed for killing, for the purpose of ripping through flesh and bone. It is not a glorification of military service, but an underlining of a tool used to reap its bloody costs. The artwork also highlights what happens after the 'event' of war as the memorial makes reference to the fact that returning Aboriginal and Torres Strait Islander soldiers were not given land as compensation for their service, unlike their white brothers in arms, widening the distance towards reparative justice for First Nations people and illustrating in explicitly material terms the injustice inherent in elevating military service as a national ideal in a patriarchal, settler colonial context.

Memorials such as *Yininmadyemi* do not represent normative accounts of war, but they do point to the uneven and unjust distribution of attachments to nation through the idealisation of the soldier figure. In a settler state, this also means refusing to acknowledge genocide against Indigenous populations, especially evident in memorials like the Australian War Memorial in Canberra, as it does not sit comfortably with the idealised figure of the soldier (Nicoll 2013, 267). With so much violence and atrocity going unaccounted for in the interests of preserving this figure and the attachments it forms, there is no space to consider questioning the necessity and inevitability of war, only to think of it in terms of unavoidable tragedy or, to bring forward an anachronism, manifest destiny. In other words, war memorials promise more war.

War memorials are also in conversation with one another. Consider the topography of physical buildings, monuments and memorials in Washington DC. The National Mall neighbours the White House and Congress and is described by the Parks Service as 'America's Front Yard', connoting its global significance. It is built to impress US power upon its visitors. Its memorials are placed deliberately in line of sight to these powerful, global institutions. Moreover, there is a straight line connecting the US's favourite wars: the Washington Monument (representing the American Revolution), the World War II Memorial and the Lincoln Memorial (representing the Civil War). Inscribed on a stone slab of the World War II Memorial is the following:

Here in the presence of Washington and Lincoln, one the eighteenth century father and the other the nineteenth century preserver of our nation, we honor those twentieth century Americans who took up the struggle during the Second World War and made the sacrifices to perpetuate the gift our forefathers entrusted to us: A nation conceived in liberty and justice.

The memorial situates the war it is representing as the 20th century's iteration of the US national myth. It tells a war story which reinscribes the principles of the nation's founding, embodied in the figure of the American soldier. It is selective about how and to whom these principles are applied as there is no mention of the atrocities committed by the United States in its contributions overall to the war, such as the atomic bombings of Hiroshima and Nagasaki. The purpose is not to accurately portray history, but rather to display a story of American exceptionalism.

Not positioned on the straight line between the Washington Monument and Lincoln Memorial are memorials of their less favoured wars: the Korean War Veterans Memorial and the Vietnam Veterans Memorial. While both are on the National Mall grounds, they are surrounded by foliage and less visible. Sitting much farther away is the American Veterans Disabled for Life Memorial. Though it is identified on maps dotted around the Mall, it is not located on the Mall grounds. There is sparse available information in the Mall about this particular memorial. As the only memorial I visited which described the traumatic experiences in warzones suffered and carried by American soldiers in any substantive, material depth, its tucked-away location is darkly ironic and telling in its relative inaccessibility. There is an intentionality, a logic to the placement of memorial sites. The proximity and visibility of memorials to one another, as well as their proximity and visibility to institutions of power responsible for waging war, are symbolic. The most prominent war memorials in the National Mall are those which neighbour powerful institutions or which sit on a line as if in conversation with one another. The rest sit more or less in the shadows, muted.

The Vietnam, Korean, and Disabled for Life memorials partially resist the promise of more war. It is therefore necessary to consider these sites if we want to change how we practice war memorialisation. In recent decades, there have been war memorials constructed to provide a different account of war, one which complicates popular understandings of war or of specific conflicts. Additional examples include the Vietnam Women Memorial in the National Mall and the Women in Military Service for America Memorial on the Potomac River at Arlington Cemetery. The American Veterans Disabled for Life Memorial gives an account of the scars carried by returning American soldiers, particularly the discomfiting physical scars such as the destruction of limbs, that traditional war memorials rarely recognise in their inscriptions, let alone their sculptures. One inscription by a soldier named Dean Winters uncharacteristically refuses to offer hope, ending on this sobering note: 'Since the war, I've been confined to a wheelchair and have tried to live a good life. However, I relive the war every day.' The inscription also resists conventional narratives of war as event, protracting the way that war is experienced as ongoing, *re*living, again and again. However, in spite of such inscriptions, the memorial is still interested in appropriating these experiences into a narrative of nationhood, which should perhaps not come as a surprise for a state-sponsored project (National Parks Service 2019). An inscription by Horace H. Shaw reads:

The strongest ties between human beings are not cemented in safety, luxury, and comfort. It is the sharing together of the scanty covering, the insufficient shelter, drinking from the same cup, eating from the same plate, the dividing by a hungry soldier with a hungrier comrade the last morsel of meat or the remnant of a cracker; the binding up of each other's wounds, the lending of courage from one heart to another: these are what create the strongest bonds between human beings.

What is striking about this inscription is how, when situated within the larger landscape of Washington DC as the centre of American global hegemony and military dominance, it reformulates the war struggle, the material struggle over things like 'insufficient shelter', 'drinking from the same cup', sharing a 'remnant of a cracker', into a representative narrative of national character. These struggles, we are urged to think, are necessary for the creation of 'the strongest bonds between human beings'. They are a necessary condition for the formation of attachments between civilians and their nation. Therefore, even though the American Veterans Disabled for Life Memorial offers an alternative glimpse into war, it also reproduces the assumption that the maintenance of these affective bonds requires that we must always be at war. In this formulation, the war memorial more generally is not interested in *ending* the reproduction of these material scars, but in regenerating a need for them, becoming part of a larger war machine that needs bodies 'preordained for injury and maiming' (Puar 2017, 65). In this formulation, the scar is not a warning, a klaxon for stopping war, but a badge of masculine strength and honour, an impetus to seek out more scars. This affective discourse idealises and valorises war service, reinforcing the assumption that war, while tragic, is unavoidable and inevitable.

A FEMINIST STRATEGY FOR FEMINIST MEMORIALISING

War memorials are not objects designed to dissuade people from war; rather they individually and collectively underscore the inherent necessity of using state power to go to war. They abstract war and render popular understandings of it as immutable. Through these abstractions, they deflect accountability for horrors caused, preserve the scope of the sponsoring institutions and reproduce attachments to nation. There may be exceptions and resistances to this model of telling war stories but even these stories are massaged or appropriated by the state's interest in conveying war making or war partaking as a net good for the world. By presenting war in this way, the national war memorials I explored in this chapter are sites where deep reflection and radical counternarrative is possible. I seek to challenge the assumption that there will (must) be more war.

What, then, would a feminist strategy for memorialising war look like? Current memorialising practices by the state mark boundaries on stolen land as the site of a memorial, creating sites to elevate military service to the plane of the sacred and ideal, with the figure of the soldier (usually white, usually male) as its embodiment. A feminist strategy requires a coalition of movements to address this. A strategy might include, drawing inspiration from the global climate change protest model, confronting how the materials used to construct war memorials are procured. It would make obvious that this is dependent on global supply chains maintained and regulated through military force. A feminist strategy would confront the settler state's authority to mark out land and consecrate it as the site of a memorial project. A feminist strategy could also challenge the state's authority to tell war stories, by protesting on proposed and existing memorial sites. Activists could peacefully disrupt events held on these sites, events such as Anzac Day, to challenge the re-enactments of idealisations featured in memorials. In these confrontations and disruptions, this coalition would need to foreground the multitude of accounts of war that are usually relegated to the shadows, that do not feature the heroic soldier figure as the only body whose experience of war counts.

Such strategies are already taking shape. The Make It Right Project is a collaboration 'dedicated to working with multiple groups – activists, artists, historians and media outlets – to remove Confederate monuments and tell the truth about history', the history of slavery and white supremacy in the United States (Holloway 2018). A feminist strategy for memorialisation would need to operate from an ethical orientation of *standing with* (TallBear 2014) a coalition of movements resisting and refusing the settler state's authority to indiscriminately wage war. At the heart of the coalition should be resistance to state acquisition of stolen lands used to memorialise war. Adopting theoretical frameworks as praxis, frameworks like Plumwood's shadow places, would include making visible the shadow places unseen in memorials. This solution demands we reproduce attachments to the human and the more than human devastated by war. Feminists must showcase the myriad ways war permeates everyday life, in order to make visible how state-sponsored memorialisation perpetuates war. This solution is motivated by and unified with ecological and social justice movements. To challenge how war is memorialised is to push back against attachments to nationhood.

REFERENCES

Note: All URLs last accessed May 2020.

Australian War Memorial (n.d. a) About the Australian War Memorial. Available at: www.awm.gov.au/about
Australian War Memorial (n.d. b) Corporate operations. Available at: www.awm.gov.au/about/organisation/corporate/annual-report-2014-2015/corporate-operations
Australian War Memorial (2018) *Australian War Memorial Annual Report 2017–2018.* Available at: www.awm.gov.au/about/organisation/corporate/annual-report-2017-2018
Boeschenstein, Nell and Mennel, Eric (2012) BackStory: Heyward Shepherd Memorial. *99% Invisible.* Available at: https://99percentinvisible.org/episode/episode-60b-backstory-heyward-shepherd-memorial/

Braxton, Toni and Line, Bill (n.d.) National Mall and Memorial Parks little-known facts. National Park Service. Available at: www.nps.gov/nationalmallplan/Documents/Media/NAMA%20Fact%20Sheet.pdf

Daley, Paul (2018) A $500m expansion of the war memorial is a reckless waste of money. *The Guardian*, 9 April. Available at: www.theguardian.com/australia-news/postcolonial-blog/2018/apr/09/a-500m-expansion-of-the-war-memorial-is-a-reckless-waste-of-money

Foley, Gary (2007) The Australian Labor Party and the Native Title Act. In: Aileen Moreton-Robertson (ed.) *Sovereign Subjects*. Crows Nest: Allen and Unwin.

Godfrey, Miles (2014) Muslim protest at Lakemba War Memorial: Veterans furious over misuse of sacred site. *Daily Telegraph*, 19 September. Available at: www.dailytelegraph.com.au/news/nsw/muslim-protest-at-lakemba-war-memorial-veterans-furious-over-misuse-of-sacred-site/news-story/70bd78b6456a7400d1fcd4e026e81ca3

Greene, Andrew (2018) Underground Australian War Memorial expansion tipped to top $500 million. *ABC News*, 6 April. Available at: www.abc.net.au/news/2018-04-07/underground-war-memorial-expansion-tipped-to-top-500-million/9627910

Holloway, Kali (2018) Announcing the launch of the Make It Right Project', *Independent Media Institute*. Available at: https://independentmediainstitute.org/make-it-right-project-announcement/

McPhedran, Ian (2015) Government spending more than $8800 for every digger killed during WW1. *news.com.au*, 3 September. Available at: www.news.com.au/national/government-spending-more-than-8800-for-every-digger-killed-during-ww1/news-story/34808367386af87773c8e4326d2a46e8

National Parks Service (2015) The memorial in context. Available at: www.nps.gov/wwii/learn/historyculture/the-memorial-in-context.htm

National Parks Service (2019) American veterans disabled for life. Available at: www.nps.gov/nama/planyourvisit/american-veterans-disabled-for-life.htm

Nicoll, Fiona (2013) War by other means: The Australian War Memorial and the Aboriginal Tent Embassy in national space and time. In: Gary Foley and Andrew Schaap (eds) *The Aboriginal Tent Embassy: Sovereignty, Black Power, Land Rights and the State*. Abingdon: Routledge.

Perkins, Hetti (n.d.) 'Yininmadyemi thou didst let fall', City of Sydney. Available at: www.cityartsydney.com.au/artwork/yininmadyemi-thou-didst-let-fall/

Plumwood, Val (2008) Shadow places and the politics of dwelling. *Australian Humanities Review* 44.

Puar, Jasbir K. (2017) *The Right to Maim: Debility, Capacity, Disability.* Durham, NC: Duke University Press.

Samuel, Stacy, Van Sant, Shannon and Schwartz, Matthew S. (2019) A U.S. Army tweet asking 'How has serving impacted you?' got an agonizing response. *NPR*, 27 May.

Simmon, Scott (2012) 'Let There Be Light' (1946) and its restoration. National Film Preservation Foundation. Available at: www.filmpreservation.org/userfiles/image/PDFs/LetThereBeLight_ProgramNote.pdf

Simpson, Audra (2014) *Mohawk Interruptus: Political Life Across the Borders of Settler States.* Durham, NC: Duke University Press.

TallBear, K. (2014) Standing with and speaking as faith: A feminist-Indigenous approach to inquiry. Research note. *Journal of Research Practice* 10(2): article N17. http://jrp.icaap.org/index.php/jrp/article/view/405/371

Terry, Jennifer (2017) *Attachments to War: Biomedical Logics and Violence in Twenty-first-century America.* Durham, NC: Duke University Press.

10

Engage with Combatants as Interlocutors for Peace, Not Only as Authorities on Violence

Roxani Krystalli

This chapter advocates engaging with combatants as interlocutors for peace as a solution for ending war. Peace processes involve contestations over authority. Participants in peace processes engage in negotiations not only about how to formally end armed conflict in the form of a peace accord, but also about the fundamental meanings of peace and violence. In addition to laying out the terms for the cessation of hostilities, peace accords (and the justice mechanisms that precede or succeed them) set the time periods of violence that are formally recognised as armed conflict, determine which actors and harms are considered conflict-related, and delineate potential remedies for the populations who suffered harm and sanctions for those who perpetrated them. All of these distinctions have significant implications for those involved in or affected by violence: The designation of time periods draws an official – if often artificial – line between 'armed conflict' and 'peacetime', while the delineation of conflict-related actors and harms formally defines certain actors as victims or perpetrators. In other words, peace processes are exercises in distinction.

In this chapter, I examine who gets to make these distinctions and with what implications. I argue that meaningfully ending war requires us to engage with combatants as interlocutors for peace, not only as authorities on violence. This, in turn, requires two concrete shifts in engagement with combatants during peace processes, each of which I analyse in detail in the sections that follow. First, peace

152

processes and their accompanying justice mechanisms need to better reflect the terms by which combatants understand their own identities and roles in the armed conflict, as well as their processes of transition out of armed groups, rather than assigning them labels that do not reflect their experiences. Second, and relatedly, the act of accurately reflecting the names and identities by which combatants understand themselves requires those engaged in peace processes to view combatants as political subjects.

Why are these feminist concerns and how might they contribute to ending war? The proposed shifts in how peace processes engage with combatants reflect an ongoing feminist preoccupation with the meanings of political subjectivity in war and peace (Baines 2017; Enloe 2014). Relatedly, engaging with combatants in ways that better align with the terms through which they understand themselves can further feminist commitments to respecting the agency of actors involved in war and their narratives about their identities, relationships, and politics (MacKenzie 2009; Parashar 2009).

These feminist considerations matter for ending war. As existing work in Colombia (Rettberg and McFee 2019; Theidon 2009; Ugarriza 2013) and elsewhere (Jelin 2013; McMullin 2013a; MacKenzie 2009; Sriram et al. 2012) has suggested, former combatants' political aspirations affect the success of their transition to civilian life. Political aspirations, in this context, do not refer exclusively to whether former combatants form political parties or participate in official, electoral politics. Rather, politics also refers to 'determinations about what constitutes power and where power operates' (Krystalli and Enloe 2019, 7), as well as to 'the process of contestation over what is human and what is not' (Baines 2017, 13). When the experience of leaving armed groups fails to engage with combatants' understanding of politics (Crane and Vallejo 2018), it may jeopardise the building of a sustainable peace.

The rest of this chapter proceeds as follows: I begin by providing an overview of my methods and defining key concepts. Next, drawing from my in-depth qualitative research in Colombia, I discuss some of the terms by which combatants make sense of their identities and experiences in order to highlight how peace processes can better reflect those understandings. I then turn to combatants' understandings of politics and political subjectivity, and the obstacles they face in fully engaging as political subjects after leaving armed groups. I conclude by summarising the implications of this discussion for peace processes.

TERMS, SCOPE AND METHODS

In this chapter, I take an intentionally broad approach to the understanding of peace processes. Consistent with existing feminist research, I do not consider peace processes to be limited to formal peace talks that aim to result in a settlement or accord, nor do I view such processes to pertain only to those actors formally recognised as peace negotiators (Cockburn 2007; De Alwis 2009; Duncanson 2016; Lederach 2017). While my analysis includes the above actors and processes, it also transcends them to explore the making of peace as more spatially and temporally fluid. That is, I understand peace processes to (a) involve a range of actors, some of whom have no formal or official power and are not necessarily represented at the peace table; (b) unfold in a variety of spaces, not all of which are official sites of negotiation; (c) spill past the temporal horizons of 'war', 'peace talks', and formally declared 'peace' to include the work of peace-building that does not tidily fit into such a linear, teleological understanding of violence and its endings.

I focus my analysis specifically on combatants in non-state armed groups, as opposed to state armed forces. Even in cases when the governing authority of the state is contested or questioned (Arjona 2016), and even when the state itself has perpetrated acts of violence against its citizens (Sandoval Rojas 2013), few would dispute the participation of state actors as key interlocutors in peace processes. In fact, the state – both through its armed forces and through its civilian leadership – often exercises more agency over the design of peace processes, dictating other actors' terms of participation in them. The implications of this authority are central to my argument about the significance of seeing combatants as interlocutors for peace, and not only as specialists in violence. The language by which to refer to combatants is itself a site of debate (Kinsella 2011). I refer to these individuals and groups by a variety of names – ranging from combatants to insurgents to *guerrilleros* or *guerrilleras* – and critically analyse the significance of these practices of naming in the discussion that follows.

For this discussion, I rely on in-depth qualitative research in Colombia between 2010 and 2018. Specifically, I draw from 57 semistructured interviews and life stories with women combatants who were in various states of transition from armed groups, ranging from recently having laid down their weapons to having lived as civilians for over two decades at the time of the interview. My interlocutors had been members of different armed groups throughout the Colombian territory, including members of the Revolutionary Armed Forces of Colombia (FARC), the 19th of April Movement (M-19), the Popular Liberation Army (EPL), and the National Liberation Army (ELN). Recognising that not all combatants transition out of armed groups by participating in state-run processes of Disarmament, Demobilisation, and Reintegration (DDR), I have also engaged with those who laid down their weapons and sought to transition into civilian life more informally (Mazurana et al. 2017). I conducted all interviews in Spanish myself and refer to all interlocutors by pseudonym.

My focus on the experiences of women combatants is not born out of a gender essentialist, erroneous impression that women are 'inherently' or 'naturally' more peaceful. Nor is this motivated by a misguided belief that a feminist approach to ending war and building peace requires exclusively female interlocutors. Instead, I recognise that women do not always get to exercise full agency over the kinds of interlocutors they get to be on matters of war and peace. This relates both to which women are allowed to speak about conflict and peace, and to the topics on which they are invited to share their authority and with regard to which women are considered experts (Theidon 2012). Women's narrative remit in war is often confined to victimhood or, more specifically, to the narration of having experienced sexual violence. As Erin Baines writes (2017, 4), the sexually violated woman 'rarely appears as a subject. Instead, her body and her experience are the object of contending political projections, quests for justice, and justifications for war.' Similarly, analyses of women excombatants' experiences often focus on the dimensions of forced recruitment or captivity, enforcing what Nimmi Gowrinathan (2018) calls 'an analytical blackout' that does not allow us to see women combatants' power or politics. I am interested in accounts of women's experiences that allow complicated moments of agency to come to the fore and that shed light on how women themselves experience, embody, and make sense of politics.

I complement the insights from these interviews with ethnographic observation at sites of transition for combatants, including observations at designated transition zones for those who had recently disarmed (November–December 2017), as well as observations at workshops facilitated by international organisations, Colombian state agencies, and Colombian non-governmental organisations (NGOs) for former combatants (January–April 2010; July–August 2013; July–August 2016; January 2018). I have used an interpretive framework in designing, analysing, and writing up this research, paying particular attention to narratives, language, emotions, and the meanings my interlocutors assigned to their experiences (Wedeen 2010; Wibben 2010).

NAMING THE PROCESS OF TRANSITION AND ITS SUBJECTS

It is a Saturday afternoon in December 2017 and I am sitting with Maria in her prefabricated accommodation in one of the transition zones for combatants in Colombia who have recently laid down their weapons. The walls do not go all the way up to meet the tin roof. When the wind blows, it rains dust on Maria's bed.

The painted road sign at the entrance to this zone declares the area to be a called 'transitional zone of normalisation'. The programme for formally disarming combatants had had many names, and so did the geographies that correspond to it. These spaces have been called, variously, zones of 'reinsertion', 'reintegration', 'reincorporation' (Rettberg and McFee 2019). Though the nouns themselves change, the politics hide in the prefix: 're'. What is the 're' available to these former combatants in a life marked by ruptures? They lived through the rupture of joining an armed group, the ruptures of a war, the often-ignored ruptures of leaving an armed group that, for some, supplied not only a livelihood, but also a sense of protection, politics, community and self. Perhaps normalisation is the honest term, after all. It renders effort visible – the effort of making something normal – even as it conveniently sidesteps the question of what normalcy might be.

Maria tells me that she misses living in the jungle. 'Not the war, not the weapon. The jungle.' This is a common theme in my conversations with combatants laying down their weapons, who resist the reduction of all sentimental attachments to their lives in armed groups to a form of mere 'weapons nostalgia'.

I ask Maria whether a return to the jungle is a possibility for her, for her life 'after'. 'Could you go back to the jungle to live? Once your … process here is complete?' Everyone seems to use the word 'process' in Colombia to refer to any bureaucracy related to the war, but there is something uncomfortable about it, like using 'journey' as a euphemism for a difficult pregnancy or a recovery from cancer. 'Could you go back after your demobilisation is complete?' I try again.

Maria's face contracts. 'I am not demobilised,' she tells me, raising her voice. 'Demobilisation is a castration. I am disarmed and will stay disarmed. But, in my heart, in my politics, I am still a *guerrillera*.'

What does it mean to still want to be a *guerrillera* in a world that requires that side of a combatant to be 'normalised'? For Maria, and for many women like her, it means a refusal to let go of the terms by which she knows herself, her social bonds and her political activities, even if she has chosen to lay down her weapons. My conversation with Sandra, a former member of the M-19 guerrilla group, further illustrates this point.

'I call myself an insurgent,' Sandra told me in an interview in February 2018, three full decades after she had stopped being a member of an armed group.

> Insurgency, to me, is a political project to transform inequality. It could be armed or not – but it does not *have to* be armed. Leaving behind the arms does not mean leaving the political project. I now work on insurgent memory initiatives, but I insist that they call me an 'insurgent', not an ex-*guerrillera*.

When I ask Sandra what she dislikes about the language of 'ex', she says: 'It's the same thing I dislike about the language of demobilisation. They want us to stay quiet, to lose our mobilisation.' I interrupt her to clarify who 'they' are. 'The state, the international NGOs, those who call us "demobilised"', Sandra responds. She continues to explain her objections to this language:

> For us, mobilisation is a social and political practice. It can trans- form from armed to unarmed. Many groups in the history of this country – and in the global history of armed conflict and revolution, if you take a look at it – have made the choice of that transfor- mation. But to call us 'demobilised' or to refer to our process as 'reintegration' has a different meaning. To me, reintegration means 'they are going to be good again' [*se van a volver buenos*]. It is a denial/negation of politics. We need to recognise that by naming things we give them meaning.

I am not suggesting here that all combatants share a single preferred way to describe themselves, their identities and their process of tran- sition out of armed groups. Rather, I posit that a sustainable peace *necessarily* requires this process of naming to be context-dependent and to treat former combatants as meaningful interlocutors in their own identification. When peace processes privilege the ease of the DDR acronym over a sustained discussion with former combatants about which identities they are leaving behind and which they carry forward into civilian life, they risk jeopardising a lasting, meaning- ful peace. The risk to peace here lies in the fact that the identities that peace processes make permissible for former combatants do not always track with their own understanding and experiences, thus potentially leading to combatants' disillusionment with civilian life, to stigmatisation in their relationships with other civilians (McMullin 2013b; Theidon 2009), and to the potential choice to re-enter armed groups. The burden of narration here does not lie exclusively with peace negotiators. Combatants themselves must articulate what it means to be a '*guerrillera*' in peacetime and how those meanings might differ from their wartime connotations.

It may seem paradoxical to claim that treating combatants as inter- locutors for peace, and not only as authorities on violence, requires allowing them to potentially carry forward some of the identities and names by which they understood themselves in a wartime context.

I would argue, however, that this is indeed a feminist commitment – consistent with other feminist commitments to reflect the terms by which people know themselves and narrate the ways in which violence affects their lives (Kinsella 2011). Feminist scholars and other critical analysts have rightfully emphasised the importance of allowing victims, survivors, human rights defenders and civil society leaders to define themselves in their own terms, as such a self-definition can be an act affirming agency and dignity (Gatti 2017; Krystalli 2019; McLeer 1998; Naples 2003). Sandra reminded us: 'We need to recognise that by naming things we give them meaning.' As I discuss in the next section, extending that practice of recognition to combatants acknowledges that their naming conventions are not exclusively tied to the *means* of violence; rather, these identities are also informed and inflected by multiple meanings of politics (Crane and Vallejo 2018).

POLITICAL SUBJECTS AND INTERLOCUTORS
ON FEMINIST PEACE

It started with a phone call. Luciana called me on a January morning in 2018 to let me know that the collective of female ex-combatants of which she had been a founding member was having a meeting. 'We are having a meeting for all those who are studying us,' she told me. Her framing reversed the typical direction of the gaze of research, allowing those who were the subjects of research to set the terms of the engagement.

I had first met Luciana in 2010, when I was working as a gender and peace-building practitioner. At the time, I was assisting a Colombian NGO to incorporate a gender lens into its programs for combatants leaving armed groups. In the years that Luciana and I had known each other, the interest in female former combatants in Colombia, and particularly (but not exclusively) in those who had been members of FARC, had surged. The collective of which Luciana had been a founding member drew together women who had been part of three different armed groups and whose experiences spanned over thirty years of the Colombian armed conflict. 'You are having a meeting with all those who are studying you?' I repeated back to

Luciana during our phone call. 'Haha yes,' she laughed. 'There are an awful lot [*un montón*] of people who want to talk to *guerrilleras* these days.'

This interest was materially observable at the meeting itself. When I arrived in the attic of the Bogotá NGO that had allowed the collective of former combatants to use its space, I was greeted by 5 women who had been members of different armed groups and 13 researchers (ranging from Colombian undergraduate students to international postgraduate students conducting fieldwork for their PhDs). In the middle of the table, in lieu of a centrepiece, there were seven recording devices, ranging from digital voice recorders to iPhones. Over the course of the meeting, each time one of the members of the collective spoke, the chorus of recorders would travel closer to her. If someone started speaking before all the devices were in place in front of her, one of her colleagues would remind her to wait. My own recording of the day is filled with invocations to 'speak louder, the recorder won't be able to hear you'.

This choreography suggests a keen awareness on the part of these women that they were being studied. Luciana made this explicit in her welcome remarks. 'We are here because you are studying us. I am speaking in terms of "you" and "us"', she began. 'For us, your questions and research topics are sources of reflection. I would like to remind you: We are not objects of study. We are people, with voice, with politics. We are interlocutors. We are participatory subjects.' Everyone in the room nodded vigorously.

'It does not interest us to be passive. We are interested in how our work is reflected in the academy, in the sense you make of us,' Luciana continued. 'We are public women in the best sense of the word. We want to be cited, we want to be recorded, we want to have our photo taken. Don't be shy.'

I do not relate this information so it can merely serve as 'background' or 'scene-setting'. Rather, the above reflections and dynamics are an integral part of how these women made sense of themselves and the power dynamics they enacted and challenged, both within armed groups and after their exit from them. Their understanding of the kinds of political subjects they wanted to be inflected both the design of their interactions with researchers and the content of those conversations.

Pertinently to this analysis, the women lamented that social imaginations about former combatants as political subjects did not permit their engagement with peacetime feminism. 'I am more of a peace activist than an ex-combatant in my identification,' Cecilia said. 'Me too,' Luciana agreed. 'We have been working for peace far longer than we have been involved in war.' Despite these self-identifications, participation in feminist peace-building spaces remains challenging. 'Whenever there is a forum or dialogue on women's participation in peace, they do not know where to put us,' Cecilia said. Alexandra added:

> When I find myself among civil society feminist women, I generally remain in silence. Whenever I make an intervention, there is not enough trust for anyone to contradict me. Among themselves, they [civil society feminists] argue all the time. But when I make an intervention, it ends there. My opinion is not considered normal.

Lightening the atmosphere, Mariana intervened, 'or maybe you are so brilliant, nobody contradicts you'. But Alexandra disagreed:

> Not at all. It is simply not an equal exchange. I remain in silence and it is a silence of exclusion. Among feminists, that costs me a lot. We cannot speak of 'the feminism'. There are many feminisms. Feminism in Colombia carries with it the stereotypes of pacifism. Women like us are contaminated by war.

These women were not suggesting that they have been excluded from all spaces altogether – rather, they pointed out that their participation had been limited to an expectation that they narrate gendered harms. 'You should see the questions we get from journalists, even from women journalists,' Lina said. 'Did they rape you? Have you shot a gun? And what do you do when you get your period in the jungle?'

I followed up with Luciana in an interview after this event to better understand what a broader engagement with combatants as interlocutors for peace might look like. Her starting point, echoing the earlier analysis, was that 'demobilisation is depoliticisation'. What, then, is meaningful political engagement? 'To be a political subject means to participate in civil and political life,' Luciana said. In a different interview, Vanessa offered a similar understanding. 'Political subjects make interventions on what it means to live as a collective, on the organising principles of society. This does not always have to pass through talking about the war.' In other words, Vanessa was empha-sising the importance of directing broader questions about life in armed groups at former combatants, as well as having wider curiosity about the meanings and practices of politics and peace, as opposed to only wanting to know about the violations that women may have experienced within armed groups. The discussion at the ex-combat-ants' collective elaborated on this theme:

> What is the political? What does the political mean? It means col-lective action for social transformation. [...] Women's participation in politics is political. The environment is political. The family is political. We, in general, are political – our life, action, words are political. Taking up arms is political, leaving arms is political.

A key theme in this analysis, therefore, is the importance of engaging with women combatants as political subjects and as full interlocutors for peace. This type of engagement would require actors engaged in peace-building and conflict resolution to recognise that women combatants are not only suitable interlocutors about viola-tions they experienced or about experiences of coercion. They are also authorities on agency, volition and various subjects of politics, including both formal/electoral politics and the politics of everyday life. Importantly, I am not claiming that combatants should receive this treatment in peace processes while other participants (including many civil society actors) remain excluded from formal and informal peace negotiations (Dayal and Christien 2020). Rather, I am arguing that this fuller engagement should extend to all people involved in and affected by war, including combatants, rather than elevating com-batants above other groups due to their prior involvement in violence.

In other words, the shift I advocate in this chapter requires that we acknowledge that combatants' previous experiences in armed groups do not render them unknowledgeable about the making of peace. Rather than treating combatants' membership in armed organisations as invalidating any expertise beyond violence, peace processes would benefit from engaging with them as complicated interlocutors (Baines 2017), with a variety of sources of knowledge, authority and expertise, and diverse visions on war, peace and politics.

CONCLUSION: CHALLENGES AND OPPORTUNITIES

A number of challenges are likely to arise through engaging with combatants as interlocutors for peace, not only as authorities on violence. First, combatants themselves will need to openly and fully recognise the harms they and the groups of which they were a part perpetrated. Without such a recognition, civil society – and, in particular, victims/survivors of these harms – are likely to see any demands for more meaningful interlocution with combatants as an attempt to evade accountability or to deny participation in violence. Second, such a process of meaningful engagement with combatants will likely require difficult conversations within feminist peace organisations. For many feminist groups, pacifism is a key tenet of their political priorities; engagement with armed actors, therefore, may seem antithetical to both the mission of the organisation and to their interpretation of feminism. Third, combatants themselves are likely to have different interpretations of the meanings of peace and politics. Combatants may have different perspectives on their preferred identities, and a differing sense of themselves and the processes of war and peace making. Reflecting this diversity of perspectives and experiences in the mechanisms of peace-building will require in-depth, long-term, context-sensitive engagement.

In this chapter, I have proposed expanding the frame of engagement with combatants in processes of ending war and building peace. An expanded frame is an invitation. It is a call to orient our curiosity in different directions and to see a range of actors and practices we may have otherwise missed. In practice, this means neither invalidating former combatants' perspective as peace-builders because of their potential involvement in violence nor elevating their expertise on peace on account of them being perceived as authorities on war.

REFERENCES

Arjona, Ana (2016) *Rebelocracy*. Cambridge: Cambridge University Press.

Baines, Erin (2017) *Buried in the Heart: Women, Complex Victimhood and the War in Northern Uganda*. Cambridge: Cambridge University Press.

Cockburn, Cynthia (2007) *From Where We Stand: War, Women's Activism and Feminist Analysis*. London: Zed Books.

Crane, Emma Shaw and Vallejo, Catalina (2018) Remaking subjects in the aftermath of war: Colombia's postconflict. *Social Science Research Council, Items Series*. Available at: https://items.ssrc.org/from-our-fellows/remaking-subjects-in-the-aftermath-of-war-capitalism-personhood-and-colombias-postconflict/ (accessed 1 June 2020).

Dayal, Anjali Kaushlesh and Christien, Agathe (2020) Women's participation in informal peace processes. *Global Governance: A Review of Multilateralism and International Organizations* 26(1): 69–98.

De Alwis, Malathi (2009) Interrogating the 'political': Feminist peace activism in Sri Lanka. *Feminist Review* 91(1): 81–93.

Duncanson, Claire (2016) *Gender and Peacebuilding*. Cambridge: Polity.

Gatti, Gabriel (ed.) (2017) *Un mundo de víctimas*. Barcelona: Anthropos.

Enloe, Cynthia (2014) *Bananas, Beaches and Bases: Making Feminist Sense of International Politics*. Berkeley, CA: University of California Press.

Gowrinathan, Nimmi (2018) On the myth of Stockholm syndrome and women guerrilla fighters. *LitHub*, 16 November. Available at: https://lithub.com/on-the-myth-of-stockholm-syndrome-and-women-guerrilla-fighters/

Jelin, Elizabeth (2013) Militantes y combatientes en la historia de las memorias: Silencios, denuncias y reivindicaciones. *Meridional: Revista Chilena de Estudios Latinoamericanos* 1: 77–97.

Kinsella, Helen M. (2011) *The Image before the Weapon: A Critical History of the Distinction between Combatant and Civilian*. Ithaca, NY: Cornell University Press.

Krystalli, Roxani (2019) *'We Are Not Good Victims': Hierarchies of Suffering and the Politics of Victimhood in Colombia*. PhD dissertation, Fletcher School of Law and Diplomacy, Tufts University, Medford, MA.

Krystalli, Roxani and Enloe, Cynthia (2019) Doing feminism: A conversation between Cynthia Enloe and Roxani Krystalli. *International Feminist Journal of Politics* 22(2): 289–298.

Lederach, Angela J. (2017) 'The campesino was born for the campo': A multispecies approach to territorial peace in Colombia. *American Anthropologist* 119(4): 589–602.

Mazurana, Dyan, Krystalli, Roxani and Baaré, Anton (2017) Gender and disarmament, demobilization, and reintegration. In: Fionnuala Ní Aoláin, Naomi Cahn, Dina F. Hayes and Nahla Valji (eds) *The Oxford Handbook of Gender and Conflict*. Oxford: Oxford University Press.

McLeer, Anne (1998) Saving the victim: Recuperating the language of the victim and reassessing global feminism. *Hypatia* 13(1): 41–55.

McMullin, Jaremey (2013a) *Ex-combatants and the Post-conflict State: Challenges of Reintegration*. Basingstoke: Palgrave Macmillan.

McMullin, Jaremey (2013b) Integration or separation? The stigmatisation of ex-combatants after war. *Review of International Studies* 39(2): 385–414.

Naples, Nancy A. (2003) Deconstructing and locating survivor discourse: Dynamics of narrative, empowerment, and resistance for survivors of childhood sexual abuse. *Signs: Journal of Women in Culture and Society* 28(4): 1151–1185.

Parashar, Swati (2009) Feminist International Relations and women militants: Case studies from Sri Lanka and Kashmir. *Cambridge Review of International Affairs* 22(2): 235–256.

Rettberg, Angelika and McFee, Erin (2019) *Excombatientes y acuerdo de paz con las FARC-EP en Colombia: Balance de la etapa temprana*. Bogotá: Ediciones Uniandes-Universidad de los Andes.

Sandoval Rojas, Nathalia (2013) La movilización social en tiempos de la Constitución: Feministas, indígenas y víctimas de crímenes de Estado ante la Corte Constitucional colombiana. *Colombia Internacional* 79: 191–217.

Sriram, Chandra Lekha, García-Godos, Jemima, Herman, Johanna and Martin-Ortega, Olga (eds) (2012) *Transitional Justice and Peacebuilding on the Ground: Victims and Ex-combatants*. Abingdon: Routledge.

Theidon, Kimberly (2009) Reconstructing masculinities: The disarmament, demobilization, and reintegration of former combatants in Colombia. *Human Rights Quarterly* 31.

Theidon, Kimberly (2012) *Intimate Enemies: Violence and Reconciliation in Peru*. Philadelphia, PA: University of Pennsylvania Press.

Ugarriza, Juan Esteban (2013) La dimensión política del postconflicto: Discusiones conceptuales y avances empíricos. *Colombia internacional* 77: 141–176.

Wedeen, Lisa (2010) Reflections on ethnographic work in political science. *Annual Review of Political Science* 13: 255–272.

Wibben, Annick T.R. (2010) *Feminist Security Studies: A Narrative Approach*. Abingdon: Routledge.

11

Recognise the Rights of Nature

Keina Yoshida[1]

This chapter argues that the protection of, and living in harmony with, nature is a key feminist solution to conflict prevention. The destruction of the natural environment and resource scarcity is a major root cause and catalyst of conflict. Women's participation as leaders in this process is vital to preventing conflict and securing sustainable peace. This is not a new solution: women from around the world, including many Indigenous communities, have long called for the protection of land, forests, rivers, oceans and traditional ways of life. Peace activists have also called for disarmament on the basis that the military-industrial complex is one of the greatest culprits that pollutes our environment, and ecofeminists and *feminismos territoriales* have drawn attention to the nexus between the exploitation of women and the exploitation of land (Ulloa 2016). It is therefore important to recognise that this solution is built upon the histories, struggles and knowledges of many peoples, including groups from around the world who have long advocated for environmental protection (Matsui 1999).

As we approach the 20th anniversary of the United Nations' (UN) Women, Peace and Security framework (WPS), many women's rights groups have increasingly called upon states to recognise the 'slow violence' of climate change as a threat to international peace and security (George 2014). There have also been calls to include the environment within the WPS framework, in recognition that the environment plays a key role in conflict prevention and peace-build-

1 This research was funded by the Arts and Humanities Research Council as part of the Feminist International Law of Peace and Security Project at the London School of Economics.

ing efforts (Kronsell 2018; Yoshida 2019). The UN's peace-building architecture recognises that development, peace and security, and human rights are interlinked and mutually reinforcing, but fails to include the environment within this formulation. Yet, the protection of the natural environment, biodiversity, and species survival and diversity is clearly an integral part of conflict prevention. As Christina Voigt (2015) has argued, the 'protection and preservation of the natural environment, integrity of ecological systems, and the survival of species are positive conditions for peace'. The question then becomes: How do we guarantee those positive conditions for peace? How do we guarantee the integrity of the ecosystems which sustain us? How do we prevent drought, deforestation, and the social and political instability that is amplified by climate-related security risks?

In this chapter, I suggest integrating the rights-of-nature approach in the WPS agenda as a tangible and necessary move towards recognising that sustainable peace also includes environmental peace. This perspective means adopting a lens which is intersectional. Intersectional theory draws attention to the multiple and often overlapping forms of oppression and 'brings women into view' along with other forms of social category or status to consider their lived experiences (Ní Aoláin and Rooney 2007; Cespedes-Baez and Yoshida 2021). This approach to intersectionality also demands a move away from an anthropocentric worldview (Quadros de Magalhães and Ribeiro de Souza 2013) and instead embraces a framework which includes:

protecting environmental rights defenders;
recognising the rights of nature;
guaranteeing nature's regeneration;
developing the conception of environmental reparations.

Protecting and living in harmony with nature is identified as a feminist solution to ending war, and the integration of the rights of nature is offered as a specific articulation of this solution. In exploring this solution, this chapter draws on a variety of feminist perspectives, including Indigenous and ecofeminist scholarship. It also engages with the ideas of the rights of nature, and environmental conflict and environmental peace. Before we examine how to integrate a rights-of-nature approach in the WPS agenda and discuss why the rights of nature are integral to preventing global conflict, the following section outlines why there can be no peace without environmental peace.

ENVIRONMENTAL CONFLICTS AND
ENVIRONMENTAL PEACE

Environmental degradation, climate change, the destruction of 'the Earth, our home', the extinction of species and ways of life, have all resulted in increasing calls for action beyond the multilateral talks on carbon reduction. All over the world, there is growing advocacy to protect the environment given the climate emergency in which we live. There is recognition of widespread governmental and corporate neglect of ecological wellbeing, where these powerful entities have prioritised profit before sustainable livelihoods and ecosystems. Increasingly, human rights organisations are drawing attention to how environmental harm and extractivism, including the demand for minerals, raw materials and hydrocarbons, are disproportionately affecting the human rights of certain communities (Raftopoulos 2017).

But how are environmental protection and climate change connected to conflict prevention? The environment relates to conflict in multiple and complicated ways. The environment is a direct target in war, with examples including napalm and biological weapons being dropped to kill people and erase vegetation, as well as weapons and toxins affecting the natural environment. Pipelines which are blown up in forests cause pollution affecting the livelihoods of local people, who are dependent on forests and rivers, and the burning of oil fields causes environmental harm. At the same time, precious resources are commodified and geographical areas become targeted on the basis of these resources which are extracted to fund conflict. The environment therefore may be targeted to sustain conflict. Environmental wellbeing is an integral part of successful post-conflict settlements.

Desertification, disasters, extreme weather, deforestation, the destruction of biodiversity, the scarcity or abundance of 'natural resources' – all are implicated in creating conditions of insecurity and undermining sustainable peace. According to Stockholm International Peace Research Institute's (SIPRI) policy brief on *Climate Change, Peacebuilding and Sustaining Peace*, 'international efforts to build and maintain peace are not yet taking these emerging challenges systematically into account' (Krampe 2019). These challenges are considered in an emerging field of practice and scholarship known as 'environmental peacebuilding', which has been described as centring the core challenges of violent conflict and adverse environmental change (Ide 2020). While there has been a rise and acknowledgement of the importance of the environment in relation to ensuring sustainable peace, there has been little gender analysis in that field of literature and practice (Fröhlich and Gioli 2015).

The environmental peace-building literature and practice explains that, if the environment forms part of the conflict matrix, it should also be part of the solution in creating conditions of peace. This can be via environmental justice in the form of equity (including concepts such as intergenerational equity), equal distribution and benefit sharing, and access to justice via participation in decisions or consultation around natural resources and natural entities. Thus, for example, the Inter-American Court on Human Rights has confirmed that states must ensure that Indigenous communities are consulted prior to any licences being granted to companies which would affect their territories and livelihoods. Furthermore, any such licences or contracts should ensure that the Indigenous community receives a reasonable benefit from any developments and that no such developments should take place until there is a prior and independent environmental and social impact assessment. Environmental justice might also be through the special protection of zones of environmental importance prior to and during conflict, including Indigenous lands (Jacobsson and Lehtonen 2020). Or it might be through more radical concepts which consider that unsustainable consumption and extractive practices must be halted given the impact on the environment and on Indigenous and women's rights (Herrero et al. 2014).

For example, in 2017, following eleven years of community advocacy, El Salvador decided to ban the El Dorado mining project which presented a risk to the Lempa River, a water source for 77 per cent of the Salvadoran population. Antonia Recinos, an activist at the heart of the struggle, is reported as commenting:

Mining is irreversible death. Experiences in other countries where mining projects are developed have shown that the greatest damage is upon the bodies and lives of women. (cited in Platero and Malik 2017)

Recinos' comment signals how mining is death, in the literal sense, for women environmental rights defenders who are targeted and killed for protecting their land and territories from development and also in a metaphorical sense, with Indigenous and other women speaking out about the spiritual and ecological violence which is caused by extractive industries and how this affects women's rights as guardians of knowledge about the land.

In addition to inter-state, international and civil wars, other types of conflicts occur within state boundaries in the form of social-environmental or ecological conflicts. These conflicts often concern the tension between the state, corporate activities and communities with large-scale and mega-development projects, affecting the rights of local and Indigenous communities to their ancestral lands and ways of life. This tension has led to the murder and deaths of many environmental land defenders around the world who have sought to protect forests, rivers and their homes (Cajete 2000; Norman 2017). These protests have been met with a 'zero tolerance policy' by governments and authorities, who have been complicit in vilifying and stigmatising those protecting the environment, even labelling environmental activists as 'terrorists' (Raftopoulos 2017), or complicit in their failure to protect.

Some of the literature on human rights and social-environmental conflicts has emphasised that extractive industries and the development of mega-projects have the effect of mutating conflicts, displacing populations and polluting natural entities. There is a 'political ecology' of war (Le Billon 2001), and social conflicts occur when there is injustice and profit is placed above biodiversity and worldviews which take spiritual and cultural links with nature seriously. The types of large-scale projects associated with extractive industries result in myriad human rights abuses, including gender-based violence against women and trafficking in human beings (UN Special Rapporteur on Trafficking 2018). Despite the development and 'greening' of human rights, people on the frontline continue to see their human rights, including the right to a healthy environment and their rights to culture, violated frequently and egregiously.

These tensions raise questions around what 'peace' means for biodiversity and the environment following agreements to cease hostilities in internal or international armed conflicts. In Colombia, as part of the debate on the 2016 peace accord, human rights lawyers have argued that 'there will be no peace without environmental peace' (Rodriguez Gavarito quoted in McNeish 2017). Subsequently, academic literature and reports of non-governmental organisations (NGOs) have recorded in Colombia and in other countries:

The links between mining, internal displacement and trafficking for sexual exploitation;

The use of paramilitaries to suppress protest by environmental rights defenders;

The targeting, smear campaigns and criminalisation of environmental rights defenders, including through the use of civil litigation suits against them;

Human rights violations, including a difficulty accessing justice around environmental rights violations (Menton and LeBillon, 2021).

While unsustainable extractivism, unequal distribution of land and income, limited democratic participation and environmental destruction can be a cause of conflict, the environment is also an important factor which brings communities together and which can create the conditions for peace. This must include peace for all peoples who seek to protect biodiversity and the rights of natural entities themselves. The rights of nature cannot be legally protected on one hand, while those who attempt to protect those rights are targeted and have their human rights violated. One simple solution to preventing conflict is to ensure that states respect, protect and fulfil their human rights obligations towards environmental rights defenders who are attempting to protect their livelihoods, and also nature. Further, states should ensure that there is access to justice and that concepts such as environmental justice are taken seriously.

WPS AND THE RIGHTS-OF-NATURE APPROACH

While many feminist scholars have called for a human rights approach and an approach which takes into account socioeconomic rights and justice as a condition for peace, it is important to ensure that environmental justice and rights are also included within the theory and practice of conflict prevention. This is because the environment sits at an important intersection of the lives of the vast majority of people, including women. Women who live in the forest, women who are responsible for water management, rural women, have expertise and understanding of the intersections of environmental and gender justice as fundamental to the conditions of peace. Peace activists such as Helen Kezie-Nwoha have argued that food and water security are central to women's concerns and conceptions of peace and yet these are not prioritised within frameworks such as the WPS framework. The concerns over food and water insecurity are being exacerbated by climate change, which in turn makes populations vulnerable to conflicts over resources which are scarce.

As the Committee on the Elimination of Discrimination against Women (CEDAW) has recently noted, women and girls experience greater risks, burdens and impacts of climate change and disasters; and women and girls in conflict situations are particularly exposed to these risks. These disasters compound pre-existing inequalities, limiting women's access to water, food, land and agricultural inputs. Women and girls are therefore more likely to face losses related to their livelihoods, and negative gender stereotyping means that they are less able to adapt to climatic conditions (CEDAW 2018). Further, it is recognised both in the environment and development literature, and in the international human rights law framework, that environmental degradation is differentially experienced on the basis of gender (Gururani 2002).

Practically, there is increasing recognition that while the environment and women are vulnerable to being targeted in conflict, women are often excluded when it comes to making decisions about natural resource and environmental management. Women's participation as leaders in answering these questions is therefore vital to preventing conflict and securing sustainable peace. As the CEDAW Committee has emphasised, the 'participation of girls and young women in the creation, development and implementation and monitoring of policies and plans on climate change and disaster risk reduction is essential, as these groups are often overlooked despite the fact that they will experience the impacts of these phenomena throughout their lifetimes' (CEDAW 2018, para. 32). Participation also includes valuing and respecting local traditional knowledge held by women in agricultural regions and by Indigenous populations.

In practice, this has led to programmes which focus on ensuring greater participation of women in natural resource management in post-conflict situations. This mirrors what Shubhra Gururani has described as 'a veritable industry of "gender and environment" scholars, experts and planners committed to the empowerment and uplift of rural women' (2002, 230). She argues that this has not resulted in an understanding of the complexities that shape gender relations, also due to a lack of understanding of how nature is also 'socially made and remade'. In other words, it is insufficient to transform society towards 'greener' conditions if we do not challenge the power relations and assumptions that are being made both about gender and nature itself.

While General Recommendation No. 37 by the CEDAW Committee provides states with important guidance in relation to their obligations, some scholars have queried the role of international law in protecting the environment and promoting peace. Across the conflict spectrum and in so-called peacetime, many different legal regimes often apply concurrently to regulate the actions of states and non-state actors. The International Law Commission (ILC) has recently produced a number of reports examining the topic and enacting a number of draft principles which are aimed at enhancing protection of the environment, including through 'preventative measures for minimising damage to the environment during armed conflict' and also through 'remedial measures'. The ILC encourages states to designate areas of major environmental and cultural importance as protected zones. Significantly, the principles recognise the special relationship between Indigenous peoples and the protection of the environment. While the draft principles signal an important reminder that states must do more to ensure that measures are taken before a conflict begins, many scholars have queried and criticised the role that international law plays with respect to environmental protection. As Christine Voigt (2015) has noted:

> The sheer number of existing laws, principles, case law, regulations, standards and so on that address environmental protection already constitute a vast and complicated apparatus of international legal norms. Yet, with environmental degradation, political stress and conflict continue to rise despite such norm density.

The point here is not that there are insufficient laws to protect the environment, but rather that too many laws already exist which primarily see nature as a resource for wealth generation (Borràs 2017) or to be managed by sovereign states in the manner that it sees fit, (as long as it does not harm other states). As Usha Natarajan and Kishan Khoday (2014, 573) have argued 'international environmental law and general international law are structured in ways that systemically reinforce ecological harm'. Christine Chinkin and Mary Kaldor (2017, 89) have explained that recent scholarship in international law has demonstrated 'its complicity in silencing and reconstructing the subaltern, supporting assertions of title to colonised territories and legalising colonial exploitation of peoples and resources'.

Therefore, some international lawyers have called for an approach to recognise the rights of nature and the greater protection of ecosystems (Gianolla 2013). This framing rejects an anthropocentric view of the world and recognises the intrinsic value of natural entities such as forests, rainforests, rivers and wildlife. Feminist approaches to the international law of peace and security have also called for a new approach to the international framework which advances 'positive peace rather than militarism, and ensure[s] environmental sustainability rather than degradation' (Otto 2018, 2). It is part of what David Boyd (2017), the current UN Special Rapporteur on the Environment and Human Rights has termed a 'legal revolution' with respect to recognising these natural entities as legal persons. It is an approach which is Earth-centred and which emphasises our interdependency with nature. This is the rights-of-nature approach.

The rights-of-nature approach has gained constitutional status in some countries, with the Constitution of Ecuador being the first to include it (Boyd 2017; Article 71 of the Constitution of Ecuador). Within these rights, which grant legal personhood to natural entities such as rivers, forests and lakes, there is also a right for nature's regeneration. The Constitution of Ecuador acknowledges that nature has a right to exist, persist, maintain and regenerate its vital cycles. It is not simply property for exploitation by those who hold power within the country or by multinational companies. This is important since many conflicts relate to grievances around natural resource distribution and destruction. For the environmental defenders in Honduras, Brazil, Colombia and in many other countries, there is no peace while their lands and environment are being destroyed.

It is instructive to consider examples of how the rights of nature can be invoked in practice. Rather than conceiving of the environment as a subset of human rights law, the rights of nature acknowledges the intrinsic value of nature. In Colombia, a number of legal decisions have granted protection to natural entities, in the context of mining, such as the Atrato River case (T-622 of 2016). In this case the Constitutional Court of Colombia ordered the protection of the rights to life, health, water, food security, a healthy environment, culture and territory. The judgment provides: 'Recognition of the Atrato River, its basin, and tributaries as an entity subject to rights of protection, conservation, maintenance and restoration by the State and ethnic communities.' As a result, a government representative and community representative were put in charge of the legal representation of the river's rights, making them 'the guardians of the river'. Legal cases such as the Atrato River case demonstrate an awareness of security which is linked to human rights and environmental rights, rather than militarisation and securitisation.

In addition to this exciting development, which creates obligations to combat illegal mining and measures the socio-ecological impacts of mining, there have been a number of other cases recognising the rights of rivers and the right to protect them from pollution (Herrera-Santoyo 2019). In a significant case, the Colombian Supreme Court declared the Colombian Amazon as a subject of rights and as such the state was required to reduce deforestation (Ardila Sierra 2019). Specifically, in the post-conflict or post-peace agreement context, the investigative branch of the Colombian Jurisdiction for Peace (JEP) has found that nature was a victim of the Colombian conflict (Cespedes-Baez and Yoshida 2021).

While the judgments recognising the rights of nature are an important step towards reconceiving a legal conception of the environment, questions remain as to why the death rates and targeting of environmental defenders remain so high when local communities are simply trying to protect against environmental degradation and protect nature rights. These socio-environmental conflicts require peaceful solutions, and feminist solutions, in order to ensure that there is sustainable and equitable peace.

THE SOLUTIONS

So far in this chapter, we have discussed the importance of women's participation and valuing women's expertise and knowledge with respect to the environment. As a part of this solution, we need to make sure that women's groups, particularly Indigenous women, forest dwellers and those who have a spiritual relationship to the land not only participate but are also consulted in post-conflict contexts about how the Earth and their territories can best be repaired. Too often the environmental and gender action plans that follow in post-conflict settings are run separately and without any awareness of how the environment intersects with women's livelihoods. A more integrated approach would therefore recognise that gender equality measures must include environmental protection, and environmental protection should ensure that gender is adequately budgeted and accounted for. In such a way, local populations, including women's groups, will be able to share their knowledge and expertise on how to integrate the rights-of-nature approach, thus far excluded from WPS action plans, in a manner which is consistent with their own entangled relationship with nature.

We have also seen how legal systems can reconceive their relationship to natural entities such as forests and rivers moving from a lens of property ownership to one which takes into account other world-views that respect nature's rights to regenerate. We have touched on the importance of concepts such as environmental justice, which include equity and distribution of benefits derived from natural resources. We have also discussed how states must respect their human rights obligations and protect, rather than target, environmental human rights defenders. These are all part of the feminist solutions to conflict prevention, since conserving a healthy environment is important for the wellbeing of all of us, and to ensure that socio-environmental and other conflicts over natural resources do not develop or escalate. Integrating a rights-of-nature approach in the WPS framework in an intersectional way means respecting and protecting ancestral and Indigenous lands. It also involves a deeper integration of environmental peace-building projects with WPS planning, beyond a focus on the management of natural resources. Focusing on the rights of nature provides an important shift away from a state-centric and anthropocentric standpoint and instead recognises nature as its own agent. It challenges us to listen to the trees, rivers, flora and fauna, and to the people who dwell most closely with them. It is a feminist solution to ending war because it forms part of feminism's utopian challenge to imagine a better world, to decentre the capitalist extractivist patriarchy, and to live in harmony with others.

CONCLUSION

As we reach the 25th anniversary of the *Beijing Declaration and Platform for Action*, it is important to recall that it recognised 'women's experiences and contributions to an ecologically sound environment must therefore be central to the agenda for the twenty-first century'. In the same way, women's leadership on an ecologically sound environment is a key solution for conflict prevention given the intersections between environmental destruction, conflict and gender inequality. As I have argued, the failure to place gender equality at the heart of environmental peace-building risks entrenching gendered power structures and fails to take into account women's leadership and expertise on the environment (Yoshida 2019). This chapter develops that thought further to suggest a solution to the problem. Instead of simply adding gender to the environmental peace-building pot, in order to create the conditions for peace and to prevent conflict, we must adopt a radical and transformative approach to the ways in which we protect our planet. One solution could be to integrate the rights-of-nature framework into the WPS agenda. This would provide an Earth-centred approach to conflict prevention and help to join up frameworks which currently remain siloed.

REFERENCES

Notes: All URLs last accessed between 23 March and 11 April 2020.

Ardila Sierra, S. (2019) The Colombian government has failed to fulfill the Supreme Court's landmark order to protect the Amazon. Dejusticia Blog. Available at: www.dejusticia.org/en/the-colombian-government-has-failed-to-fulfill-the-supreme-courts-landmark-order-to-protect-the-amazon/

Borràs, S. (2017) New transitions from human rights to the environment to the rights of nature. *Transnational Environmental Law* 6: 585–585.

Boyd, D.R. (2017) *The Rights of Nature: A Legal Revolution That Could Save the World.* Toronto, ON: ECW Press.

Cajete, G. (2000) *Native Science: Natural Laws of Interdependence.* Santa Fe, NM: Clear Light Publishers.

CEDAW (2018) General recommendation No. 37 on gender-related dimensions of disaster risk reduction in the context of climate change. 7 February, CEDAW/C/GC/37.

Cespedes-Baez, L. and Yoshida, K. (2021) The nature of Women, Peace and Security: A Colombian perspective. *International Affairs.*

Chinkin, C.M. and Kaldor, M. (2017) *International Law and New Wars.* Cambridge: Cambridge University Press.

Fröhlich, C. and Gioli, G. (2015) Gender, conflict, and global environmental change. *Peace Review* 27: 137–146.

George, N. (2014) Promoting Women, Peace and Security in the Pacific Islands: Hot conflict/slow violence. *Australian Journal of International Affairs* 68: 314–332.

Gianolla, C. (2013) Human rights and nature: Intercultural perspectives and international aspirations. *Journal of Human Rights and the Environment* 4: 48–78.

Gowers, J. (2018) Sussex researchers funded to investigate violence against environmental defenders. University of Sussex. Available at: www.sussex. ac.uk/broadcast/read/46365

Gururani, S. (2002) Forests of pleasure and pain: Gendered practice of labour and livelihood in the forests of the Kumaon Himalayas, India. *Gender Place and Culture: A Journal of Feminist Geography* 9(3): 229–243.

Herrera-Santoyo, H. (2019) The rights of nature (rivers) and constitutional actions in Colombia. Global Network for the Study of Human Rights and the Environment (GNHRE) Blog. Available at: https://gnhre. org/2019/07/08/the-rights-of-nature-rivers-and-constitutional-actions-in-colombia/#_ftn3

Herrero, Y., Cembranos, F. and Pascual, M. (eds) (2014) *Cambiar las gafas para mirar el mundo*. Madrid: Libros en acción.

Ide, T. (2020) The dark side of environmental peacebuilding. *World Development* 127: 104777.

Jacobsson, M. and Lehto, M. (2020) Protection of the environment in relation to armed conflicts: An overview of the International Law Commission's ongoing work. *Goettigen Journal of International Law* 10(1): 27–46.

Krampe, F. (2019) *Climate Change, Peacebuilding and Sustaining Peace*. Stockholm: SIPRI.

Kronsell, A. (2018) WPS and climate change. In: S.E. Davies and J. True (eds) *The Oxford Handbook of Women, Peace, and Security*. Oxford: Oxford University Press.

Le Billon, P. (2001) The political ecology of war: Natural resources and armed conflicts. *Political Geography* 20: 561–584.

Matsui, Y. (1999) *Women in the New Asia*. London: Zed Books.

McNeish, J.-A. (2017) Extracting justice? Colombia's commitment to mining and energy as a foundation for peace. *International Journal of Human Rights* 21: 500–516.

Natarajan, U. and Khoday, K. (2014) Locating nature: Making and unmaking international law. *Leiden Journal of International Law* 27: 573–593.

Ní Aoláin, F. and Rooney, E. (2007) Underenforcement and intersectionality: Gendered aspects of transition for women. *International Journal of Transitional Justice* 1(3): 338–354.

Norman, E.S. (2017) Standing up for inherent rights: The role of Indigenous-led activism in protecting sacred waters and ways of life. *Society & Natural Resources* 30: 537–553.

Otto, D. (2018) *Queering International Law: Possibilities, Alliances, Complicities, Risks*. Abingdon: Routledge.

Platero, D.M. and Malik, L. (2017) The women behind El Salvador's historic environmental victory. *AWID*. Available at: www.awid.org/news-and-analysis/women-behind-el-salvadors-historic-environmental-victory

Quadros de Magalhães, J.L. and Ribeiro de Souza, T. (2013) On the right to peace and the environment. *Critical Legal Thinking*. Available at: https://criticallegalthinking.com/2013/02/18/on-the-right-to-peace-and-the-environment/

Raftopoulos, M. (2017) Contemporary debates on social-environmental conflicts, extractivism and human rights in Latin America. *International Journal of Human Rights* 21: 387–404.

Ulloa, A. (2016) Feminismos territoriales en America Latina: Defensas de la vida frente a los extractivismos. *Nomadas* 46: 123–139.

UN Special Rapporteur on Trafficking (2018) *Report Presented to the General Assembly on Trafficking in Persons, Especially Women and Children*, A/73/171, 17 July. Available at: www.ohchr.org/en/issues/trafficking/pages/annual.aspx

Voigt, C. (2015) Environmentally sustainable development and peace: What role for international law? In: C.M. Bailliet and K.M. Larsen (eds) *Promoting Peace through International Law*. Oxford: Oxford University Press.

Yoshida, K. (2019) The nature of Women, Peace and Security: Where is the environment in WPS and where is WPS in environmental peacebuilding? LSE Centre for Women, Peace and Security Working Paper Series. Available at: www.lse.ac.uk/women-peace-security/assets/documents/2020/WPS22Yoshida.pdf

12

Create Just, Inclusive Feminist Economies to Foster Sustainable Peace

Carol Cohn and Claire Duncanson

War cannot be ended without transforming the conditions that are at the root of wars, including – centrally – the currently dominant economic model, which exacerbates inequalities and drives environmental crises. In this chapter, we argue that building inclusive, just and sustainable economies is an important feminist solution to ending war.

Although there is a rich feminist scholarship that outlines alternatives to the currently dominant economic model of extractivist, neoliberal capitalism (see e.g. Balakrishnan et al. 2016; Bauhardt and Harcourt 2018; Leach 2015; Raworth 2017), this literature rarely addresses matters of war and peace. In this chapter, we make those links, while drawing on the insights of feminist economists, feminist political ecologists and feminist development scholars. We see building inclusive and sustainable economies as crucial to ending war in *all* contexts, a global, general solution if you like. But here our focus will be specifically on countries emerging from war, and on the policies and practices they could adopt to produce a more inclusive, just and sustainable peace.

We focus on post-war countries, in particular, because they are in some ways the hardest case. Wars typically reorient and distort economies, and often leave the infrastructure of the pre-war economy in tatters. The economic resources needed for remedy, repair, rebuilding and transformation at the end of a war are massive and urgent, even while the country's coffers are likely to be depleted. And post-war countries are infamously in danger of slipping back into war (Mason 2019; Walter 2011); even in 'peace', physical and structural violence remain.

Yet post-war contexts also present us with 'windows of opportunity' (Rees and Chinkin 2015). The period immediately following a
war's political settlement can be a moment of great potential: large
amounts of external support flow in; constitutions are drafted; infrastructure is (re)built; economic plans are drawn up; and the social,
political and economic arrangements that will structure the post-war
society are being set. The United Nations (UN) has recognised this to
some extent with its advocacy of 'building back better'. (UNDP 2008)
Here we argue for something much more transformative than the UN
has in mind, and we draw on the feminist economics and feminist
political ecology literature to suggest not so much improvements to
capitalism but radical alternatives. Nothing less is required, we think,
in order to end war and achieve gender-just and sustainable peace.
And the alternatives developed in these contexts can be models with
much greater applicability in countries which are 'stable' but which
suffer from the same neoliberal, extractivist economic system.

A key part of building inclusive, just and sustainable economies is
a transformation in the ways care and nature are valued in post-war
economies. To make this argument, we first introduce key critiques
that feminist economists and ecologists have made of dominant
post-war economic recovery models. In the second section, we
introduce feminist theorising about the importance of organising
economies around the values of care and provisioning, and the difference this would make to post-war recovery. In the third, we draw
attention to the ways feminist ecologists prioritise care of nature
and value ecological sustainability over extraction and depletion of
resources, and we argue this must be central to sustainable peace. The
fourth section suggests some practical ways to achieve inclusive, just
and sustainable economies, including progressive ways of generating
revenue, and the creation of an active state that is participative, transparent and accountable, and that prioritises social provisioning and
environmentally sustainable forms of development.

FEMINIST PERSPECTIVES ON DOMINANT
POST-WAR ECONOMIC RECOVERY MODELS

Right now, the economic recovery policies imposed on states
emerging from armed conflict are a recipe for repeatedly falling back

into armed violence, rather than a solution to war. The economic recovery prescriptions of the donor community – international financial institutions (IFIs), banks, governments in the global North – most often rely on the large-scale extraction and export of natural resources, along with privatisation and the shrinking of the public sector as part of post-war economic rebuilding. While they posit that these measures will lead to economic growth, that economic growth will lead to jobs and rising incomes, and that this will contribute to building peace and preventing relapse into war, too often the promised jobs and gains in living standards fail to materialise at a meaningful scale (see Cohn and Duncanson 2020; Mlinarević et al. 2017). Although these policies may lead to aggregate economic growth of GNP, they tend to concentrate wealth and deepen inequalities, while at the same time depleting and degrading the ecosystems upon which lives and livelihoods depend. Any profit that is achieved is the result of downloading the costs onto women and other marginalised groups, and onto the planet; the peace, if any, that emerges is thus superficial and precarious.

The analyses of feminist economists and ecologists can be used to help us understand how and why these economic recovery policies can fall so far short and have such deleterious effects – because their analyses illuminate the distortions and exclusions built into the foundational economic theory upon which the recovery prescriptions are based. Feminist economists and ecologists critique not only the neoliberal version of capitalism, driven by powerful economies and IFIs since the 1970s; more deeply, they critique the fundamental assumptions of capitalism found in classical and neoclassical economic thought.

One of their fundamental insights is that capitalism privileges the monetised aspects of the economy while ignoring the sphere of social reproduction or unpaid work, which includes both subsistence production (particularly significant in much of the developing world) and the unpaid care work (for family, friends and neighbours) that keeps the social fabric together (Bauhardt and Harcourt 2018; Benería et al. 2015). A second element of their critique notes that capitalism is not geared towards universally meeting human needs, but to generating profits, which is accomplished, in part, by producing and then meeting an endlessly proliferating set of human wants – among the subset of the population with sufficient resources to pay. Third, capitalism ignores the dangerous consequences of its degradation of the environment and fails to acknowledge the benefits for human wellbeing that societies derive from the ecosystems we inhabit. Its measure of success, ever-increasing GDP, is a measure which is disastrous for the environment (Philipsen 2015).

In sum, capitalism is a model which prioritises profit generation from the exploitation of 'surplus' value from labour and from the planet; an extractivist approach to both humans and the natural world, rather than an approach focused on human sustenance, the repair and recovery of the social fabric, or ensuring adequate and sustainable livelihoods for all. An approach to post-war countries that focuses on the recovery of the capitalist economy, then, will be quite different from one directly focused on the recovery of the people and ecosystems that have been ravaged by war (Cohn and Duncanson 2020). In the next sections, we draw on some of the key insights of feminist economic thinking to provide a roadmap for doing things differently.

TRANSFORMING ECONOMIES BY REVALUING CARE, AND THE IMPLICATIONS FOR SUSTAINING PEACE

A key approach of feminist economics has been to point out that a vast range of things are as important as paid work in determining the wellbeing not only of individuals and families, but also of the economy itself (Folbre 2001). Centrally, there is care work. What may first come to mind as 'care work' is taking care of children, sick people and the elderly. This work is not only carried out mostly by women but is also considered to be 'women's work' (Budlender 2010). In capitalist and patriarchal societies that makes it easy to take this work for granted when it takes place, unpaid, within the family (Benería et al. 2015; Waring 1988), and to devalue and pay low wages for it when it takes place in the paid economy.

But feminists also think of care work more expansively, as caring not just for people and the varied needs we each have (not only to have good health, but for example, to learn, to grow, to feel safe and secure), but also for our homes, our communities and our planet. We also mean it to include the entire economic, social and physical infrastructure that makes all those kinds of work possible. The myriad types of care work required to sustain society have been brought into sharp relief by the 2020 coronavirus pandemic; for example, caring for one's family in the home cannot be done without the people working in supermarkets and pharmacists; many of those workers, as well as workers in health care, cannot be present to provide that care without childcare centres and schools for their children; community health cannot be safeguarded when workers lack paid sick leave and thus must keep working even when they are ill and perhaps contagious; and without substantial unemployment insurance or guaranteed minimum incomes, the most basic elements of care – shelter, running water, and food on the table – are beyond the reach of many.

Feminists point to the oft-neglected insight that all of us are from the start interdependent – as people who need, give and receive care (Tronto 1993). Care needs to be acknowledged as a central aspect of human life and valued as such:

> Care is not a parochial concern of women, a type of secondary moral question, or the work of the least well off in society. Care is a central concern of human life. It is time we began to change our political and social institutions to reflect this truth. (Tronto 1993, 180)

Feminists thus advocate for a fundamental reorientation of our economies to facilitate this broad understanding and prioritisation of care. This includes a rethink of how paid employment and unpaid care and domestic work are organised, with responsibilities for unpaid care and domestic work more evenly distributed between women and men, and between households and society. It also includes everything from changes to urban planning, including water and energy provision, to how we conceive of and structure education, and how we structure and deliver social services (see UN Women 2015).

How might this key insight of feminist economics – the importance of valuing care, and of reorienting economies to facilitate care

– transform the priorities of post-war economic recovery policy? And how would this transformation help avoid a return to war, and lead to peace that is more sustainable?

Space does not permit a comprehensive account, but even if we restrict our analysis here to just one sphere of care work, health care, the benefits of an approach to post-war economies that privileges care – and the infrastructure to support it – are obvious and at least threefold.

First, providing universal, easily accessible state-funded health care is crucial for building equitable, just and sustainable peace because health care needs at the end of a war are likely to be acute, numerous, widespread and, of course, gendered (see e.g. DeLargy 2013; Rai et al. 2019). In addition to the pent-up need for medical services which were not available or accessible during the war, the specific health sequelae of war include not only direct, and some-times gender-specific, wounds (such as amputations, traumatic fistula, effects of chemical weapons, psychological trauma), but also unvaccinated populations, the spread of contagious diseases, and poverty- and malnutrition-related ill-health. But while the needs are great, access to health care is likely to be minimal. War destroys vital health infrastructure, both physical (clinics) and social (death and displacement of doctors and nurses). To the extent that health care facilities still exist, access is still likely to be undermined by security concerns, lack of mobility, and destroyed roads. As we have noted, women often shoulder the burden of care for wounded and disabled family members in the absence of health services. Thus, they not only face their own health needs, but also increased care work, which in turn restricts their livelihood and employment opportunities. Providing state-funded, easily accessible health care would thus improve the lives of caregivers, as well as the lives of those directly needing care, and of their families as well.

Second, investing in health care in post-war contexts offers plen-tiful rewarding job opportunities and, with explicit consideration to recruiting both men and women at all levels, an opportunity to break down the gendered inequalities and stereotypes, prevalent in all societies, which result in expectations that women will undertake the bulk of caring labour. Generating employment opportunities is a crucial element of peace-building. It gives ex-combatants and civilians alike a stake in the peace (see e.g. del Castillo 2016). As it is, employment post-war is often variously absent, degraded, depleted, unavailable, or precarious due to a range of factors: assets, resources and markets have been destroyed or stolen during fighting, labour has been displaced, disabled or is required for caring for the injured; there may be an influx of recently demobilised soldiers, internally displaced persons (IDPs) and refugees all looking for work. Lack of job opportunities for men can lead to psychological difficulties, higher levels of domestic violence, or (re)recruitment into armed groups or criminal gangs; and lack of job opportunities for women can reinforce pre-existing gendered inequalities and precariousness. Generating employment opportunities for both men and women is thus central to ensuring that peace is gender-equitable, just and sustainable.

Third, building an economy around care can contribute to a new social contract, which can enhance the legitimacy of the post-war state, contributing to the sustainability of the peace. While there is not an automatic or linear relationship in this respect, improved health services can increase trust in government and thus modestly contribute to reinforcement of the authority and legitimacy of the post-war state. This is especially so when the health service also offers opportunities for employment and training, citizen oversight of health programmes, and participatory monitoring mechanisms (Haar and Rubenstein 2012).

The cruel irony we see when we look at health – that war prevents the meeting of human needs and produces horrific new problems, while it simultaneously destroys the means for responding to those needs – is repeated in similarly complex gendered ways vis-a-vis each of the other crucial services which make up the social infrastructure of the state: education, childcare, social security, justice systems. So too for the physical infrastructure encompassing roads, water, energy, housing and so on. In all cases, war has destroyed the services on which people rely, at the same time people are in need of a particularly enhanced level of provision in gender-specific ways. Building an economy around care – in its broadest sense that is, not just physical and mental health care but social care, education, childcare – offers a route to transforming this situation, to ending wars and building equitable, just and sustainable peace. We will come on to the issue of how such a transition might be financed, but first, will introduce the second crucially important aspect of feminist thinking: the valuing of nature.

TRANSFORMING ECONOMIES BY REVALUING NATURE, AND THE IMPLICATIONS FOR SUSTAINING PEACE

As well as recognising the importance of orienting economies to support care, broadly conceived, feminist economists, and particularly feminist political ecologists, argue that sustainability and respect for the planet need to be put at the heart of our economic models (Leach 2015; Raworth 2017). A commitment to sustainability, they argue, requires recognising the connections between rising income inequality, conspicuous consumption, and the acceleration of fossil fuel and natural resource extraction (Benería et al. 2015), acknowledging environmental limits to growth, and realising the need for a 'safe operating space for humanity' (Rockström 2009).

Feminist political ecologists' and economists' prescriptions for alternatives to capitalism share much with some of the Green New Deal thinking now evident in many political parties, think tanks and international organisations (Tienhaara 2019). But for feminists, green economies are not just about lowering carbon emissions; they must be inclusive, sustainable and restorative; they replace the logics of 'extract and use-up' with ideas of circularity and regeneration (Bauhardt 2014; Harcourt and Nelson 2015; Leach 2015). Feminist green economies have inherent in them a challenge to masculinist values: growth, efficiency and extraction; dominion over nature and its unruliness; and costly, ambitious technical solutions to the problems we've created. They involve rethinking and understanding humans' relations to nature and ecosystems, and the purposes of life, noting that what constitutes a good life is not acquiring more things but the quality of your relationships and time in nature. A resource-light life embraces 'time wealth'; it values sufficiency more than efficiency.

How might this second key insight of feminist ecologists – that nature, like unpaid labour, also needs to be revalued, to be recognised as both encompassing and sustaining all of life, including humanity – transform the priorities of post-war economic recovery policy? And how would this transformation help avoid a return to war, and lead to peace that is more sustainable?

Reframing our understandings of the goals of the economy – from growth of GDP and 'efficient' extraction of resources, to the goals of sustainability and sufficiency – would transform the priorities of post-war economic recovery, enabling post-war countries to truly 'build back better'. Indeed, as climate crisis and mass extinction become ever more acute and apparent, and as we increasingly recognise the ways in which climate change exacerbates violent conflict and undermines human security, the need to integrate policies and practices that address and arrest climate change and biodiversity-collapse into peace-building has never been clearer (see Cohn and Duncanson forthcoming).

These policies and practices will need to involve all spheres of the economy, including key sectors such as agriculture and land use, natural resources, energy, transport and urban planning. Taking inspiration from, learning from and giving more power and resources to Indigenous and other local communities, post-war countries could, for example, adopt a whole new approach to land. There is an opportunity for post-war countries to ban large-scale industrialised agriculture and develop instead regenerative agriculture, massive reforestation, peatland and wetland restoration, and rewilding, all of which would contribute to climate and biodiversity restoration after war (see IPCC 2019). Large-scale industrialised fishing could be replaced by more sustainable, locally owned fisheries. Renewable energy could replace fossil fuels, and ways to limit energy use, required to address climate change, could be devised in fair and equitable ways. Food production and distribution, urbanisation and transport systems could be designed to be as energy-efficient as possible.

Policies regarding infrastructure, too, would require a significant rethink and transformation. Currently, post-war states are advised to prioritise massive physical infrastructure projects that can facilitate the efficient export of extracted goods, even while they download the costs onto people and nature, and exacerbate inequalities. Instead, *physical* infrastructure could be designed to support a circular, restorative economy – a web of provisioning, rather than corridors of extraction. This, along with the substantial investment in *social* infrastructure designed to support care, wellbeing and harmony with nature, would go far to reduce the causes of structural violence and war itself.

Taken together, these feminist policies revaluing nature would have three clear benefits in terms of their contribution to sustaining peace and preventing relapse into war. First, the creation of circular, restorative economies involves a shift away from a reliance upon fossil fuels and other high-value mineral resources, resources which have infamously fuelled violence and corruption in many countries (see e.g. Lujala and Rustad 2012; UNEP 2009). The potential profit of extraction, under capitalism, makes the exploitation of natural resources worth displacing people off their land, looting and killing. From almost every corner of the globe, there are reports of people being uprooted for access to the land under which minerals, oil and gas can be found, and terrorised, tortured and killed (Global Witness 2020). Women and other marginalised groups are targeted for rape and sexual violence by armed groups, including at times paramilitaries acting at the behest of transnational corporations (see Cohn and Duncanson 2020; Méndez Gutiérrez and Carrera Guerra 2015). A move away from extractivism to feminist green economies has the potential to end this violence.

Second, similar to investing in care, the creation of circular, restorative economies could contribute to addressing the inequalities, injustices and alienation that have been so central to driving war through the provision of employment opportunities for diverse sectors of the population – for ex-combatants, as well as for those whose lives and means of livelihood were harmed by the war, and those who lacked decent livelihoods pre-war. Sustainable agriculture and land use, sustainable use of natural resources, renewable energy, sustainable transport systems, reforestation and peatland restoration projects, rewilding and eco-tourism could provide plentiful rewarding employment and livelihood opportunities. Crucially, if you de-carbonise farming, for example, or de-carbonise the heating and powering of homes and workplaces, and put specific policies in place to ensure that the new opportunities for employment are distributed fairly and that the work is decently rewarded (see Braunstein and Houston 2015), these climate and biodiversity-friendly policies can be a crucial element of building inclusive, gender-just peace after war.

Third, circular, restorative economies must be understood as integral to peace. Such economies are fundamental to human wellbeing: from maintaining the ecosystems in which humans farm and forage for their subsistence and livelihoods; to maintaining healthy habitats for the pollinators on whom our food security relies; to avoiding the eco-system destruction that leads to zoonotic epidemics and pandemics; to maintaining healthy air and the water cycle; to providing sources for the development of new medications to alleviate human suffering; to meeting human needs for recreation, pleasure and health. In this sense, there is no peace without functioning ecosystems – only immiseration, starvation and conflict.

GETTING FROM HERE TO THERE

Such a transition is not impossible. Many post-war countries in poorest regions of the world have comparative advantages in renewable energy, for example, and have the opportunity to leapfrog to climate-friendly transport and urbanisation strategies (Klasen 2013). Nonetheless, the financial and governmental challenges for post-war states can look overwhelming.

So how do we get from where we are now to where we want to be? How do we create just, inclusive, sustainable economies which prioritise infrastructures of care that sustain both people and our planet's ecosystems? This feminist solution to ending war requires not only a transformation in our understanding of the purposes of economic activity; it also requires financial resources, and a strong, effective, accountable state which understands its primary function as ensuring social welfare, rather than ensuring conditions that enable the unfettered freedom of capital.

Financial resources

The repair of war's harms, and transition to an economy that transforms the inequalities underlying armed conflicts, will require substantial financial resources. But given war's destruction of the productive capacity of the economy, the entrenchment of war economies, and the distorting effects of an influx of internationals in the post-war period, any post-war state faces serious challenges in generating revenue. Prior to the war itself, it is likely that state revenue will already have been limited, as a legacy of colonialism and donor-driven economic policies oriented to avoiding debt defaults. Then, war compounds the problem: resources will not just have been destroyed, they will have often been captured by military or criminal elites.

The most commonly advocated options for generating revenue, such as attracting inward investment, privatisation of state-owned assets and exporting natural resources or goods, have the effect of exacerbating inequalities, including gendered inequalities. They also often fail to generate anticipated revenues, due to elite capture, whereby those who have amassed power and wealth during the war years are best able – through fair means and foul – to benefit from the deals and opportunities on offer. Aid, which can spike to 50 per cent of GDP in post-war periods (in countries receiving aid more generally, it is between 1 and 10 per cent) (del Castillo 2017), can be hard for any post-war government to manage, and is also subject to capture by criminal and political elites. Post-war states thus provide challenging contexts in which to embark on creating inclusive and sustainable green economies, with their ambitious plans for the provision of public goods and employment creation, outlined above.

And yet feminist economists and ecologists have solutions. They draw attention to a range of mechanisms through which the creation of just, inclusive and restorative economies could be financed. First, it would be possible for post-war governments to spend more on building an infrastructure of care if the way aid expenditure is classified were changed. Aid transfers to post-war countries are significant but currently – due to International Monetary Fund (IMF) rules – restrictions apply which preclude post-war governments from spending it to support a substantial infrastructure of care. But if a change were made to classify spending on social infrastructure was as 'investment' rather than 'consumption', so as to recognise its 'public goods quality', post-war states could invest more freely without infringing IMF limits on public debt (see Seguino 2016). Second, more resources for an infrastructure of care and for restoration of nature would also be available if donors decided to forgive odious debts, an appropriate action especially because those debts were often racked up by the corrupt regime a war was fought to overthrow (Ndikumana and Boyce 2011). Third, transforming taxation practices offers multiple opportunities: controls could be applied to cross-border short-term capital flows (e.g. Financial Transaction Tax); tax loopholes could be closed and more progressive tax regimes enacted – corporate tax dodging costs poor countries at least $100 billion every year (see Oxfam 2019). Fourth, redirecting just a fraction of the resources spent worldwide on militaries and military equipment, some $1.7 trillion in 2018 (SIPRI 2018), to support the recovery of post-war countries could enable significant investment in the transition from extractivism to an economy of restoration and care (WILPF 2018).

A strong (role for the) state

It will be clear from our account above that feminist just, inclusive and restorative economies assume a strong role for the state. In post-war settings, however, as we note above, states are often weak, fragmented and beset by corruption. While IFIs have partly recognised this with their push for good governance, they tend to mean little more than providing a stable environment for markets, whereas for us good governance should mean an active, interventionist state that puts care and the restoration of nature at its heart.

Advocating for a strong state can be uncomfortable territory for many feminists. States, especially colonial settler states, have often been the source of gendered insecurities and oppressions. But when thinking about the needs of people in post-war contexts, the requirement for a well-resourced and well-managed social infrastructure to support care, and the need to find a new way to respect and live with nature, it seems clear to us that the state has to be part of the solution. It is the state – if transparent, accountable and responsive – that has the legitimacy and scope to deliver the inclusive and sustainable economy we have argued for here (see Braunstein and Houston 2015; Tickner 2018).

How do you build strong states which prioritise social provisioning and environmentally sustainable forms of development? It is perhaps especially challenging in post-war countries where the state has been weakened by decades of structural adjustment policies, austerity measures and warfare, and where patriarchal patronage relations have been privileged over public services – but most of those characteristics are not limited to post-war states. So more generally, what elements could foster this transformation of the state? Civil society groups and social movements will need resources and support to hold the state accountable (Rai et al. 2019; UNDP 2008). Tools such as gender impact analyses, participatory budgeting and independent audits of government can all contribute. Civil society groups and international bodies can use the UN's International Covenant of Economic and Social Rights to hold post-war governments and the donor community to account: economic recovery policies must contribute to the progressive realisation of economic and social rights, and this legal provision can be used to push states and donors to fund the social infrastructure required for an economy organised around care, sufficiency and sustainability (Rees and Chinkin 2015). Mechanisms to ensure representation of women and other marginalised groups in all levels of government will also be central to countering vested interests and developing progressive policies for social provisioning and environmental sustainability.

CONCLUSION

In this chapter, we have argued that building inclusive, just and sustainable economies is an important feminist solution to ending war. Ending war cannot be achieved without addressing the root causes of wars, including – centrally – the currently dominant global capitalist economic model, which exacerbates inequalities and drives environmental crises.

We have focused specifically on post-war countries because they so often slip back into armed violence. Also, the aftermath of war presents especially daunting challenges, even while it also presents windows of opportunity. But we believe that the solution we have been outlining – a feminist approach to the building of inclusive, just and sustainable economies – is equally applicable to countries which do not have armed warfare in their recent past; that it is necessary if we are to end the many forms of physical and structural violence that characterise countries which are 'at peace', as well as to prevent future wars.

It strikes us that when international architects of post-war economic policy think about economic recovery policy, they start from above, with a model of the purpose of an economy, the meaning of a 'healthy' economy, and steps that need to be taken to reach that goal (which typically include targeting inflation, export-oriented growth, tackling public deficits, and so on). In contrast, feminists start from the ground up. If we want economic recovery policy to contribute to ending war and building peace – to ameliorate the inequalities and exclusions that underlie armed conflict, and to make the lives of the country's inhabitants more secure – we need to start by looking at the conditions in which people live their lives at the war's end, for those are the conditions that will need to be transformed.

Starting, as feminist economist and ecologists do, with people's lives, not abstract economic models, alerts us to the needs that people have for care – broadly defined – and for a healthy environment in which to recover and live. The feminist revaluing of care and nature can provide the basis of a radically different approach to post-war recovery, to ending war, and to building peace that is sustainable. This approach, through building just, inclusive and sustainable economies, would transform the conditions underpinning wars. Putting care at the heart of the economy would meet the needs of people after war, has the potential to provide employment in fair and inclusive ways, and can contribute to a new social contract. It would also recognise and prioritise the relationships which make our lives possible and give them depth and meaning. Shifting from an extractivist approach to valuing nature would bring an end to the violence fuelled by extractivism, could provide quality and inclusive employment opportunities, and is imperative for ensuring the healthy functioning of ecosystems on which our lives and sustainable peace depend.

REFERENCES

Note: All URLs checked on 15 April 2020.

Balakrishnan, R., Heintz, J. and Elson, D. (2016) *Rethinking Economic Policy for Social Justice: The Radical Potential of Human Rights*. Abingdon: Routledge.

Bauhardt, C. (2014) Solutions to the crisis? The green new deal, degrowth, and the solidarity economy: Alternatives to the capitalist growth economy from an ecofeminist economics perspective. *Ecological Economics* 102: 60–68.

Bauhardt, C. and Harcourt, W. (eds) (2018) *Feminist Political Ecology and the Economics of Care: In Search of Economic Alternatives*. Abingdon: Routledge.

Benería, L., Berik, G. and Floro, M. (2015) *Gender, Development and Globalization: Economics as if All People Mattered*, 2nd edn. New York: Routledge.

Braunstein, E. and Houston, M. (2015) Pathways towards sustainability in the context of globalization: A gendered perspective on growth, macro policy and employment. In: M. Leach (ed.) *Gender Equality and Sustainable Development*. Abingdon: Routledge, pp. 34–55.

Budlender, D. (2010) *Time Use Studies and Unpaid Care Work*. New York: Routledge.

Cohn, C. and Duncanson, C. (2020) Whose recovery? IFI prescriptions for postwar states. *Review of International Political Economy* 27(6), doi: 10.1080/09692290.2019.1677743.

Cohn, C. and Duncanson, C. (forthcoming) Women, peace, and security in a changing climate. *International Feminist Journal of Politics*.

DeLargy, P. (2013) Sexual violence and women's health in war. In: C. Cohn (ed.) *Women and War*. London: Polity Press, pp. 54–79.

del Castillo, G. (2016) Economic reconstruction and reforms in post-conflict countries. In: A. Langer and G.K. Brown (eds) *Building Sustainable Peace: Timing and Sequencing of Post-conflict Reconstruction and Peacebuilding*. Oxford: Oxford University Press, pp. 51–71.

del Castillo, G. (2017) *Obstacles to Peacebuilding*. Abingdon: Routledge.

Folbre, N. (2001) *The Invisible Heart: Economics and Family Values*. New York: New Press.

Global Witness (2020) *Defending Tomorrow: The Climate Crisis and Threats against Land and Environmental Defenders*. Available at: www.globalwitness.org/en/campaigns/environmental-activists/land-and-environmental-defenders-annual-report-archive/

Haar, R.J. and Rubenstein, L.S. (2012) *Health in Postconflict and Fragile States*. US Institute of Peace. Available at: www.jstor.org/stable/resrep12275.

Harcourt, W. and Nelson, I.L. (eds) (2015) *Practising Feminist Political Ecologies: Moving beyond the 'Green Economy'*. London: Zed Books.

IPCC (2019) Summary for policymakers. In: *Climate Change and Land: An IPCC special report on climate change, desertification, land degradation, sustainable land management, food security, and greenhouse gas fluxes in terrestrial ecosystems*. Available at: www.ipcc.ch/site/assets/uploads/sites/4/2020/02/SPM_Updated-Jan20.pdf

Klasen, S. (2013) Gender, growth and adaptation to climate change. In: B. Cela, I. Dankelman and J. Stern (eds) *Powerful Synergies: Gender Equality, Economic Development and environmental sustainability*. New York: UNDP, pp. 49–59. Available at: www.undp.org/content/undp/en/home/librarypage/womens-empowerment/powerful-synergies.html

Leach, M. (ed.) (2015) *Gender Equality and Sustainable Development*. Abingdon: Routledge.

Lujala, Päivi and Rustad, Siri Aas (eds) (2012) *High-value Natural Resources and Post-conflict Peacebuilding*. Abingdon: Routledge.

Mason, T.D. (2019) Sustaining the peace after civil war: What do we know about peace failure versus peace duration? In: *Oxford Research Encyclopedia of Politics*, doi: 10.1093/acrefore/9780190228637.013.1689.

Méndez Gutiérrez, L. and Carrera Guerra, A. (2015) *Clamor for Justice: Sexual Violence, Armed Conflict and Violent Land Dispossession*. Guatemala: Equipo de Estudios Comunitarios y Acción Psicosocial (ECAP).

Mlinarević, G., Isaković, N.P., True, J., Chinkin, C., Rees, M. and Svedberg, B. (2017) *A Feminist Perspective on Post-conflict Restructuring and Recovery: The Case of Bosnia and Herzegovina*. WILPF. Available at: https://wilpf.org/wp-content/uploads/2017/08/Feminist-political-economy-ENG-FINAL.pdf

Ndikumana, L. and Boyce, J.K. (2011) *Africa's Odious Debts: How Foreign Loans and Capital Flight Bled a Continent*. London: Zed Books.

Oxfam (2019) *Public Good or Private Wealth?* Briefing Paper. Oxford: Oxfam GB. Available at: https://oxfamilibrary.openrepository.com/bitstream/handle/10546/620599/bp-public-good-or-private-wealth-210119-en.pdf

Philipsen, D. (2015) *The Little Big Number: How GDP Came to Rule the World and What to Do about It*. Princeton, NJ: Princeton University Press.

Rai, S.M., True, J. and Tanyag, M. (2019) From depletion to regeneration: Addressing structural and physical violence in post-conflict economies. *Social Politics: International Studies in Gender, State & Society* 26(4): 561–585.

Raworth, K. (2017) *Doughnut Economics: Seven Ways to Think like a 21st-century Economist*. White River Junction: Chelsea Green Publishing.

Rees, M. and Chinkin, C. (2016) Exposing the gendered myth of post-conflict transition: The transformative power of economic and social rights. *New York University Journal of International Law and Politics* 48(4): 1211–1226.

Rockström, J. et al. (2009) Planetary boundaries: Exploring the safe operating space for humanity. *Ecology and Society* 14(2): 32.

Seguino, S. (2016) *Financing for Gender Equality in the Context of SDGs*. Working Paper Series No. 426. Amherst, MA: Political Economy Research Institute.

SIPRI (Stockholm International Peace Research Institute) (2018) Global military spending remains high at $1.7 trillion. SIPRI, 2 May. Available at: www.sipri.org/media/press-release/2018/global-military-spending-remains-high-17-trillion

Tickner, J.A. (2018) Rethinking the state in International Relations: A personal reflection. In: S. Parashar, J.A. Tickner and J. True (eds) *Revisiting Gendered States: Feminist Imaginings of the State in International Relations*. Oxford: Oxford University Press, pp. 19–32.

Tienhaara, K. (2019) The Green New Deal is going global. *The Conversation*, 6 May.

Tronto, J. (1993) *Moral Boundaries: A Political Argument for an Ethic of Care*. London: Psychology Press.

UN Women (2015) *Progress of the World's Women 2015–2016: Transforming Economies, Realizing Rights*. New York: UN Women.

UNDP (United Nations Development Programme) (2008) *Crisis Prevention and Recovery: Enabling Local Ingenuity*. Available at: www.undp.org/content/undp/en/home/librarypage/crisis-prevention-and-recovery/crisis-prevent-recovery-report-2008-post-conflict-economic-recovery.html

UNEP (United Nations Environment Programme) (2009) *From Conflict to Peacebuilding: The Role of Natural Resources and the Environment*. Available at: https://wedocs.unep.org/bitstream/handle/20.500.11822/7867/pcdmb_policy_01.pdf?sequence=4&isAllowed=y

Walter, B.F. (2011) *Conflict Relapse and the Sustainability of Post-conflict Peace*. World Development Report Background Papers. Washington, DC: World Bank.

Waring, M. (1988) *If Women Counted: A New Feminist Economics*. New York: Harper & Row.

WILPF (Women's International League for Peace and Freedom) (2018) Move the money from war to peace. Available at: www.wilpf.org/move-the-money/

13

Change How Civilian Casualties are 'Counted'

Thomas Gregory

This chapter suggests changing the way we count civilian casualties as a feminist solution to war. The chapter begins by acknowledging that body counts are an important tool in the fight against forgetting the costs of war as they provide some information about the number of people injured or killed as a consequence of this violence. Yet it also draws attention to the politics of counting – or not counting – civilian casualties. It will examine cases where the military has sought to downplay or deny the violence they cause by refusing to count civilian casualties or deliberately undercounting the number of civilians killed. Against those who suggest that the solution is to ensure that militaries count civilian casualties and that these counts are conducted correctly, this chapter argues that these numbers are insufficient when it comes to accounting for pain and suffering experienced by civilians and holding militaries accountable for the death and destruction they cause.

Drawing on the work of feminist theorists, such as Sally Engle Merry and Adriana Cavarero, it argues that body counts fail to contest the dehumanising logic that reduce human beings to mere statistics. Moreover, these numerical indicators can reinforce a very clean and sterile image of war that is utterly devoid of the dead and injured bodies left strewn across the battlefield and the emotional experiences of those who have to live with its devastating effects.

As a solution to this problem, this chapter proposes a more relational response to the suffering of civilians, which foregrounds the individual lives that are lost and the circumstances surrounding their deaths. Rather than simply counting civilian casualties, it argues that we need to name those who are killed or injured, we need to find ways of telling their stories – not just stories about their grisly demise but also stories about who they were as individuals and the lives that they left behind. The solution, therefore, is not to devise more accurate or precise ways of counting civilian casualties but to look for alternative modes of accounting for the pain and suffering that is inflicted during these wars. As such, it takes seriously the feminist call to foreground the everyday in global politics and to listen to those who are so often relegated to the margins.

COUNTING CASUALTIES

During Operation Desert Storm in Iraq, General Norman Schwarzkopf was asked to comment on the number of civilians killed by coalition troops, but claimed he had 'absolutely no idea what the Iraqi casualties are'. He also seemed reluctant to correct this oversight, announcing that 'if I have anything to say about it, we're never going to get into a body-counting business' (quoted in Cushman 1991). Describing this as a form of pre-censorship, Margot Norris (1991: 225) argued that the military was actively trying to de-realise the devastating effects of war by ensuring that the dead and injured bodies of Iraqi civilians remained completely invisible and totally unknowable. This refusal to count civilian casualties not only denies us a:

> numerical inventory of the enemy dead, but also the willingness to reckon with the meaning and significance of such vast numbers of the killed in an accounting of the purpose, necessity ... and human cost of their violent destruction. (Norris 1991, 237–8)

Without accurate information about the number of civilians who were killed as a consequence of these military operations, we have no way of knowing whether they were conducted in accordance with the dictates of international humanitarian law, which requires belligerents to discriminate between combatants and non-combatants, ensure any anticipated civilian harm is proportionate to the expected military gains, and that appropriate precautions are taken to reduce the likelihood of civilian deaths. (Norris 1991, 238)

Similar concerns were raised during the early stages of Operation Enduring Freedom in Afghanistan after General Tommy Franks announced to reporters that 'we don't do body counts' (quoted in Broder 2003). Although coalition casualties were counted with meticulous accuracy, Jessica Hyndman (2003, 8) argued that there was an 'audible silence' about the civilians killed by coalition bombs. This enabled the military to portray the conflict as a surgical strike against the enemy – with minimal impact upon the civilian population – even though many of these bombs missed their targets and killed civilians in the process (Hyndman 2003, 9). Others also expressed concern about this refusal to count civilian casualties, with John Sloboda et al. (2013, 54) arguing that: 'there can be no justification for insulating ourselves from knowledge of war's effects'. At a minimum, they insist that militaries have an obligation to record – and release – basic facts about who was killed, where they were killed and when they were killed, insisting that there can be 'no moral justification for refusing to record war deaths by every available means' (Sloboda et al. 2013, 54). This is echoed by Daniel Mahanty and Alex Moorehead (2019), who argue that people cannot participate in debates about the legitimacy of war if they are kept in the dark about the impact they are having on innocent civilians.

This reluctance to count civilian casualties has prompted various non-profit organisations to keep a running tally of the civilians killed, drawing on a variety of sources – from international media reports through to local witness reports. Airwars (2019), for example, estimates that between 8,148 and 13,097 civilians have been killed in coalition airstrikes in Iraq and Syria since August 2014, which is significantly more than the 1,321 deaths that coalition forces have admitted killing. Similarly, a joint investigation with Amnesty International (Amnesty Internaitonal 2019) concluded that coalition forces had killed more than 1,600 civilians during a four-month campaign in the Syrian city of Raqqa, which reduced entire neighbourhoods of the city to mounds of rubble. These body counts are obviously important when it comes to holding militaries accountable for the damage that they cause to both people and places, drawing attention to the disconnect between rhetoric and reality.

Even though coalition commanders challenged people to 'find a more precise air campaign in the history of warfare' – insisting that their goal is 'always zero human casualties' – these independent assessments revealed that civilian casualties were significantly higher than the official figures acknowledged, raising important questions about the heavy-handed tactics that were being used by coalition forces and the adequacy of their battlefield damage reports (Lieutenant General Stephen Townsend, quoted in Amnesty International 2019).

Even when militaries do count civilian casualties, there is no guarantee that their data is accurate. Official figures released by the UK Ministry of Defence, for example, claimed that more than 4,000 enemy combatants had been killed by the Royal Air Force (RAF) in approximately 1,700 bombing raids across Iraq and Syria and that only one civilian had been killed as a consequence of these operations. Data collected by various non-profit organisations suggested that these official figures were simply not credible, with Airwars noting that the RAF dropped over 4,000 munitions – mostly 500lb bombs – on densely populated residential areas. As the executive director of Action on Armed Violence Iain Overton put it, the suggestion that there was only 'one civilian casualty against 4,315 enemies must be a world record in modern conflict' (quoted in Barnes and Hall 2019). These discrepancies could be the product of deliberately undercounting the civilians killed but they might also arise as a consequence of methodological choices about how these counts are conducted and what is included in these counts (see Sebolt et al. 2013).

When it comes to counting civilian casualties, it is important for us to consider whether these counts are being conducted and what is at stake when the military simply refuses to count those it kills. It is also important to pay attention to how these counts are conducted and what is included in these counts because these methodological decisions will have a significant bearing on the accuracy of the figures eventually produced. However, we should also be cautious about how these numerical indicators shape our understanding about the violence inflicted on the battlefield. As we shall see in the following section, feminists have warned that body counts create a very clean and sterile image of war, erasing the horrifying effects of this violence while presenting its victims as mere objects – things that can be counted rather than human beings with specific stories to tell.

THE LIMITATIONS OF COUNTING CIVILIAN CASUALTIES

The previous section focused on concerns about the refusal to count civilian casualties and problems with how these counts are conducted, which suggests that a potential solution would be to ensure that civilian casualties are counted and that these counts are conducted properly. Feminists argued that militaries were actively trying to avoid counting civilians or downplay the number of civilians killed in order to present a simple and clean image of the battlefield – one that is completely devoid of the chaos and the carnage experienced by civilians on the ground. There are obvious parallels with the 'technostrategic language' used by nuclear strategists that actively seeks to evade the catastrophic consequences of a nuclear strike, as Ray Acheson demonstrates in her chapter. This section will argue that simply counting civilian casualties and ensuring these counts are accurate is not enough to disrupt the dehumanising logic that transforms civilians into mere statistics – in some cases, counting civilian casualties might actually reinforce the problem.

The previous section focused on those occasions where militaries have refused to count civilian casualties or have deliberately undercounted those they have killed, either by design or because of the methodological decisions taken before conducting their counts. One obvious solution to this problem would be to ensure that militaries not only count civilian casualties but that every civilian casualty is counted. Yet simply documenting these deaths fails to disrupt the dehumanising logic that renders the civilian population profoundly disposable because it reduces civilians to mere statistics while also erasing the devastating effects of the violence that is inflicted upon their bodies. Although she was critical of coalition attempts to conceal the death and destruction inflicted upon the Afghan people, Jessica Hyndman warned that simply counting these casualties cannot do justice to the individuals who lost their lives or capture the grief experienced by those left behind. She argues that while 'counting is an important device for remembering, it is also flawed in the way it transforms unnamed dead people into abstract figures' (Hyndman 2007, 38).

Feminists have also expressed broader concerns about the unintended consequences of counting civilian casualties. Elsewhere, I have argued that body counts can disguise the full horrors of war by producing a strangely disembodied account of the violence inflicted in war, which tells us very little about what actually happens to the people when they are hit by falling bombs or struck by stray bullets (Gregory 2014). The process of counting these casualties cleanses them of any blood and gore, transforming them into numerical indicators that can be tabulated into neat little rows or converted into pretty little graphs. As the horrifying effects of this violence – not to mention the emotional distress it causes to those left behind – is completely erased from view, there is no sense that the primary 'purpose of the event described is to alter (to burn, to blast, to shell, to cut) human tissue' (Scarry 1985, 64). As such, these body counts can reproduce the 'technostrategic language' described by Ray Acheson in her chapter on nuclear weapons, as it enables us to talk about this violence without ever confronting the devastating effects of what happens to the people involved.

Cristina Masters (2007, 44–5) is also ambivalent about the way in which body counts have been used by the military as a technology of war – a metric that can be used to measure progress in wars without a continuous front, or as a propaganda tool that can be used to remind people about the 'necessity' of a particular conflict. She argues that dead bodies cannot simply speak for themselves and there is always politics at play when it comes to representing the dead. The bodies that are counted by coalition forces – the bodies of soldiers who have been killed or injured in the line of duty – are not used to illustrate the awfulness of war, but deployed within a gendered narrative of sacrifice designed to reinforce masculinist notions of protection (Masters 2007, 48–9; see also Young 2003). When civilian casualties are counted, these figures are not necessarily used to highlight the horrors of war, but can also be used to demonstrate the 'technological prowess' of the military or the surgical precision of its strikes, by emphasising how few civilians died in that particular operation (Masters 2007, 47). The dead bodies that do appear in these body counts are not necessarily grieveable bodies, whose deaths can be publicly commemorated or mourned, but as bodies that have been thoroughly dehumanised, devalued and disqualified (Masters 2007, 55).

Although she does not write about body counts per se, the work of Sally Engle Merry on what she terms the 'seduction of quantification' is particularly useful here as it provides a specific set of conceptual tools for thinking about how these numerical indicators work to make violence more or less visible. She argues that quantification is seductive because it appears to offer us concrete statistical information about the world around us, creating simple metrics that can be used to measure, rank and compare different processes while helping people to make difficult decisions in the absence of more detailed contextual information. Yet she argues that:

> the process of translating the buzzing confusion of social life into neat categories that can be tabulated risks distorting the complexity of social phenomena [because ...] counting things requires us to make them comparable, which means that they are inevitability stripped of their context, history and meaning. (Merry 2016, 1)

Some of these concerns are technical, although she reminds us that the political often hides behind the technical. While numbers have an aura of objectivity, she argues that decisions will have been made about what is counted and what is not counted, who is authorised to conduct these counts and how these counts should be conducted – what methods will be used to accumulate this data and what methodological assumptions have informed these decisions – and what categories need to be constructed in order to make sense of the social world (2016, 14).

There are some obvious lessons here for those of us interested in counting civilian casualties in terms of who is counting, what is counted and how these counts are conducted. While the categories of combatant and non-combatant may seem relatively stable and self-evident, Helen Kinsella (2011) argues that they are inescapably gendered, with women and children coming to be viewed as the quintessential innocent civilian while the status of combatant is reserved almost exclusively for men. These gendered distinctions can be deadly for anyone that falls into the category of a 'military age male' in contemporary conflicts – irrespective of whether they are actually involved in the conflict – because fitting this description can be sufficient to transform someone into a legitimate target (Carpenter 2013). At the same time, the distinctions can also be significant when it comes to counting and categorising the victims of a particular incident or operation, where gender might be one technique used to determine whether the victims were combatants or non-combatants (Wilcox 2017).

Counting casualties is an important weapon in the fight against forgetting. Feminists have resisted this forgetting and drawn attention to the problematic assumptions that shape how these counts are conducted. While body counts may appear to provide an objective and politically neutral measure of the death and injury inflicted in any given conflict, the figures that circulate within the public sphere quickly become detached from the specific methodological decisions that went into producing this data and the politics that informed these decisions. As Merry explains:

> rather than objective representations of the world, such quantifications are social constructs formed through protracted social processes [yet …] once established and recognized, they often circulate beyond the sphere envisioned by their original creators and lose their moorings in specific methodological choices and compromises. (2016, 5)

There are 'technical' dilemmas that raise important questions about who and what gets counted. Should investigators only focus on recorded deaths and risk underestimating the total number of casualties or should they use sample techniques to estimate the total number of deaths and risk overstating the number of casualties? Should they focus only on the direct harm caused by conflicts or should they also consider indirect deaths caused by unexploded ordinance, unstable buildings and the toxic remnants of war, the health problems caused by disease, malnutrition and the difficulties accessing basic medical

care, and the harm that is caused by the disintegration of a community's infrastructure and the displacement of peoples?

Feminist concerns about the quantification of social life is also
evident in the work of Diane Nelson, who claims that counting is
both 'essential *and* insufficient, dehumanizing *and* reparative, necessary *and* complicated' (2015, 24). Conscious that numbers play
an important role in highlighting the devastating effects of contemporary violence, drawing attention to the clandestine cemeteries
overflowing with dead bodies and the hidden hospitals that are filled
with the victims of war, she nevertheless argues that numbers can
mask as much as they reveal, stripping away much of the horror and
the heartache of these conflicts (Nelson 2015, 81). As Peter Greena-
way argues, 'counting is like taking aspirin – it numbs the senses and
protects the counter from reality [because it …] makes even hideous
events bearable' (quoted in Nelson 2015, 17). The process of counting
bodies dissociates them from their context, transforming them into
just another thing that needs to be quantified, enumerated, calculated. There is no guarantee that simply counting the casualties of
war will do anything to disrupt the martial logic that renders this
killing permissible in the first instance, no guarantee that keeping a
running tally of casualties will make the horrors of war intelligible to
those of us watching from afar, no guarantee that the publication of a
daily body count will make the victims seem any more real, any more
human. As Wilcox reminds us, 'the enumeration of deaths does not
necessarily constitute a politics of re-humanizing or "subjectivizing"
those who have been made into "mere bodies"' (2015, 163).

FROM DATA TO EXPERIENCE

Although it is fraught with various methodological conundrums
– conundrums that are intensely political – most feminists would
argue that accumulating data on civilian casualties is the absolute
bare minimum that needs to be done, a small but essential step that
can be taken to ensure that there is some level of accountability for
the harm that is inflicted and that the victims receive some recognition for their suffering. Yet this demand that the victims are counted
should always be accompanied by a reminder that numbers are insuf-

ficient because so much is left on the cutting-room floor. A feminist solution to war would not dispense with these body counts, but it would also look for a more relational mode of address that does not erase the human lives that are lost. In short, feminist scholarship reminds us that body counts should be the beginning of the conversation about the costs of war and not the goal. A feminist solution cannot treat people like 'stick figures' to be classified and counted but human beings with feelings, thoughts and emotions (Sylvester 2011).

The insufficiency of numbers becomes clear when you consider the testimony of Zubair and Nabila ur Rehman – two Pakistani children who were injured in a drone strike that killed their 67-year-old grandmother Mamana Bibi and injured four of their cousins. The children had been invited to Washington DC to talk about the impact drones were having on their community, although only a small handful of lawmakers bothered to attend the session. Zubair, who was only 12 at the time of the attack, describes how he was picking okra with his grandmother when he heard drones hovering overhead, telling members of Congress that neither of them felt afraid at first because neither of them were militants. When the first drone opened fire, he describes how 'the whole ground shook and black smoke rose up [making ...] the air smell poisonous' (quoted in McVeigh 2013). His younger sister, who was only eight at the time of the attack, was also picking okra when she heard the 'dum dum noise' from the drones above. She describes the moment the first missile struck, telling lawmakers that 'everything was dark and I couldn't see anything. I heard a scream – I think it was my grandmother but I couldn't see her' (quoted in McVeigh 2013). Once the dust had settled, she describes how she ventured back out to search for her grandmother, eventually finding her shoes before discovering 'her mutilated body a short time afterwards'. It had been 'thrown quite a long distance away by the blast and it was in pieces [so...] we collected as many different parts from the field [as we could find] and wrapped them in a cloth' (quoted in Amnesty International 2013, 19).

Simply quantifying the harm inflicted on this fateful morning would inevitably mean that much of this context would be stripped away. The names of the victims would almost certainly be lost in the process, even if some of their demographic details might remain, and the unimaginable terror experienced by the children as they fled the scene of the attack – not to mention the unthinkable horror of having to piece together the charred and dismembered remains of their dead grandmother – would be rendered invisible within the dataset. It is unlikely that the victims would register as human beings with a unique and rather shocking story to tell because they would simply be classified as one dead woman and six injured children when entered into the database. The process of quantification also means that these specific figures would quickly be subsumed into a much bigger dataset, which only adds to distance between the victims and those of us who rely on these body counts, further desensitising us to their pain. When looked at in isolation the number of civilians harmed in this single strike seems rather stark – one dead and at least six children injured – but it does not take long before these casualties are simply some of the 39 to 70 people who are thought to have been killed or injured by drones in Pakistan that month, or the 312 to 622 people who are thought to have been killed or injured by drones in Pakistan that year, or the 3,677 to 5,775 people thought to have been killed or injured by drones in Pakistan since records began (Bureau of Investigative Journalism 2019).

Data on civilian casualties certainly help to reveal the scale of the violence and the sheer number of people affected, but they paint a very abstract and strangely disembodied view of war, and one that is remarkably devoid of human beings with feelings or thoughts. The testimony of Zubair and Nabila shows that a feminist solution to counting casualties would need to create space for the voices of ordinary civilians, so that they can explain how their lives have been affected by this conflict. On the one hand, this testimony works to remind us just how brutal war can be, particularly when it comes to the destruction or decimation of the human body. While body counts provide us with some sense of how many bodies have been killed or injured in war, they do not tell us what war actually does to these bodies, the fact that many – like the body of Mamana Bibi – are literally blown to smithereens. The work of the Italian feminist theorist Adriana Cavarero (2011, 2) is instructive here as it reminds us that: 'while violence against the helpless is becoming global in ever more ferocious forms, language proves unable to renew itself to name it; indeed, it tends to mask it'.

FEMINIST SOLUTIONS TO THE BODY COUNT

The trouble with body counts is they do not create space for this horror to be seen – in fact they may inadvertently conceal it by transforming these broken bodies into neat and tidy statistics that retain almost no trace of the human beings they are supposed to count. Cavarero argues that the *language of horror* can provide us with a conceptual framework that can make sense of this suffering, drawing attention to the dehumanising effects of this violence, the fact that this violence seems to overshoot the more 'elementary goal of taking a life and dedicates itself to destroying the living being as a singular body' (2011, 12). For Cavarero, contemporary practices of violence do not simply kill their victims, but leave them unrecognisable as human beings by reducing them to pieces of flesh and bone that first have to be collected, sorted and then reassembled before their relatives can give them a proper funeral or burial (see also Gregory 2016).

At the same time, the testimony of Nabila and Zubair reminds us that any feminist solution to war would need to make visible the heart-wrenching experiences of those touched by war, drawing attention to the ways in which this violence impinges upon their lives in ways that cannot be captured by numerical measurements alone. As well as drawing attention to the way in which these particular modes of thought work to obscure the horrors of war, Cavarero also points out that they work to objectify, devalue and ultimately dehumanise the victims by obscuring any sense of their status as singular beings.

The reason this matters to feminists like Cavarero is that it highlights the violence that is inherent within traditional modes of thinking, which often focus on *what* someone is rather than *who* they are. When it comes to counting civilian casualties, it is clear that any attempt to quantify the deaths and injuries caused by war will end up erasing the stories of those who are killed or injured, along with the stories of those who have lost loved ones as a result of these actions. These statistical measures are not interested in the stories of those who have been harmed, but only in what they are – they rely on categorising individuals based on whether they are combatants or non-combatants, and whether the victims were killed or merely injured. There is no space within these spreadsheets for any discussion about the people who are actually affected by this violence, which is why feminist attempts to make these stories visible is so important. Even though few people bothered to show up to hear Zubair and Nabila tell their story, their mere presence at the congressional hearing can be seen as a kind of performative contradiction, a moment when attempts to reduce people to what they are come unstuck and we get a glimpse – albeit a very brief one – of who they are and how this violence affects their lives.

Some non-profits have already started to supplement their statistical assessments with more detailed information about the individuals who were killed, including their name and profession, details of their deaths and photographs of the scene. When they are unable to find a name for those listed in their database, they include photographs of their personal effects – including bloodstained backpacks, dusty shoes and tattered identity cards – to help humanise the data, providing us with a brief glimpse of the individual lives lost as a result of these operations. Although the voices of those killed remain inaudible, these representations give us an opportunity to reflect on the violence that is inflicted during war. A feminist approach to counting casualties would enable us, therefore, to build a more complete picture of the pain and suffering experienced by civilians, enabling us to hold militaries more accountable for the death and destruction they cause.

CONCLUSION

Civilian casualty data presents feminists with a bit of a dilemma. On the one hand, there is no denying that this data is an important weapon in the fight against forgetting, as it provides us with basic information about the costs and consequences of war. At the same time, feminists are acutely aware that counting anything – including casualties – is an intensely political act. When attempting to count the costs of war, it is imperative that we pay attention to what is counted and what is not counted, because the refusal to count certain costs or include certain costs in the count is one way that the pain and suffering inflicted on civilians is camouflaged, erased or obscured. We must also pay close attention to who is conducting these counts and how these counts are conducted, examining how certain methodological choices can work to make this violence more or less visible. At the same time, this chapter has warned about how the quantification of these costs can objectify, devalue and dehumanise the victims of war by transforming them into mere statistics. A feminist solution to war needs to move beyond this obsession with quantifying casualties by finding novel and creative ways to acknowledge the individual lives lost and the horrifying circumstances surrounding these deaths. A feminist solution to war needs to find a way of re-humanising these debates by reminding people that every single statistic is an individual who has a unique and irreplaceable story to tell (Dauphinee 2007).

REFERENCES

Airwars (2019) US-led coalition in Iraq and Syria. Available at: https://airwars.org/conflict/coalition-in-iraq-and-syria/

Amnesty International (2013) Will I be next? US drone strikes in Pakistan'. Available at: www.amnestyusa.org/files/asa330132013en.pdf

Amnesty International (2019) War in Raqqa: Rhetoric versus reality. 25 April. Available at: https://raqqa.amnesty.org/

Barnes, C. and Hall, R. (2019), UK claims it has killed just one civilian in 1,700 bombing raids on Iraq and Syria. *The Independent*, 7 March. Available at: www.independent.co.uk/news/world/middle-east/syria-iraq-uk-airstrikes-civilian-deaths-raqqa-mod-a8811781.html

Bureau of Investigative Journalism (2019) Drone strikes in Pakistan. 13 September. Available at: www.thebureauinvestigates.com/projects/drone-war/pakistan

Broder, J. (2003) US military has no count of Iraqi dead in fighting. *New York Times* 2 April. Available at: www.nytimes.com/2003/04/02/world/nation-war-casualties-us-military-has-no-count-iraqi-dead-fighting.html

Carpenter, C. (2013) *'Innocent Women and Children': Gender, Norms and the Protection of Civilians.* Aldershot: Ashgate.

Cavarero, A. (2011) *Horrorism: Naming Contemporary Violence.* New York: Columbia University Press.

Cushman, J. (1991) 'Pentagon seems vague on the Iraqis' death toll. Available at: www.nytimes.com/1991/02/03/world/war-in-the-gulf-the-casualties-pentagon-seems-vague-on-the-iraqis-death-toll.html

Dauphinee, E. (2007) The politics of the body in pain: Reading the ethics of imagery. *Security Dialogue* 38(2): 139–155.

Gregory, T. (2014) Body counts disguise the true horror of what wars do to bodies. *The Conversation*, 10 November. Available at: https://the conversation.com/body-counts-disguise-the-true-horror-of-what-wars-do-to-bodies-31416

Gregory, T. (2016) Dismembering the dead: Violence, vulnerability and the body in war. *European Journal of International Relations* 22(4): 944–965.

Hyndman, J. (2003) Beyond either/or: A feminist analysis of September 11th. *ACME: An International E-Journal for Critical Geographies* 2(1): 1–13.

Hyndman, J. (2007) Feminist geopolitics revisited: Body counts in Iraq. *Professional Geographer* 59(1): 35–46.

Kinsella, H. (2011) *The Image Before the Weapon: A Critical History of the Distinction between Combatant and Civilian.* Ithaca, NY: Cornell University Press.

Mahanty, D. and Moorehead, A. (2019) Costs of war can't be assessed without official civilian casualty estimates. 3 April. Available at: www.justsecurity.org/63488/costs-of-war-cant-be-assessed-without-official-civilian-casualty-estimates/

Masters, C. (2007) Body counts: The biopolitics of death. In: E. Dauphinee and C. Masters (eds) *The Logics of Biopower and the War on Terror: Living, Dying, Surviving.* Basingstoke: Palgrave Macmillan, pp. 43–57.

McVeigh, T. (2013) Drone strikes: Tears in Congress as Pakistani family tells of mother's death. *The Guardian*, 29 October. Available at: www.theguardian.com/world/2013/oct/29/pakistan-family-drone-victim-testimony-congress

Merry, S.E. (2016) *The Seductions of Quantification: Measuring Human Rights, Gender Violence and Sex Trafficking.* Chicago: University of Chicago Press.

Nelson, D. (2015) *Who Counts? The Mathematics of Death and Life After Genocide.* Durham, NC: Duke University Press.

Norris, M. (1991) Military censorship and the body count in the Persian Gulf War. *Cultural Critique* 19(autumn): 223–245.

Scarry, E. (1985) *The Body in Pain: The Making and Unmaking of the World.* Oxford: Oxford University Press.

Sebolt, T., Aronson, J. and Fischhoff, B. (eds) (2013) *Counting Civilian Casualties: An Introduction to Recording and Estimating Nonmilitary Deaths in Conflict.* Oxford: Oxford University Press.

Sloboda, J., Dardagan, H., Spagat, M. and Hsiao-Rei Hicks, M. (2013) Iraq body count: A case study in the uses of incident-based conflict casualty data. In: T. Sebolt (eds) *Counting Civilian Casualties: An Introduction to Recording and Estimating Nonmilitary Deaths in Conflict.* Oxford: Oxford University Press, pp. 53–75.

Sylvester, C. (ed.) (2011) *Experiencing War.* Abingdon: Routledge.

Young, I.M. (2003) The logic of masculinist protection: Reflections on the current security state. *Signs* 29(1): 1–25.

Wilcox, L. (2015) *Bodies of Violence: Theorizing Embodied Subjects in International Relations.* Oxford: Oxford University Press.

Wilcox, L. (2017) Embodying algorithmic war: Gender, race and the posthuman in drone warfare. *Security Dialogue* 48(1): 11–28.

14

Listen to Women When Creating Peace Initiatives

Laura J. Shepherd

Women have always been centrally involved in peace and war work. Despite being systematically overlooked and erased through Western Anglophone accounts of peace and war, history includes multiple separate, interwoven narratives of women's work in making, and ending, war. In the early 20th century, the efforts of a number of women to end war were crystallised in the formation of the Women's International League for Peace and Freedom (WILPF) at The Hague in 1915. Drawing on, and inspiring, many decades of related peace activism, WILPF's work towards ending war is well documented (see, for example, Confortini 2012). In 2000, members of WILPF and others were instrumental in advocating the need for feminist perspective on conflict within the international body charged with the maintenance of peace and security: the United Nations Security Council. WILPF's successful advocacy led to the adoption of a resolution on gender and conflict, centring gender violence as a matter of concern to international security. This resolution became the cornerstone of a thematic agenda on Women, Peace, and Security (WPS) at the UN Security Council. There are now ten related resolutions documenting the ways in which gender matters to peace and security.

The originary impetus of the WPS agenda – to demilitarise the international system and end war – often seems to be forgotten (though this forgetting, in turn, can often be read as a wilful forgetting, or act of deliberate erasure). In this chapter, I explore what we learn when we listen to women by providing a reading of the WPS agenda as an artefact of feminist knowledge. Focused on the WPS agenda, this chapter offers 'listen to women,' as a simple but profound solution for ending war, one which recognises sustained feminist activism and theory as central to creating peace and reiterates the importance of taking women's perspectives on peace and war seriously.

In this chapter, I begin by providing a brief outline of the WPS agenda. I then elaborate on three things we can usefully learn from listening to women, from attending closely to women's activities and the knowledge claims that women make, drawn from the experience of working on and with the WPS agenda for two decades. The first of these three lessons coheres around feminist mobilisation and maximisation of strategic opportunities for political change. The feminist peace activists who advocated for the WPS agenda operated from the principle that women *know* war in particular ways – ways that have historically been excluded from discussions about how to bring about war's end – and that this knowledge should be taken seriously in order to end war.

The second opportunity to learn relates to collaborative activism and the importance of coalition-building. If we listen to, and learn from, the way that women *organise*, we can filter this knowledge towards a solution for ending war. The third, and final, element resides in learning from the way feminists *make connections*, not only between people but also between different issue areas, and kinds of activity. The WPS agenda is sustained by a network of activists, advocates and academics, policy-makers, politicians and practitioners; this network values different kinds of knowledge and facilitates connections drawn across theory and practice as well as diverse fields of activity. War is complex and unbounded, extending across time and space, with plural effects that impact individuals and communities, as well as relations between states. Our ability to find ends to war will be enabled through our ability to grasp its complexity; ending war begins with recognising the intimate and intricate connections that together constitute the whole.

THE WOMEN, PEACE AND SECURITY AGENDA

As mentioned above, the WPS agenda is formally articulated in a series of ten UN Security Council resolutions, a sequence that began in 2000 with the adoption of UN Security Council Resolution (UNSCR) 1325. The organisation of the agenda is usually described in terms of three or four 'pillars': the *participation* of women in peace and security governance; the *protection* of women's rights and their bodies; the *prevention* of violence; and a mandate for gender-responsive *relief and recovery* programming. Beyond the formal architecture, however, there is a multitude of implementation, advocacy and policy practices that also constitute the agenda as a 'known object' in contemporary world politics: from NATO's Bi-Strategic Command Directive 40-1, which explains how the WPS resolutions should be implemented across NATO activities; to the National Action Plans (NAPs) or NAP-like documents that articulate a commitment to implementation in 81 states; to the extensive civil society advocacy networks that nurture, support and challenge the development of the agenda across the world. Knowledge claims manifest not only in the stories that we tell about the WPS agenda but also in the provisions and principles of the agenda itself, and the practices that are its mode of reproduction.

The WPS agenda is, in origin and practice, a product of feminist activism and feminist theory, and it is, in essence, concerned with the prevention of conflict – with ending war. I think we can read the WPS agenda, in its totality, as an embodiment of feminist activism and theory; the agenda would not have come into being without the dedicated efforts of feminist peace activists, and it is an artefact of feminist theory because it is motivated by a set of feminist ideas about how the world works – how security can be achieved and how wars can end. If the WPS agenda, and its attendant provisions and principles, were resourced and supported, then the international system would be closer to effective conflict prevention. Within the WPS agenda are tools and resources to foster peace and security: the emphasis on participation within the agenda, for example, is based on recognition of the simple fact that including women in peace negotiations produces material differences in the kinds of peace achieved. Women's influence in negotiations may result in the elaboration and promotion of women's rights in transitional justice processes, or increased support for women's land ownership. Meanwhile, the emphasis on women's engagement in conflict prevention values the peace-building and violence prevention work that women do, often informally and at the community level, as part of the process of bringing about an end to war more globally. In order to develop feminist solutions for ending war, I thus propose that we listen to women.

There are many ways in which listening to women will move us closer to solutions for ending war. In this section, I propose that we should listen to women because women *know* (about peace, war, and everything in between and outside of these often arbitrary categories), women *organise* (formally and informally, in politics, peace-making, and post-conflict reconstruction and beyond), and women *make connections* (across and between communities of all different kinds: intellectual, geographical, and those based on kinship). These ways of knowing and doing are integral to creating meaningful peace.

Women know

Preceding the formalisation of the WPS agenda, women have developed and mobilised knowledges – often marginalised, feminist, Indigenous and subaltern knowledges – about peace and security. These knowledges have routinely and consistently been undervalued, systematically *de*valued, through and as a result of the imbrication of racialised and gendered power in the institutions that validate and sustain knowledge. As Chandra Talpade Mohanty explains, subaltern knowledge is positioned as Other, as lesser; the producers of such knowledge – 'third-world women' – are positioned as objects to be gazed upon by 'Western eyes', rather than agents of knowledge production:

> in the context of the hegemony of the western scholarly establishment in the production and dissemination of texts, and in the context of the legitimating imperative of humanistic and scientific discourse, the definition of 'the third-world woman' as a monolith might well tie into the larger economic and ideological praxis of 'disinterested' scientific inquiry and pluralism which are

the surface manifestations of a latent economic and cultural colonization of the 'non-western' world. (Mohanty 1988, 82)

The subjugation of *kinds of knowing* cannot be separated from the use and application of *ways of knowing* to shore up systems of domination through time. 'The ways in which scientific research is implicated in the worst excesses of colonialism remains a powerful remembered history for many of the world's colonized peoples' (Tuhiwai Smith 2012, 1). The reproduction of binary oppositions – researcher/researched, knower/known, subject/object – through the production of knowledge in service of 'Western civilization' (Tuhiwai Smith 2012, 62–7) creates subject positions in which coloniser and colonised are interpellated and from which it is, or is not, possible to speak with authority and have one's story heard. It is to this reproductive knowledge economy that Gayatri Chakravorty Spivak gestures when she proposes that 'the subtext of the palimpsestic narrative of imperialism be recognized as "subjugated knowledge"' (1988, 25).

We must quiet the will to dominate the conversation about peace and war, recognise different knowledges and ways of knowing, and listen attentively to those historically subjugated knowledges and subordinated subjects. In doing so, we will learn – not only about peace and war but about *power*, because 'it takes resources and access to be "heard" when and where it matters', and 'the actual amount and amazing variety of powers that are required to keep the voices on the margins from having the right language and enough volume to be heard in the centre … are never fully tallied' (Enloe 1996, 187–8). Without an understanding of power in knowledge production and the perpetuation of claims about the validity of certain kinds of knowledge over others, we cannot begin to identify the problems of war, let alone form its solution. And we can learn about power, and knowledge, from listening to women.

From listening to women, we can learn about how to mobilise feminist knowledges and strategically mobilise to challenge 'pale, male, and stale', hierarchically organised, blinkered, and gender-blind security organisations such as the UN Security Council. We can learn about how to value and amplify different forms of knowledge, to think differently about expertise. One of the foundational assumptions embedded in the WPS agenda is the fact that women – diverse women – *know* peace and security differently. Their expertise on peace and security cannot be 'tacked on' to existing, state-centric, narrow and militarised visions of what peace and security means, because to recognise the validity of their knowledge claims is to espouse a thoroughly transformed and transformative vision of peace and security.

Up until the adoption of UNSCR 1325, the UN Security Council had not paid any attention at all to the fact that gender matters to peace and security concerns. Carol Cohn explains that 'the SC is at the center of UN power. Not coincidentally, it is also an overwhelmingly male and masculinist domain, devoted to the "hardcore" issue of military threats to international peace and security' (2008, 186). The story of the WPS agenda, therefore, is a gendered story of women pushing at the door of 'the master's house' (Lorde 1984, 110). Cohn and others elaborate persuasively on what a significant achievement it was for advocates to get the issue of 'women and peace and security' on to the agenda of the UN Security Council at the turn of the 21st century. Those involved have written about how the women – as individuals and as representatives of civil society organisations from across the world – mobilised feminist knowledges to disrupt the conservative space of the Security Council. Sanam Naraghi Anderlini, for example, recalls: 'We were offering an alternative, or a new opening as a pathway to adapt the institutions better to the changing nature of warfare: *Women in civil society build peace. They can make a difference. Work with them*' (Naraghi Anderlini 2019, 43, emphasis in original).

Relatedly, from women's activism around the WPS agenda, we can learn about how to strategically seize political opportunities, to identify and work with allies, and to lobby, canvas and advocate not only for the big things – like the new mechanisms of international governance, or new forms of national policy – but also for the little things, like making sure that gender isn't used as a synonym for women in those policy documents. Feminists historically have been admirably strategic in their forms of political engagement, taking advantage of moments of possibility and using those moments to leverage lasting change. Scholars of political change refer to 'political opportunity structures' to describe those windows of opportunity that open, politically, to enable new perspectives to inform existing debates or areas of political practice. The efforts of allies demanding the Security Council take seriously the WPS agenda took place in the broader context of shifting ideas about security at the UN and beyond.

At the end of the 20th century, critical interventions by the above-mentioned bearers of marginalised knowledges challenged the international community's focus on traditional notions of state-centred security (where the state is also seen in conventional terms as a territory with defined borders and a population to be governed). This 'state-centric' view shifted towards the idea of 'human security', which focused on the different forms of *in*security that exist in the world. Human security sees the referent object of security – the thing that needs to be made secure – as the human individual rather than the state. Human security discourse and practice was the result of the international community taking seriously women's knowledge about (in)security. Those feminist activists working on the nascent WPS agenda recognised the political significance of this shift in security thinking. They identified this moment as an opportunity to integrate long-held concerns for women's human rights in conflict and conflict-affected settings with ideas about how to prevent further violence and insecurity in those contexts. Recognising that the UN Security Council – and the UN more broadly – was 'primed' to listen to ideas about women's rights in relation to discussions about peace and security was an integral part of successful advocacy for what became the WPS agenda.

Women organise

One of the key things that we are learning from listening to women, and carefully observing their political activism, is that they have sophisticated and powerful modes of organising for peace. The adoption of UNSCR 1325, and the subsequent development of the thematic agenda item on 'women and peace and security' into a complex governance system that we have come to know as the WPS agenda, relied on mobilisation and maximising political opportunities. There is no doubt that this represented significant, and concerted, collective effort. Even if we limit the window of historical enquiry to just the few weeks prior to the adoption of UNSCR 1325, we can identify multiple forms and vectors of collaboration: between female civil society representatives and their constituencies within their countries of origin; between those representatives and staff at UN Women; between all of those people and the staff at various country missions (notably the missions of Jamaica, Namibia and Bangladesh) at the UN in New York. These people – all involved in ways large and small with the drafting and eventual adoption of UNSCR 1325, all of whom had identified that this was the right time to be pushing this agenda forward and to be seeking to effect real political change in the field of peace and security – organised around this issue because they felt a sense of real investment, of ownership. One such activist explains: 'SCR 1325 is our tool, the tool of women's peace activists and human rights non-governmental organisations (NGOs). It was our idea, not the Security Council's, and it is our efforts that have given it life since its adoption' (Ruby 2014, 181).

We can learn from women's organisations, from their political movements. We can learn about how to work collaboratively and effectively even where there are profound differences of perspective and priorities, and we can learn how to respect and harness those differences to create better policy and advocacy platforms. The working group of NGOs that cohered around the WPS issues that they wanted to see embedded in a Security Council resolution were by no means united on all of those issues, nor were the demands of the communities they represented necessarily aligned, but they found a way to work together to achieve something that they could all believe in. In surfacing the possibility of learning from women's organising, I do not mean to erase the many tensions and vectors of exclusion that inform and shape women's movements globally and historically. Much disservice is done to the struggles for voice and representation within cis-heteronormative and racist institutions if idealised myths about harmony within feminist peace activism are perpetuated. For example, the 'origin stories' of the adoption of UNSCR 1325 frequently exclude the formative and profound influence that African women and women's organisations had on the emergent agenda.

The agenda is frequently traced back to the Fourth World Conference on Women in Beijing in 1995 and the outcome document, the *Beijing Platform for Action*; the *Platform for Action* included a chapter on gender and armed conflict, which is often sighted and cited as the foundation of UNSCR 1325. What is frequently missing from the citation and recitation of the *Beijing Platform for Action* as a linchpin of the WPS agenda, however, is any acknowledgement that 'Africa was the source and venue for the establishment of the type of principles and policies articulated in UNSCR 1325 even before the emergence of this UN resolution on women' (Diop 2011, 173). While mention is made in the origin story of the WPS agenda of the influence of the Windhoek Conference, held in Namibia in May 2000, the subsequent Declaration, and the Namibia Plan of Action on Mainstreaming a Gender Perspective in Multidimensional Peace Support Operations, it does not enjoy nearly as central a role in the narrative as the *Beijing Platform for Action*. Moreover, the Windhoek Declaration is articulated as part of the documentary heritage of UNSCR 1325 in the Preamble of the resolution itself but, unlike the *Beijing Platform for Action*, is never mentioned again in the policy architecture of the agenda.

In combination with the elision of time between March and October in many narratives of UNSCR 1325, the writing-out of Windhoek and the failure to cite the African Platform for Action (adopted in 1994) as the primary inspiration for the *Beijing Platform for Action* represents place and race in the WPS story in not altogether unproblematic ways; although Beijing was a 'world conference', it took place at a time at which some feminist collectives and organisations in the global South were expressing concern 'about the imposition of what is perceived as an external agenda, and about whose interests are served by the [gender] mainstreaming project' (Baden and Goetz 1997, 10). Further, differences in political preparedness and positional authority meant that women of colour in Beijing were not necessarily able to contribute to the deliberations and the outcome document as fully as other groups of women (Dutt 1996, 527). Thus, the incantation of Beijing invokes not only a particular policy platform – and it is important to remember that the *Platform for Action* was ultimately negotiated by government representatives – but a temporal linkage to the other UN conferences in the series, a spatial linkage through attachment to the UN, and a racialisation of the agenda that positions African feminists as supplicants to the UN Security Council rather than drivers of this agenda.

But we can learn from this whitewashing of the WPS agenda's history. We can recognise the need to organise differently, and more inclusively, in order to make space for different perspectives and to make visible different knowledges. It is essential that the 'we' here is an inclusive collective, mindful of differences between women and their experiences – differences that do not, importantly, preclude collective political action, as I elaborate below. This is not a new challenge for feminist knowledge and praxis. Feminist philosophers have often questioned the integrity and coherence of the subject of 'woman'. Contestation over who counts as a woman, and on whose behalf rights as a woman can therefore be claimed, has been a feature of the landscape in feminist theory for over two centuries; as Lisa Tilley reminds us, 'within white feminism the category of "woman" has always been a tightly bordered one' (2018, n.p.). Transgressing those borders and thinking about women in an inclusive, intersectional way that is respectful of all modes of self-identification can form the basis of a feminist politics. Until we recognise the instability and mutability of the subject of 'woman', however, we risk carrying with us in our peace work a residual essentialism that reproduces particular configurations of overlapping and interconnected white, cis, hetero and male privilege. The demand for a coherent subject on whose behalf rights are claimed can be a way of undermining feminist political movements. Celebrating diversity and, at times, incoherence can be a way of finding unity in difference.

Diverse need not mean divided, and the acknowledgement of women's differences is a necessary precondition for the meaningful participation of women in politics. Mobilising this knowledge can create new collectives, new forms of organisation, and new political possibilities, including the possibility of finding solutions to end war. Activists and WPS advocates are vigorously organising to challenge the idea that descriptive representation is enough in peace-making, peace-building, and post-conflict reconstruction. The questions of *which* women are present, and how they substantively represent the

interests and priorities of their communities, are of primary significance. We are learning how to avoid the assumption that just because
a woman is female-identified by medical discourse, she herself
identifies as a woman, and, further, can speak for all women. Coalition-building, and collective action involving the collaboration of
diverse women in respectful and inclusive ways is a challenging way
of doing political work, but it is essential to learn how to know and
organise differently if we are going to achieve different outcomes
than have been achieved throughout history. Thinking about the
subject of 'woman' in an inclusive, intersectional way that is respectful of all modes of self-identification can draw from feminist theory
and practice.

Women make connections

Thinking carefully, and empathetically, about difference, involves
– perhaps seemingly paradoxically – making connections across
communities, across borders both physical and intellectual. While
'organising' is action-focused, making connections is about the
process of 'joining the dots', a process for which feminists – being so
attuned to the workings of multiple forms of power – have a particular talent. Feminist peace research has, for many decades, charted the
establishment and consolidation of connections across intellectual,
ethnic, community and national boundaries by women working for
peace and resolution to conflict.

The challenge is to see how differences allow us to explain the
connections and border crossings better and more accurately, how
specifying difference allows us to theorise universal concerns more
fully. It is this intellectual move that allows for my concern for women
of different communities and identities to build coalitions and soli-
darities across borders (Mohanty 2003, 505).

Thus, third and finally, from women's advocacy for the WPS agenda
(which again I am reading here as an artefact of feminist activism and
theory), I think we can learn how to make the connections between
different forms of inequality, different forms of injustice, and different forms of violence.

Activists and researchers working on WPS issues are, for example, making the connections between domestic violence policy-setting agendas within the state – the reduced funding available for effective programme development and delivery, and the deprioritisation of domestic violence as a political issue during the average election campaign cycle – and that same state's commitments to, and lavish funding of, violence prevention in conflict-affected settings overseas. This example is specifically grounded in critique of the UK government's reduction in funding allocated to domestic violence crisis centres across the UK, which happened in tandem with the much-publicised (and expensive) Global Summit to End Sexual Violence in Conflict held in London in June 2014, part of the Preventing Sexual Violence Initiative championed by former Foreign Secretary Lord William Hague and UN Special Envoy Angelina Jolie. British feminists and others are mobilising and organising, drawing these connections and holding those in power accountable for the outcomes that flow from these policy decisions.

Women doing peace work also build coalitions and draw connections across issue areas. Ending war means ending war economies, and so peace work has to take into consideration not just the reconfiguration of formal and informal political institutions but also the redistribution of resources, including rights to land and water, support to engage in small- and large-scale economic activity, and education. At the transnational level, WPS advocates are connecting the WPS agenda to other important platforms: first, the Convention on the Elimination of all forms of Discrimination against Women (CEDAW) – General Recommendation 30 of which now requires states to report to the CEDAW Committee on the work they are doing to support women's rights in conflict and conflict-affected areas – and secondly, the Sustainable Development Goals (particularly Goal 5 on gender equality and Goal 16 on peace, justice, and strong institutions). Nationally, regionally and internationally, women working for peace are using social media and digital technologies to foster and strengthen connections.

Activists and researchers working on WPS issues are beginning to understand, and work to mitigate, the gendered, racialised and sexualised exercise of power that perpetuates hierarchies of authority in peace and security governance. They are drawing attention to exclusions of people and their lived experiences – for example, the lack of consideration given to lesbian, gay, bisexual, and trans people in the majority of WPS policy actions. Activists also flag exclusionary themes and issues – for example, the omission of reproductive rights from the core of the WPS agenda, even though the protection of these rights is essential for bodily autonomy and integrity. There are numerous examples of WPS activists, advocates and researchers making those connections, across national boundaries, across issue areas, and across institutions, in pursuit of ending war and preventing violence of all kinds, to all kinds: human and non-human alike. Learning from women making connections broadens our perspective on peace work and enables holistic and relational perspectives on ending war.

ENDING WAR

Preventing violence is complex, ending war much more so. A lot of violence prevention work outside of feminist spaces looks solely at disarmament, or solely at organisational power, or solely at deterrence. The feminist activism and theory that is embedded in the WPS agenda, in all its glorious diversity, is complex and clever, and draws together connections between disparate forms of violence to explore how such violence can be prevented. The meaningful and consistent participation of diverse groups of women, and the protection of the rights of all women in all circumstances, are inextricably linked to the prevention of violence. The WPS agenda renders visible those connections, across a multitude of contexts and in an endless variety of ways. These different knowledges are of critical significance. Understanding the racialised and gendered hierarchies of knowledge that have precluded the recognition of these knowledges as knowledge will help us further our engagement with the racialised and gendered discourses that perpetuate peacelessness. I would even argue that now it is difficult to think through violence prevention, to venture solutions to war ideologies and war fighting, without taking seriously the issues around which the WPS agenda coheres: without listening to women. Listening to women – paying close attention to women's knowledge claims, of all kinds – is essential to efforts at ending war. Listening to women ensures a peace that is inclusive and expansive, a peace that is attuned to the operation of power. A gender-blind, exclusionary, narrow vision of peace and security is a thin and meagre vision indeed.

REFERENCES

Baden, Sally and Goetz, Anne Marie (1997) Who needs [sex] when you can have [gender]? Conflicting discourses on gender at Beijing. *Feminist Review* 56: 3–25.

Cohn, Carol (2008) Mainstreaming gender in UN security policy: A path to political transformation? In: Shirin M. Rai and Georgina Waylen (eds) *Global Governance: Feminist Perspectives*. Basingstoke: Palgrave Macmillan, pp. 185–206.

Confortini, Catia C. (2012) *Intelligent Compassion: Feminist Critical Methodology in the Women's International League for Peace and Freedom*. Oxford: Oxford University Press.

Diop, Bineta (2011) The African Union and implementation of UNSCR 1325. In: Funmi Olonisakin, Karen Barnes and Eka Ikpe (eds) *Women, Peace and Security: Translating Policy into Practice*. London: Routledge, pp. 173–183.

Dutt, Mallika (1996) Some reflections on U.S. women of color and the United Nations Fourth World Conference on Women and NGO forum in Beijing, China. *Feminist Studies* 22(3): 519–528.

Enloe, Cynthia (1996) Margins, silences and bottom rungs: How to overcome the underestimation of power in the study of International Relations. In: Steve Smith, Ken Booth, and Marysia Zalewski (eds) *International Theory: Positivism and Beyond*. Cambridge: Cambridge University Press, pp. 186–202.

Lorde, Audre (1984) *Sister Outsider: Essays and Speeches*. Berkeley, CA: Crossing Press.

Manchanda, Rita (2017) Introduction. In: Rita Manchanda (ed.) *Women and Politics of Peace: South Asia Narratives on Militarization, Power and Justice*. London: Sage, pp. i–xl.

Mohanty, Chandra Talpade (1988) Under Western eyes: Feminist scholarship and colonial discourses. *Feminist Review* 30(3): 61–88.

Mohanty, Chandra Talpade (2003) 'Under Western eyes' revisited: Feminist solidarity through anticapitalist struggles. *Signs: Journal of Women in Culture and Society* 28(2): 499–535.

Naraghi Anderlini, Sanam (2019) Civil society's leadership in adopting 1325 resolution. In: Sara E. Davies and Jacqui True (eds) *The Oxford Handbook of Women, Peace and Security*. Oxford: Oxford University Press, pp. 38–52.

Ruby, Felicity (2014) Security Council Resolution 1325: A tool for conflict prevention? In: Gina Heathcote and Dianne Otto (eds) *Rethinking Peacekeeping, Gender Equality and Collective Security*. Basingstoke: Palgrave Macmillan, pp. 173–184.

Spivak, Gayatri Chakravorty (1988) Can the subaltern speak? In: Cary Nelson and Lawrence Grossberg (eds) *Marxism and the Interpretation of Culture*. Basingstoke: Macmillan, pp. 24–28.

Tilley, Lisa (2018) But what about the aid worker? *Al Jazeera* Opinion, 21 February.

Tuhiwai Smith, Linda (20120) *Decolonizing Methodologies*, 2nd edn. London: Zed.

Notes on Contributors

Ray Acheson

Ray Acheson is director of Reaching Critical Will, the disarmament program of the Women's International League for Peace and Freedom, one of the world's oldest feminist peace organisations. They have been involved with intergovernmental disarmament processes since 2005, providing reporting, analysis, and advocacy on nuclear weapons, the international arms trade, and more, from a feminist and antimilitarist perspective. Ray serves on the steering group of the International Campaign to Abolish Nuclear Weapons (ICAN), which won the 2017 Nobel Peace Prize for its work to ban nuclear weapons, as well as the steering committees of the Campaign to Stop Killer Robots and the International Network on Explosive Weapons. Ray has been awarded the 2020 Nuclear Free Future Award and the 2018 UN Women Metro New York Champion of Change prize. They are the author of *Banning the Bomb, Smashing the Patriarchy* (2021).

Sarai Aharoni

Sarai Aharoni is a senior lecturer in the Gender Studies Program at Ben-Gurion University of the Negev. Her research focuses on Women, Peace and Security (WPS), feminist security studies, and histories of women's policy agencies and feminist movements in Israel. She has published articles on gender, peace and conflict in Israel in various journals and co-edited the book *Where Are All the Women? U.N. Security Council Resolution 1325: Gender Perspectives of the Israeli-Palestinian Conflict* (2004). In addition to her academic work, Sarai is a long time scholar-activist. She formed the first project on UN Security Council Resolution 1325 in Israel (2003), was one of the founding members of the IWC (International Women's Commission) and has been involved in various women's initiatives to promote peace since then. Sarai is also an active member of the Haifa Feminist Institute (HFI), an independent feminist archive, library and research centre that seeks to enhance local feminist voices and histories.

Yolande Bouka
Yolande Bouka is an Assistant Professor in the Department of Political Studies at Queen's University, Canada. Her research and teaching focus on gender, African politics and security, political violence, and field research ethics in conflict-affected societies. Her current research is a multi-sited historical and political analysis of female combatants in Southern Africa. In addition to her academic work, she has extensive experience with development and security research agencies. She has worked with and offered support to USAID, the UK Department for International Development, the United Nations, the African Union, the Center for Strategic and International Studies and the United States Institute of Peace. Between 2014 and 2016 she was a researcher at the Institute for Security Studies (ISS) in the Conflict Prevention and Risk Analysis Division in Nairobi, Kenya, where she led research on peace and security in Africa's Great Lakes Region.

Carol Cohn
Carol Cohn is the founding director of the Consortium on Gender, Security and Human Rights and a Lecturer in Women's Studies at the University of Massachusetts Boston. Her research and writing has focused on gender and security issues ranging from work on the discourse of civilian nuclear defence intellectuals and US national security elites to gender integration issues in the US military, feminist approaches to thinking about weapons of mass destruction, the gender dimensions of contemporary armed conflicts, the concept of 'vulnerability' in security and humanitarian discourse, and gender mainstreaming in international peace and security institutions, including the passage of UN Security Council resolutions on women, peace and security and the ongoing efforts to ensure its implementation at the international, national and grassroots levels. In addition to her research, Cohn facilitates training and workshops for UN Security Council Resolution 1325 and has been active in the NGO Working Group on Women, Peace and Security since 2001.

Claire Duncanson
Claire Duncanson is a Senior Lecturer in International Relations at the University of Edinburgh. Prior to her academic career, she worked

for a variety of human rights and international development NGOs, including Amnesty International, Jubilee 2000 and Global Perspective. Claire's research interests lie at the intersection of international security, International Relations theory, environmental politics and gender politics. Her work applies theoretical insights about feminism, gender and, in particular, masculinities, to current international issues, such as military interventions, military transformations, peacekeeping, peace-building and nuclear proliferation. Claire is the author of two books, *Forces for Good? Military Masculinities and Peacebuilding in Afghanistan and Iraq* (2013), and *Gender and Peacebuilding* (2016). She has also published widely in academic journals, including on feminist debates over women's military participation.

Thomas Gregory

Tom Gregory is a Senior Lecturer at the University of Auckland. Tom is currently working on three projects related to conflict, violence and war. The first is a Marsden-funded book project entitled *The Politics of Killing Civilians: Counterinsurgency and the Economy of Force*, which examines civilian casualty mitigation efforts in Afghanistan and Iraq. The second project builds upon his existing work, situating contemporary debates on drones, autonomous weapons and the use of explosive weapons in populated areas within a history trajectory that reaches back to debates about expanding bullets, cluster munitions and chemical weapons. Finally, he is working on a VR (virtual reality) project with colleagues in Computer Sciences on the ethics of war, which focuses on how new technologies might be used to explore debates about ethics and war.

Eda Gunaydin

Eda Gunaydin is a graduate student in the Department of Government and International Relations at the University of Sydney. Her key research interests are in the areas of identity, and postcolonial and post-structuralist discourse theory in International Relations. Eda's doctoral research focuses on the Rojavan project, which offers an alternate vision of sovereignty and governance with the potential to challenge state-centric systems in International Relations. Her research has been published in *International Studies Quarterly, International Feminist Journal of Politics* and *Patterns of Prejudice.*

Heidi Hudson
Heidi Hudson is Professor of International Relations and Dean of the Faculty of the Humanities at the University of the Free State, Bloemfontein, South Africa. She has written extensively in the area of feminist security studies, with a specific focus on Africa. Her current research interests concentrate on discursive and material gender deficits of liberal peace-building in the postcolony. Her other area of interest is the gendering of Africa's International Relations, the African knowledge project and postcolonial/decolonial strategies of resistance. Heidi has held several fellowships through Fulbright, the Nordic Africa Institute, and the University of Calgary (Canada). In 2018, she was the Claude Ake Visiting Chair at the Nordic Africa Institute and the Department of Peace and Conflict Research in Uppsala, Sweden. She is co-editor and co-author of *Post-conflict Reconstruction and Development in Africa: Concepts, Role-players, Policy and Practice* (2013), with Theo Neethling. Heidi was a PRIO (Peace Research Institute Oslo) Global Fellow from 2014 to 2017 and currently serves on several advisory and editorial boards.

Roxani Krystalli
Roxani Krystalli is a Lecturer at the University of St Andrews School of International Relations in Scotland. Her research and teaching focus on feminist peace and conflict studies, as well as on the politics of nature and place. Roxani is particularly interested in the role of storytelling and narratives in conflict-affected settings, as well as in how the study of peace would be different if we centred experiences of love and care. Roxani has worked at the intersection of gender and peace-building as an academic researcher and humanitarian practitioner. She previously served as Program Manager at the Feinstein International Center, where she managed a portfolio aiming to increase the use of research in humanitarian policy and practice. Roxani has partnered with a variety of organisations, including Oxfam GB, Mercy Corps, the International Committee of the Red Cross, and more, to conduct and analyse research on the experiences

of conflict-affected people in Uganda, South Sudan, Syria, and the refugee crisis in Greece, Jordan and Turkey. Roxani regularly advises international organisations and NGOs on various aspects of gender, justice, and peace-building.

Megan MacKenzie
Megan MacKenzie is a Professor and Simons Chair in International Law and Human Security at Simon Fraser University. Her research examines war, security studies, post-conflict recovery and reconstruction, and military culture. Her work is broadly focused on the ways that gender matters in understanding war and insecurity, and the ways that experiences of war and insecurity are shaped by gendered norms and sexism. Megan's research considers military culture and gender integration, which includes projects on military sexual violence, the integration of women into combat roles, and military suicide. She also has worked on issues related to post-conflict transitions including projects on disarmament programmes, amnesty provisions in peace agreements, and truth and reconciliation commissions.

Diksha Poddar
Diksha Poddar is currently a Research Scholar at the Centre for South Asian Studies, School of International Studies at Jawaharlal Nehru University, New Delhi, where she is studying the processes of narrativisation around youth and peace-building in conflict areas for her doctoral thesis. She has over six years' experience of working at the praxis of grassroots peace-building, gender and development in South Asia. Diksha is associated with WISCOMP (Women in Security, Conflict Management and Peace), an initiative of the Foundation for Universal Responsibility of His Holiness the Dalai Lama, New Delhi, as a Junior Fellow. Her interest lies at the intersection of gender, youth, creative arts, peace-building, and feminist methodologies. An MPhil. in South Asian Studies, Diksha has completed her Master's in Development Studies and a postgraduate Diploma in Conflict Transformation and Peace Building from Lady Shri Ram College for Women, University of Delhi.

Jessica Russ-Smith

Jessica Russ-Smith is a Wiradyuri Wambuul woman, Social Worker, and Scientia PhD Scholar at the School of Social Sciences, University of New South Wales (Australia). Her doctoral research explores Indigenous embodiment of sovereignty based upon the Wiradyuri cosmology and the sacred Wiradyuri relationship of grandmothers and granddaughters. Her thesis is entitled *'Balayanhi Wiradyuri Garingundhi': We Are Sovereign My Granddaughter. Embodying Wiradyuri Women's Sovereignty through Wiradyuri Knowing, Being and Doing.* Jessica's research has also explored decolonising social work, Indigenous social work, ethics, activism, embodying sovereignty, working with Aboriginal children and young people, and experiences of Indigenous researchers.

Sertan Saral

Sertan Saral is a PhD candidate with the Department of Gender and Cultural Studies at the University of Sydney. He is interested in the discursive force of military service as a type of gender performativity and cultural capital; as a regulatory norm that stratifies bodies within society along identity markers; and as having a generative and inheritable quality which reproduces and perpetuates war-making. His current project is considering these ideas within two sites in the United States where militarism and democracy are entangled: memorials dedicated to military veterans in Washington DC and Mt Vernon IL, and in relation to military veterans who run for public office.

Laura Shepherd

Laura J. Shepherd is a Professor of International Relations in the Department of Government and International Relations at the University of Sydney, Australia. Laura's primary research programme focuses on the UN Security Council's Women, Peace and Security agenda. She has written extensively on the formulation of UN Security Council Resolution 1325 and subsequent Women, Peace and Security resolutions, and her research engages the motifs of violence prevention and inclusive peace that characterise debates about women, peace and security in global politics. Laura has recently concluded a research project examining advocacy around, and implementation of, the Women, Peace and Security agenda at global, national and local levels, and she is currently working on a number of projects related to the governance of violence and violence prevention. Laura is author/editor of several books, including, most recently, *Narrating the Women, Peace and Security Agenda* (Oxford University Press, 2021) and *Civil Society, Care Labour, and the Women, Peace and Security Agenda: Making 1325 Work* (with Caitlin Hamilton and Anuradha Mundkur; Routledge, 2021). She tweets from @drljshepherd and blogs occasionally for The Disorder of Things.

Shweta Singh

Shweta Singh is Senior Assistant Professor of International Relations at the South Asian University (New Delhi, India). She was recently appointed as the UN Women International Expert on populism, nationalism, and gender (Regional Office for Asia and Pacific). She is co-editor (with Tiina Vaittinen and Catia Confortini), of a Rowman and Littlefield book series titled Feminist Studies on Peace, Justice and Violence. Her recent publications include, 'In between the Ulema and local warlords in Afghanistan: Critical perspectives on the everyday, norms translation and UNSCR 1325' (*International Feminist Journal of Politics*, 2020); 'Gendering education for peace: Critical perspectives', in Tarja Väyrynen, Swati Parashar, Élise Féron and Catia Confortini (eds), *Handbook of Feminist Peace Research* (Routledge, 2021); 'Teaching gender and hydro-diplomacy in South Asia: Critical reflections' (*International Feminist Journal of Politics*, 2019).

Nicole Wegner

Nicole Wegner is a Postdoctoral Research Fellow in Gender and War in the Department of Government and International Relations and a member of the Centre for International Security Studies at the University of Sydney, Australia. Her work is broadly focused on feminist approaches to understanding gender, war and militarism, which sees gender as central to understanding how lethal violence is condoned and legitimised. She has published on feminist methodologies, militarist myths related to international peacekeeping, and Support the Troops discourse in North America, and is currently working on several collaborative projects, examining veteran suicides in NATO militaries and feminist foreign policy strategies.

Cai Wilkinson

Cai Wilkinson is an Associate Professor in International Relations at Deakin University, Australia. Cai's research focuses on societal security in the post-Soviet space, with a particular focus on LGBTQ human rights and 'traditional values' in Kyrgyzstan and Russia, as well as on interrogating the role of genders and sexualities in international politics. Methodologically, Cai utilises interpretive ethnographic approaches that foreground lived experiences and situated knowledge production. Their research has considered securitisation theory, LGBT activism in Central Asia, and fieldwork-based research methods. Cai is currently working on projects about the politics of LGBT rights in the post-Soviet space and the protection of LGBTIQ rights in the Asia-Pacific.

Keina Yoshida

Keina Yoshida is a Research Officer in the Centre for Women, Peace, and Security, where they work on the AHRC-funded project Feminist Approaches to the International Law of Peace and Security (FILPS). Keina is a member of the editorial board of *Feminist Legal Studies*. Keina is researching the links between the environment, nature, sustainable development goals, the gendered causes and impacts of violence against women, and structural inequalities in the context of international legal conceptions of peace and security. Keina is also a barrister at Doughty Street Chambers where they also form part of the Doughty Street International team. Keina has acted in a number of high-profile public law challenges in the High Court and Court of Appeal, many of which raise points under the Human Rights Act or have equality implications. Keina has acted in the European Court of Human Rights and as an intervenor in regional and international courts including before the Inter-American Court of Human Rights and the UN Committee on the Elimination of Discrimination against Women (CEDAW). They are appointed to Panel C Counsel of the Equality and Human Rights Commission (EHRC).

Index

post-conflict, 31, 34, 40, 49, 168, 173, 176, 219, 225
post-conflict reconstruction, 31, 219, 225
post-war, 5, 12, 181–4, 186–7, 189, 191–5
posttraumatic stress disorder (PTSD), 143
poverty, 38, 39, 94, 105, 186
power relations, 49, 64, 69, 125, 126, 173
prevention, 166–8, 172, 177–8, 218–9, 227–8
privatisation, 183, 192
privilege, xvi, 3, 21, 23, 94, 105, 108, 109, 158, 225
protest, 22, 50, 51, 66, 148, 171
    protests, 2–3, 44, 48, 66, 129, 170
    non-violence resistance, 48
psychological violence(s), 62, 100
public, xii, 8, 10, 40, 44, 47, 51, 55, 97–9, 124, 138–41, 144, 160, 183, 192–4, 195, 207
    public sector, 183
    public spaces, 40, 98, 138–9
    public support, 141

queer, 5, 8, 89–101, 105–6, 109–11, 113, 116–18
    queer analysis, 8
    queer International Relations (IR), 91–2
    queer security, 101
    queer vision, 100

race, xiv, 4–5, 22, 23, 69, 110, 117, 125, 128, 224
    racial, 23, 107, 117, 123, 126
    racialisation, 225
    racialized, 97, 121–3, 126, 127–9, 132, 134, 219, 227, 228
    racism, 2, 5, 12, 13, 23, 36, 94, 100, 106, 107, 116–17, 122, 125
    antiracism, xi

racist, 105, 110, 117, 123, 125, 134, 223
antiracist, 2, 23, 110, 118, 134
rape, 1, 5, 33, 49, 66, 111, 161, 190
    rape in war, 1
rebels, 49, 131
    rebel forces, 129–3
reconciliation, 40–1
reconstructing, 109, 174
recovery, 157, 182–4, 186, 189, 193, 194–5, 218
refugees, 47, 48, 187
reintegration, 156, 158
    see Disarmament, Demobilization, and Reintegration (DDR)
religion, 69, 117
religious, 79, 80, 84, 140
renewable energy, 189–91
reparations, 48, 167
reproductive rights, 228
resources, 3, 5, 19, 21, 37, 49, 82, 101, 133, 168, 169, 172, 174, 177, 181, 182–4, 187, 189–94, 218, 220, 227
Responsibility to Protect (R2P), 122, 124
restorative, xiii, 40, 41, 188, 190–1, 192, 193
revolution, 78, 80, 81, 110, 145, 158, 174
Revolutionary Armed Forces of Colombia (FARC), 155, 159

sanctions, 5, 124, 152
security, xv, 1, 2, 6, 8, 12, 29–31, 33, 35–9, 41–2, 47, 48, 65–8, 75, 84, 89–101, 106–9, 111, 113–18, 123–4, 126, 128–9, 131, 134, 144, 166–7, 172, 174, 175, 186, 187, 189, 191, 216–23, 225, 228, 229
    security theory, 38, 42
    secure, 8, 35, 38, 91, 100, 185, 195, 222
    securitisation, 100, 175
    security forces, 66–7

Thanks to our Patreon Subscribers:

Lia Lilith de Oliveira
Andrew Perry

Who have shown generosity and
comradeship in support of our publishing.

Check out the other perks you get by subscribing
to our Patreon – visit patreon.com/plutopress.
Subscriptions start from £3 a month.

The Pluto Press Newsletter

Hello friend of Pluto!

Want to stay on top of the best radical books
we publish?

Then sign up to be the first to hear about our
new books, as well as special events,
podcasts and videos.

You'll also get 50% off your first order with us
when you sign up.

Come and join us!

Go to bit.ly/PlutoNewsletter